W9-BPJ-687

Foolproof Planting

Foolproof

Planting

How to successfully start and propagate more than 250 vegetables, flowers, trees and shrubs

By Anne Moyer Halpin and the Editors of Rodale Press

A ROUNDTABLE PRESS BOOK

Rodale Press, Emmaus, Pa.

Printed in the United States of America

A Roundtable Press Book

Directors: Marsha Melnick, Susan E. Meyer
Book Designer: Martin Lubin/Binns & Lubin
Illustrator: Wendy Frost

Published by Rodale Press, Inc.

Book Editor: Paula Bakule
Cover Illustrator: Jon Ellis
Cover Designer: Jane Knutila

If you have any questions or comments concerning this book, please write Rodale Press, Book Reader Service, 33 East Minor Street, Emmaus, PA 18098

Library of Congress Cataloging-in-Publication Data

Halpin, Anne Moyer.
    Foolproof planting : how to successfully start and propagate more
than 250 vegetables, flowers, trees, and shrubs / by Anne Moyer
Halpin and the editors of Rodale Press.
        p.   cm.
    "A Roundtable Press book."
    ISBN 0-87857-876-5
    1. Plant Propagation.   2. Planting (Plant culture)   I. Rodale
Press.   II. Title.
SB119.H284   1990
635—dc20   89–10991
                                                                            CIP

Distributed in the book trade by St. Martin's Press

2   4   6   8   10   9   7   5   3   1   hardcover

CONTENTS

INTRODUCTION

This book has a twofold purpose: to provide a quick, convenient reference to planting techniques and to serve as a guide to the basics of plant propagation. Most gardeners eventually develop an interest in starting plants from seeds or by other methods. These garden hobbyists need an easy-to-use reference that both covers the basics and simplifies the complexities of plant propagation.

There are many books that explain plant propagation in great technical detail. But there is no single easy-to-use reference that provides basic planting and propagating information for many different plants. That's how this book was born.

I have often wished for just such a reference book, so that I could find the correct spacing and planting depth for plants whose nursery instructions had been lost or for seeds stored without their original packets. In the midst of a hectic growing season, which usually includes trying to find time to garden, hold down a job, care for children, run a household, and myriad other chores, many of us tend to misplace pieces of information we may need later. The idea of keeping a detailed garden journal with seed packets neatly affixed to its pages and garden plans perfectly drawn to scale and carefully updated each year has always appealed to me. But, in truth, I've never managed to find the time to do more than scribble hasty notes in a disorderly notebook. Somehow bits of helpful information get lost, and I find myself digging through a pile of books and files to find the instructions I need to plant my nicotiana seeds or start new thyme plants.

This book is my solution to these typical gardening dilemmas. *Foolproof Planting* assembles all the information gardeners need to start new plants and plant their gardens. Chapters One through Three explain how to start plants from seed (indoors and out), how to propagate plants by vegetative means, and how to plant stock purchased from local or mail-order suppliers. Chapter Four is an encyclopedia that summarizes planting and propagating information for more than 250 different plants.

This book is meant to be a quick and reliable reference guide, not an exhaustive manual of procedures. Use it to find out how far apart to plant your corn, when to take cuttings from your geraniums, or which is the best way to propagate your raspberries. Use it also to explore the many exciting options for multiplying plants. From the simple division of a clump of daylilies to bud grafting of rose bushes, *Foolproof Planting* provides easy directions for increasing your favorite plants. I hope it serves you well.

Anne Moyer Halpin

Part 1

Basic Techniques

CHAPTER ONE

Starting Plants from Seed

There are lots of reasons to grow your own plants from seed. For one thing, it's the least expensive way to get more plants. What's more, the choice, of plants and cultivars available from commercial suppliers in seed form is far greater than the number of cultivars sold as started plants. In addition, seeds are lots easier to handle than plants. Shipping dates are less of a problem; seeds can be stored until you are ready to plant them, whereas plants need to be put in the ground quickly. If weather conditions are bad, it's a simple matter to store your seeds until a suitable planting day arrives.

If you are inclined toward experimentation, you can try your hand at plant breeding, working with nonhybrid and open-pollinated varieties. You can cross-pollinate the flowers and save the resulting seeds, repeating the selection process for a few years until the plants have become genetically stable and you have a reliable crop of seeds that will produce plants with the characteristics you like. Catalogs of heirloom seeds are a good source of nonhybrid seeds to use in backyard breeding projects. For more information on seed saving or heirloom seeds, write to Kent Whealy at the Seed Saver's Exchange, RR 3, Box 239, Decorah, IA 52101. Enclose a stamped, self-addressed envelope and ask for a copy of the introductory brochure, which describes the publications and activities of the Seed Saver's Exchange.

Finally, growing plants from seed is a rewarding experience. Watching the first tiny shoots poke through the soil is a wonder, even more so when the seeds are challenging to germinate and the plants difficult to grow. These tiny shoots never fail to renew a gardener's appreciation of the miracle of growth.

The Structure of Seeds

A seed is an embryonic plant. Encased within a covering known as the seed coat are a primary root (called a radicle) and a primary shoot (or plumule). To the root and shoot are attached seed leaves (or cotyledons), which are the first leaves to form on the plant. Cotyledons do not as a rule have the characteristic shape of the plant's "true leaves," which possess the unique form and shape that identify a mature plant as a tomato or marigold or bean. Seed-bearing plants have one seed leaf (in which case they are known as monocotyledons, or monocots) or two seed leaves (dicotyledons, or dicots). A seed can nourish the tiny plant until it develops its first true leaves; then the plant must derive its nourishment from the soil.

Seeds come in many sizes. The seeds of rhododendrons are so tiny that it can take five million of them to weigh a pound. At the other end of the scale, a single coconut seed can weigh as much as 50 pounds.

How Seeds Are Produced

A plant produces seeds and fruit by a sexual process in which male flower parts fertilize female flower parts and produce an egg that becomes a seed. Fruits are the structures the plant produces to contain its seeds. The process by which fertilization occurs is called pollination.

The flowers of some plants have both male and female parts; such flowers are known as *perfect flowers* or *self-fertile flowers*. Other plants (squash, for example) have some male flowers and some female flowers; these flowers are called imperfect or self-unfertile. Some species (hollies and gingko trees are two examples) produce all male flowers on some plants and all female flowers on other plants, so both a male and a female plant are needed for pollination to occur.

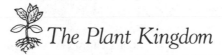 *The Plant Kingdom*

For new gardeners unfamiliar with plant reproduction, a basic introduction to the way plants are named and classified may help to provide a better context for the discussion below on how pollination occurs and how hybrids are produced.

Plants, like animals, are classified into groups according to similarities in their structure. Botany is the study of plant structure and classification, while horticulture is the science (many of us prefer to consider it an art) of plant growth. The system of botanical nomenclature used around the world was developed largely by a Swedish scientist named Carl von Linné. Like all scientific languages, botanical nomenclature is Latin, and Linné was honored by having his name latinized to Carolus Linnaeus.

Plant *families* are groups of related plants that possess certain characteristics in common. For example, the Compositae (Composite or Daisy Family) is made up of plants having compound flowers. The family contains over 15,000 species in more than 800 genera, and includes such seemingly diverse members as asters and goldenrod. Family names are Latin, end in -ae, and are printed in Roman type with an initial capital letter. Rosaceae, Umbelliferae, and Leguminosae are a few more examples.

A *genus* (plural *genera*) is a group of closely allied plant species that all belong to the same family. Members of the same genus are similar in many ways to one another and also different in many ways from other members of the family. Occasionally, a genus may contain only one species. Genus names are usually either descriptive of the plant's appearance or commemorative of the person who first named the plant. In botanical nomenclature, plants are described using two words, the first word indicating the genus and the second word indicating the species. The botanical name is printed in italics, with the first letter capitalized. The name of the snapdragon, for example, is *Antirrhinum majus*. The genus name, *Antirrhinum*, refers to the snoutlike structure of the flower.

A *species* is a plant or group of very closely related plants (called varieties or cultivars) that are alike except for small differences such as flower color, leaf variegation, or plant size (dwarf plants are usually varieties or cultivars). The species names are also descriptive of the plant. To return to the example of the snapdragon, the species name *majus* indicates that the plant is tall or upright. A very loose approximation of the snapdragon's botanical name in English might be "tall noselike flower." In the past, many species names were capitalized, but today it is generally accepted that all may be lowercase, although reference works such as *Hortus Third* preserve the capitals as a matter of historical interest. In this book the word *species* is abbreviated as spp.

A *variety* is a variation of a species that has occurred as a natural mutation. It is written in italics, following the abbreviation var., which appears in Roman type. A *cultivar* is a variety developed in cultivation; it is written in Roman type (with an initial capital letter) surrounded by single quotes.

Parts of a Flower

The male reproductive parts of a flower are the *stamens*, which are made up of long, slender stalks called *filaments* which support pollen-containing structures called *anthers*. The female reproductive structure is the pistil; it consists of a *stigma* on top of a long tube called the *style*, which has a swollen base where an ovary is located. The ovary contains ovules and, after fertilization, seeds.

At the time of fertilization, the stigma becomes sticky. Ripe grains of pollen are transferred by the pollinating agent from the anthers to the stigma, where they stick. The pollen grain germinates and sends a hollow tube down through the style into the ovary. Sperm cells, which originate in the pollen grain, are sent down the tube and into the ovary, where fertilization of the ovules occurs. Fertilization must occur in order for the seed capsules (fruit) to mature. If fertilization does not occur, the fruit drops from the plant. Some flowers (those of strawberries, for instance) contain more than one ovary and more than one stigma. In such flowers all the stigmas must be pollinated and all the ovaries fertilized or the resulting fruit will not develop evenly and will be misshapen.

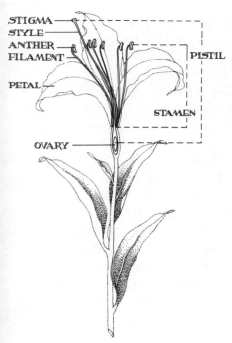

STIGMA
STYLE
ANTHER
FILAMENT
PETAL
PISTIL
STAMEN
OVARY

This illustration shows the parts of a typical flower. The female reproductive organ is the pistil, which is made up of the stigma, style, and ovary. The male reproductive organs are the stamens, which consist of anthers and filaments.

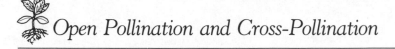

Open Pollination and Cross-Pollination

Most pollination occurs naturally. Pollen is carried by bees, moths and butterflies, birds, wind, or water. When flowers are pollinated naturally, without human intervention, the process is known as *open pollination*. Open-pollinated varieties are those that are able to reproduce themselves by natural means.

Cross-pollination requires two parent plants—one that donates the pollen and one that receives it. The resulting seeds contain a combination of the genes of both parents and grow into plants known as F_1 (first generation) hybrids. Hybridization can occur in nature, but it is usually induced by plant breeders seeking to blend the traits of related plants to produce offspring that are superior to both parents. Breeders work to develop plants with such characteristics as disease resistance, larger fruit, more colorful flowers, double-petaled flowers, or a greater degree of cold-hardiness.

In order for cross-pollination to occur, the pistils of one plant must be receptive to the pollen of the other plant, allowing the pollen grains to germinate on the stigma and send the pollen tube down the style to the ovary. Generally speaking, varieties of the same species are easy to cross, although some popular fruit crops are exceptions to this rule. Species of the same genus can be crossed in some genera but not in others. Intergeneric hybrids—crosses between two genera—are rare, but do exist. One plant family boasting a number of intergeneric hybrids is the Orchid Family. The lavish flowers of the genus *Laeliocattleya* are a result of crossing *Laelia* and *Cattleya* species. The crossing of these two genera produced a new range of flower colors and differences in the form.

A flower that is self-pollinating (contains both male and female parts) can produce seeds if its stigma receives pollen from its own anthers, the anthers of other flowers on the same plant, or the flowers of other plants of the same variety. When breeders want to cross two flowers that are self-pollinating, they must remove the male organs from one flower and the female parts from the other.

Pollination is of interest to fruit growers as well as plant breeders. Edible fruits that produce perfect, self-pollinating flowers are called *self-fruitful*. Gardeners can plant a single variety of these fruits and get a crop. Blueberries, grapes, peaches, raspberries, and strawberries are all self-fruitful.

A flower that needs cross-pollination in order to produce fertile seeds must receive pollen from another variety or species. Edible fruits with this type of flower are called *self-unfruitful*. In order to get a crop, gardeners must plant the variety they want along with another variety that can supply compatible pollen. The plants must grow close together—no more than 300 feet apart in most cases.

Cross-pollination of fruits is very tricky, for not all varieties in the same species can cross-pollinate each other. In order to set fruit, the two varieties must be compatible. Apples, sweet cherries, elderberries, pears, and plums all have both compatible and incompatible varieties. There are also degrees of self-unfruitfulness. Sometimes fruits may be somewhat, but not entirely, self-unfruitful or self-fruitful. Sour cherries exhibit this perplexing characteristic. To make matters even more confusing, some varieties (Winesap apples, for instance) have sterile pollen, meaning that they cannot pollinate either themselves or other varieties.

Compatibility of pollen is not the only factor fruit growers need to consider when choosing pollinator varieties. Both plants should also bloom at the same time, and the pollinator variety should produce lots of viable pollen in order to increase the rate of success. To make efficient use of garden space, the pollinator variety should also produce edible fruit.

You can find information on pollinator varieties for individual fruits in Part 2 of this book and in nursery catalogs. You can also consult your local USDA County Extension Agent to find out about good pollinator varieties for your area.

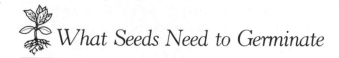

What Seeds Need to Germinate

Seeds vary greatly in terms of the conditions they need to germinate successfully. Different seeds need different combinations of light or darkness, moisture, temperature, and a length of dormancy in order to germinate. Most seeds require moisture and many need darkness to break their dormancy and germinate. But some seeds, such as the tiny seeds of wax begonia, browallia, and portulaca, need light to germinate and will not sprout if buried under soil. Other tiny seeds, like those of salpiglossis, must have darkness but must not be buried—these seeds are best germinated on top of soil in flats covered with black plastic. Some seeds need warmth also, while others, particularly those of hardy trees and shrubs, need varying amounts of cold. Some seeds need alternating periods of cold and warmth before they will sprout. Gardeners wishing to start such plants outside their native habitat or normal growing season will have to give the seeds special pretreatment to mimic the conditions in their home climate.

Seeds contain enough nutrients to supply their needs until roots have begun to grow. After that the tiny plants must take their nourishment from the surrounding environment. Seedlings need light, air, moisture, and nutrients from the soil in order to grow.

Gardeners can plant seeds either directly outdoors in the garden, in nursery beds, or in a cold frame; or indoors in pots, flats, or other containers. The method you choose will depend upon the kind of seeds you are planting. Direct-seeding is generally used for cold-tolerant and fast-growing vegetables, and for *hardy annuals*. (Hardy annuals can tolerate some frost and are usually seeded directly where they are to grow.) In northern gardens, these plants are seeded in spring; in the South, Southwest, and along the West Coast, seeds are planted in fall. Plants that do not transplant well are also usually direct-seeded. Seeds that germinate slowly, or those of plants that need a long, warm growing season to mature, are often started indoors, especially by gardeners in northern areas who need to get a head start on the outdoor growing season.

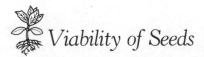 *Viability of Seeds*

Seeds don't retain their capacity to germinate indefinitely. Sooner or later they die. The length of time seeds remain viable (able to sprout) varies widely from plant to plant, from as little as a few days to hundreds of years. Lotus seeds found in the Egyptian pyramids have been germinated by scientists in this century.

The seeds of many annual flowers will last 2 to 3 years; some vegetable seeds can be stored up to 10 years under the right conditions. Some weed seeds can wait for as long as 50 years before sprouting. A seed's viability depends not only on the type of plant from which it comes, but also upon the environmental conditions under which it is stored. Most seeds keep best in a cool, dry environment.

The first step for gardeners who want to start seeds they have collected and saved themselves or stored from a previous year is to test the rate of germination.

TESTING FOR GERMINATION RATE

To test seeds for viability, place 25 of them on a damp (but not soggy) paper towel or cloth. Either roll up the towel and fasten it with rubber bands, or place it in a shallow dish and cover the dish with a lid or a second dish. Put the seeds in a warm place out of cold draft. Every day or two, give them some air, see if the towel needs to be moistened, and check to see if any of the seeds have sprouted. Wait the number of days that is average for that plant to germinate (this information is available on commercial seed packets); then wait an extra week. Count how many seeds have sprouted and multiply that number by four to arrive at the percent of germination. Most seeds packaged commercially germinate at rates of 85 to 90 percent or better. If less than 75 percent of your seeds have sprouted, it is best to buy new seed. If the seeds are rare or difficult to get, you will have to sow extra to get the number of plants you want in your garden.

Pretreatments for Seeds

Some seeds need help from the gardener in order to break their dormancy and germinate. The two primary pretreatments are providing a cold period (a process called stratification) and softening a hard seed coat by soaking, or by nicking or abrading it so that moisture can enter (a procedure called scarification).

STRATIFICATION

Many plants ripen their seeds in fall. The seeds are programmed to remain dormant throughout the cold winter and germinate the following spring, when the soil warms and growing conditions are more hospitable for the young plants. The process of stratification imitates the cold winter conditions these seeds need to sprout. They must have cold temperatures, moisture, and exposure to air.

Trees and shrubs whose seeds need stratification include fir (*Abies*), most maple species (*Acer*), birch (*Betula*), beech (*Fagus*),

Forsythia, sweet gum (*Liquidambar*), honeysuckle (*Lonicera*), *Magnolia*, and flowering cherry (*Prunus*). The seeds of some flowers need stratification also: Columbine (*Aquilegia*), bleeding heart (*Dicentra*), gas plant (*Dictamnus*), daylily (*Hemerocallis*), *Iris*, lavender (*Lavandula*), *Lobelia*, garden phlox (*Phlox paniculata*), and *Viola* are some examples. And to confuse matters still more, there are quite a few trees and shrubs whose seeds will germinate without stratification, especially if they are sown as soon as they ripen. Plants in this category include *Abelia*, Japanese maple (*Acer palmatum*), alder (*Alnus*), barberry (*Berberis*), sweet shrub (*Calycanthus*), common camellia (*Camellia japonica*), cedar (*Cedrus*), beauty bush (*Kolkwitzia*), mock orange (*Philadelphus*), sycamore (*Pieris, Platanus*), oak (*Quercus*), and *Spiraea*.

There are several ways to stratify seeds, but keep in mind that you cannot simply toss packets of seeds into your refrigerator to stratify them. If you have space in your refrigerator, you can mix the seeds with damp (but not soggy) sand, peat moss, sphagnum moss, or a mixture of equal parts sand and vermiculite, and put them in a plastic bag. Tie the bag tightly shut and put it in the refrigerator for the required length of time. Check the seeds once a week until germination time nears, to make sure the medium has not dried out—it should be kept evenly moist.

Many seeds needing stratification are large enough to be easily separated from the medium when it's time to plant. If you should find yourself needing to stratify fine seeds (for example, pansies), plant the seeds in flats of a suitable growing medium and stratify the seeds in their flat. Make sure the medium is moist after planting. Enclose the flat in a plastic bag and store it in a refrigerator or cold frame. After the required stratification time, remove the flat from the cold exposure and set it out at room temperature with the appropriate lighting as described on page 38.

If you live in a cold climate, you can also stratify seeds outdoors in a protected cold frame or unheated basement or garage. In the bottom of a wooden box about 4 inches deep, place a layer ½ to ¾ inch deep of damp peat moss or sand, then a thin layer of seeds. Repeat layers until the box is nearly full, making sure you end with a layer of sand or peat. Cover the box with plastic and place it where the temperature will stay around 40° F. Check the box regularly to maintain the moisture level.

When planting time arrives or the seeds sprout, remove the seeds from the bag or box and gently separate them from the stratification medium. Plant the seeds out in the garden or in pots or flats to start growing indoors or in a cold frame.

Some seeds need to be stratified and then germinated and nurtured indoors before being set out in the garden. To calculate the date to begin stratification of these seeds, follow this simple procedure: Add the number of days seedlings will need to grow indoors before planting out, plus the number of days from seed sowing to germination, plus the number of days required for stratification. This will give you the total number of days needed from the beginning of stratification to the proper time for setting out plants. Convert the total number of days to the number of weeks. On a calendar find the date at which you wish to set the plants out in the garden. Count back from this date the total number of weeks you've just calculated to find the date at which you should begin stratification of your seeds. Planting times and dormancy needs for trees and shrubs are given in Part 2.

HANDLING COMPLEX DORMANCY NEEDS

Some seeds need a complicated cycle of alternating cold and warm periods in order to germinate. These seeds, which are said to undergo a double dormancy, may take 2 years to sprout in nature, but gardeners can speed up the process indoors.

Collect the seeds when they ripen in fall, clean and dry them. Mix the seeds with moist (not wet) sand, peat moss, or sphagnum moss and put them in a plastic bag. Tie the bag tightly shut and put it in a warm place where temperatures are between 65 and 85° F for 4 to 6 months. The back of a kitchen shelf or cupboard or on top of the refrigerator (making sure you cover the plastic bag to keep out light) are two possible locations. Check the bag regularly to make sure the medium is damp.

At the end of 4 to 6 months, move the bag to the refrigerator, at a temperature of about 40° F, for 3 more months. Continue to check often to make sure the medium stays damp. At the end of this time the seeds should be ready to plant.

Not many plants have such complicated dormancy needs. Some that do, all of them woody, are fringe tree (*Chionanthus* spp.), *Cotoneaster* species, hawthorn (*Crataegus* spp.), dove tree (*Davidia involucrata*), silver bell (*Halesia* spp.), witch hazel (*Hamamelis* spp.), holly (*Ilex* spp.), juniper (*Juniperus* spp.), sumac (*Rhus* spp.), yew (*Taxus* spp.), and *Viburnum* species.

Flowers That Need Stratification

Seeds of the flowers listed here need stratification for successful germination. The optimum temperature and time for stratification varies. As a general rule, seeds that require 32° F can be stratified in a freezer, and seeds that require 45° F can be stratified in a refrigerator. All of the flowers listed here are perennials, with the exception of pansies, which are usually grown as annuals.

Bleeding heart (*Dicentra spectabilis*) 6 weeks at 32° F

Columbine (*Aquilegia* spp.) 3 weeks at 45° F

Daylily (*Hemerocallis* spp.) 6 weeks at 45° F

Garden phlox (*Phlox paniculata*) 4 weeks at 45° F

Gentian (*Gentiana acaulis, G. lagodechiana*) 3 weeks at 32° F

Iris (*Iris kaempferi, I. kamaonenesis*) 6 weeks at 45° F

Lobelia (*Lobelia* spp.), perennial species only, 12 weeks at 45° F

Monkshood (*Aconitum carmichaelii*) 3 weeks at 32° F

Pansy (*Viola* × *Wittrockiana*) 1 week at 45° F

Primrose (*Primula* spp.) 4 weeks at 45° F

SCARIFICATION AND SOAKING

Some seeds have extremely hard coats that have to be scraped, scratched, or softened to allow moisture to penetrate so that growth can begin. A hard coat keeps seeds from germinating during dry weather when conditions are not conducive to good growth. Some seeds with hard coats sprout when spring rains soak into the soil and soften the coats. Other seeds (those of tomatoes, for instance) contain substances that inhibit germination until the seeds have absorbed enough water to wash away the inhibitors.

Some seeds coats are so hard that they can't even take in moisture until they are broken somehow.

Scarification involves breaking into the seed coat by nicking it with a knife or file or scraping it with sandpaper. Scarification with a knife or file is practical only for large seeds. The best way to scarify smaller seeds is to roll them in sandpaper. Seeds needing scarification include false lupine (*Thermopsis*), *Camellia japonica*, smokebush (*Cotinus*), and *Wisteria*.

Stratification Times for Common Trees and Shrubs

Here are the stratification times for seeds of some commonly grown trees and shrubs.

Apple (*Malus*) 1 to 3 months

Arborvitae (*Thuja*) 2 months

Ash (*Fraxinus*) 1 to 3 months

Barberry (*Berberis*) 1 to 3 months, if seeds are not sown immediately when ripe

Beech (*Fagus*) 3 to 5 months

Birch (*Betula*) 1 to 3 months

Cedar (*Cedrus*) 1 to 2 months

Cherry, flowering (*Prunus*) 2 to 4 months

Clematis 3 months

Currant, Gooseberry (*Ribes*) 3 months

Dogwood (*Cornus*) 3 to 4 months

False cypress (*Chamaecyparis*) 2 months

Fir (*Abies*) 2 to 3 months

Forsythia 1 to 2 months

Golden larch (*Pseudolarix*) 1 month

Hemlock (*Tsuga*) 2 to 4 months

Hickory (*Carya*) 3 to 4 months

Honeysuckle (*Lonicera*) 1 to 2 months

Hornbeam (*Carpinus*) 3 to 4 months

Lilac (*Syringa*) 1 to 3 months

Magnolia 3 to 6 months

Maple (*Acer*) 2 to 4 months

Oak (*Quercus*) 3 months, if seeds are not sown immediately when ripe

Pear (*Pyrus*) 3 months

Pine (*Pinus*) 1 to 3 months

Privet (*Ligustrum*) 3 to 4 months

Rose (*Rosa*) 4 months or more

Spruce (*Picea*) 1 to 3 months

Sweet gum (*Liquidambar*) 1 to 3 months

Sycamore (*Platanus*) 2 months, if seeds are not sown immediately when ripe

Some seeds will germinate only if the seed coat has been softened. Soaking seeds in warm water softens them, as does spring rains. Redbud (*Cercis*) and honey locust (*Gleditsia*) are two plants whose seeds appreciate soaking. Place the seeds in a bowl or other container and pour very hot water (about 190° F) over them. Make sure the volume of water is five to six times the volume of the seeds—if you use less, the water will cool off too quickly and the seed coats may not be soft enough to permit germination. Leave the seeds in the water overnight.

The next day, if the seeds have swelled, remove them from the water and plant them immediately, before they have a chance to

Seeds Needing Scarification

Seeds of these plants need to be scarified in order to germinate indoors.

Camellia	Lupine (*Lupinus* spp.)
Cotoneaster	Morning-glory (*Ipomoea* spp.)
Dogwood, flowering (*Cornus florida*)	Redbud (*Cercis*)
Golden rain tree (*Koelreuteria*)	Silk tree (*Albizia*)
Hawthorn (*Crataegus*)	Sweet pea (*Lathyrus* spp.)
Holly (*Ilex*)	*Wisteria*

dry out. If the seeds have not yet swelled, leave them in the water longer and plant them when they have expanded. For information on which seeds need scarification and which need soaking, see the plant entries in Part 2.

Sulfuric acid is used to soften seed coats in commercial production, but for safety reasons home gardeners are better off sticking with soaking in water.

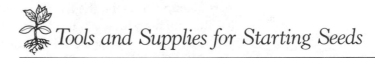 *Tools and Supplies for Starting Seeds*

If you will be starting seeds anywhere other than directly where the plants will grow in the garden, you will need something in which to grow the seedlings. You can start seeds in wooden or plastic flats, cellular plastic "six packs" and "market packs," clay or plastic pots, pots or water-expandable pellets or blocks made of compressed peat, cylinders made of rolled-up newspaper, recycled margarine and cottage cheese cups, disposable aluminum foil bread pans—practically any container that can hold soil and can have drainage holes punched or drilled into the bottom. Containers made of peat and newspaper cylinders can go into the garden with the seedlings; plants will have to be removed from the other kinds of containers.

Flats allow you to start a lot of seeds in a relatively small space, but seedlings will have to be transplanted into the garden or into individual pots when still small. Flats come in various sizes, and

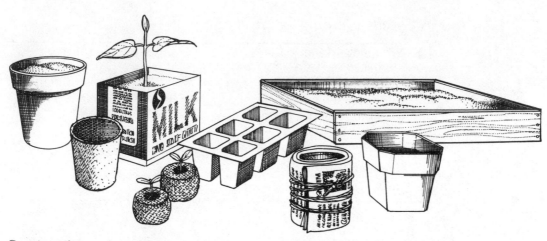

Containers that can be used for starting seeds include purchased items, such as terra-cotta or plastic pots, peat pots, peat pellets, plastic six-packs, and standard nursery flats. Recycled milk cartons or rolled-up newspapers also make handy seed-starting containers.

should be at least 2½ or 3 inches deep to allow enough space for roots. A standard size is 24 by 14 by 3 inches. Some flats are divided into compartments, each of which holds a single plant. Other flats are undivided, and seedlings are thinned by the gardener to the desired spacing.

Peat pellets and blocks that expand when they are moistened come with enough growing medium to support plants until they are a couple of inches high; other containers will need to be filled with a medium in which the seeds are planted.

Some seeds germinate best in warm soil. If you have only a flat or two of seeds, you can place them on top of your water heater or refrigerator to give them some warmth from below. If you are starting more seeds, consider purchasing electric heating cables. These cables are designed to be placed under the soil in greenhouse benches to supply even warmth for plant roots. The cables are specially made to withstand conditions underground. If you don't have a greenhouse, you could construct a large flat to serve as a propagating bed, install heating cables, and raise your seedlings under fluorescent lights in the basement. Or use heating mats, which can simply be placed on a heatproof surface with flats or pots set on top of them.

The only other tools you will need to start seeds are something to make planting holes or furrows, a device for misting or gently watering newly planted seeds and tiny seedlings, some plastic or glass to cover the flats in the beginning, and something to help you hold tiny seedlings during transplanting without damaging them.

For seeds that are neither very large nor very fine, a pencil makes reasonable planting holes. If you are planting large seeds, you can use a dibble to make the holes. You can also simply push a fingertip into the soil. Very fine seed is usually scattered over the soil surface and covered with a very thin layer of fine-textured sphagnum moss or soil—no planting holes are needed. To make small furrows to sow seeds in rows, you can use a pencil, the edge of a ruler, or a wooden tongue depressor or popsicle stick.

Newly planted seeds need evenly moist soil in order to germinate, but watering with a watering can may wash the little seeds right out of the soil. A gentler way to water is to mist the soil with a plant mister or a recycled (but clean!) pump spray bottle.

When seedlings are large enough for their first transplanting, a tongue depressor with a notch cut into one end can be a great help in holding delicate stems as you move the tiny plants to a new flat or pot.

Germination Media

Seeds are easy targets for disease pathogens, and seedlings need special care in order to grow sturdy and stocky. The advantage of starting seeds indoors is that the environment can be carefully managed, especially in terms of the growing medium. You can start seeds indoors in a sterile growing medium that is free of disease pathogens. The three most important characteristics of a good germinating medium are: (1) water retention, to provide adequate moisture for germination; (2) porosity, to allow air to circulate through the medium; and (3) sterility, to protect seeds from disease pathogens.

Seeds need moisture to germinate, so the most important quality of the medium in which a seed is planted is that it be able to hold moisture. Too much moisture, though, will encourage fungus and rot, so the medium must also have good drainage.

Soil can provide the moisture that seeds need to sprout, but many soils drain too slowly and hold too much moisture for seedlings and allow too little air to circulate. Clay soils, in which the soil particles are very small and closely packed, are generally too dense and wet to encourage good germination. Because soil by

(continued on page 28)

Growing Trees and Shrubs from Seed

Most nursery-grown trees and shrubs are propagated from cuttings, budding, and grafting. Home gardeners can also produce new plants by layering. These vegetative methods, described in Chapter 2, are the only ways to reproduce hybrid trees and shrubs. But nonhybrid varieties can be grown from seed, and in fact there are some good reasons for growing woody plants from seed, even though they grow slowly.

For one thing, seeds generally produce tougher, healthier plants than grafting. And the genetic variations of plants grown from seed sometimes result in more interesting, more vigorous, or hardier specimens that are valuable in breeding work.

The seeds of many woody plants need special pretreatments to germinate outside their natural habitat. In order to break their dormancy, they may need stratification, alternating warm and cold periods, or scarification. The type of pretreatment varies with the structure of the seed.

Winged seeds, such as those of conifers and maples, need moisture and cold stratification in order to sprout. If you want to grow these trees from seed, gather the seeds when they ripen in fall, remove those of conifers from the cones when they open, and rub off the wings if you wish (some people prefer to leave them on). Stratify the seeds over winter and plant outdoors the following spring. The exceptions in this group are maple species, such as red maple, whose seeds mature in summer. These seeds can be planted as soon as they are ripe.

Many seeds with hard coats also need to be stratified after they are separated from the fruit in which they are enclosed. Plants in this category include holly (*Ilex* spp.), *Cotoneaster* species, *Viburnum* species, and dovetree (*Davidia involucrata*). To clean the seeds, soak the ripe fruit in water for several days until the fruit starts to ferment. Then put your hand in the container of water and squeeze the fruit pulp between your fingers to separate the seeds from it. The viable seeds will sink to the bottom of the container, while the pulp and nonviable seeds float to the top. Skim off the pulp and bad seeds and drain off the water; you will be left with the good seeds.

Most of these seeds can either be sown outdoors in fall or stratified over the winter. Some of them, such as holly, viburnum, cotoneaster, and hawthorn (*Crataegus* spp.) require a double dormancy.

Fleshy seeds like those of oaks (*Quercus* spp.), chestnut, (*Castanea* spp.), and horse chestnut and buckeye (*Aesculus* spp.) are best planted as soon as possible after you collect them because they break dormancy quickly. Most of these seeds can be stored in containers in a cold place over winter if you cannot plant them in fall. Plant the stored seeds in early spring. One exception to the rule in this group is the white oak, whose seeds germinate shortly after they ripen. These acorns cannot be held over winter.

Some shrubs, such as azaleas and rhododendrons (*Rhododendron* spp.), *Hydrangea* species, St. John's wort (*Hypericum* spp.), mountain laurel (*Kalmia latifolia*), *Pieris* species, and *Spiraea* species, have very tiny seeds. You'll have to watch the ripening seed capsules closely in early fall, because if the capsules open before you can collect them it will be nearly impossible to find the dropped seeds. The best approach is to collect the seed capsules as soon as they turn brown and keep them indoors in labeled paper bags. Store the bags in a warm dry place until the capsules open.

You can plant the seeds indoors under lights in fall, or keep them until spring and plant them outdoors. If you start the seeds indoors, plant them on top of a fine-textured, acidic growing medium. One good mix is two parts of sieved peat moss and one part perlite, with a ½-inch layer of sieved sphagnum moss on top. The medium should be moist when you plant. Scatter the seeds on top of the sphagnum, mist them lightly, and cover the container with a sheet of plastic. When the first seedlings come up, remove the plastic and give the plants plenty of air and light.

itself seldom makes a good germination medium (it often lacks sufficient porosity, and soilborne disease pathogens can be a problem, especially indoors), most gardeners find that it works better to mix the soil with other materials, or to germinate seeds in a medium that contains no soil at all. Garden soil used as part of a seed starting mixture should always be pasteurized.

Soilless mixes are advantageous because they are light in weight, do not compact, hold moisture while still draining well, and are sterile. A light, loose growing medium allows roots to penetrate readily, and also makes thinning and transplanting easy. More importantly, using a sterile medium reduces the chance that *damping-off* (a fungus disease that often attacks young seedlings) or other disease problems will attack delicate seedlings. Soilless mixes also contain no weed seeds that would compete with your seedlings for moisture and nutrients. The drawback to soilless mixes is that they contain no minerals to nourish the young seedlings after the seeds sprout. All nutrients must be supplied through fertilizers, either organic or synthetic.

COMPONENTS FOR GERMINATION MIXES

You can purchase commercial seed-starting mixes if you are so inclined. But most commercial mixes contain chemical fertilizers, and it is easy to concoct your own medium—and less expensive as well. A number of different materials can be combined with one another and with soil in various formulas for germination mixes.

Peat moss, the remains of plants that decomposed centuries ago, is a component of many seed-starting mixes. Peat moss is slightly acidic and has little or no nutritive value, although it is an excellent source of organic matter. Peat can absorb and hold a great deal of water after it is moist, but it actually sheds water when it is dry. Before adding peat moss to any planting medium, make sure it is thoroughly moistened but not soggy. The best way to dampen peat moss is to knead water into it with your hands.

Sand is another useful material for germination media. Be sure you use builder's sand (also called sharp sand) instead of sand from a beach and be sure to pasteurize it first. Beach sand contains salts that could harm tender seedlings. Sand drains well and provides sturdy support for roots and shoots. When mixed with soil it adds air space, improves drainage, and generally adds body to the mix. On the other hand, sand does not absorb or hold water well, and it offers no nutrients for plants.

Vermiculite is expanded mica, sterile and very light in weight. It is porous, allowing plenty of air to circulate, and it absorbs water while still draining well. Like sand, it has no nutritional value. Vermiculite can be used by itself, but it is more often mixed with other materials in germination media.

Perlite, another mineral product, is expanded bits of volcanic rock. Like vermiculite it is sterile and drains well while still holding water. It contains no nutrients, but combines well with peat moss in seed-starting mixes.

Potting soil or *garden soil* is used in some seed-starting mixes, but it is more often included in growing media for plants that are already growing and need nutrition more than sterility. Soil by itself is too heavy and dense to make a good seed-starting medium, but it can be mixed with other materials to achieve an airy, porous planting medium. If you include garden soil in a planting mix for seeds, you should first pasteurize it to eliminate pathogens and disease organisms in the soil that could rapidly multiply and attack seedlings in a warm indoor environment.

To pasteurize soil, put it into a disposable turkey roasting bag and bake it in a low (200° F) oven for 30 minutes. Hot soil does not smell particularly pleasant, but pasteurization really is necessary if you will be using garden soil for plants grown indoors. Soil used in seed-starting mixes should be fine-textured, with no lumps or stones.

A final material that comes in handy for starting seeds is finely milled *sphagnum moss*. Several kinds of moss are known as sphagnum. All of them grow in bogs, and they are frequently quite acidic. Sphagnum moss has fungicidal properties that apparently help keep damping-off pathogens at bay. In fact, some seeds germinate best in a layer of finely shredded sphagnum moss. In any case, to help protect tiny seedlings, many growers like to put a thin layer of sphagnum moss on top of whatever germination medium they use.

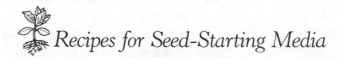 *Recipes for Seed-Starting Media*

There are several classic formulas for seed-starting mixes that are widely used. You may wish to experiment until you settle on the mix that you like best, or you might want to create your own.

A medium developed at Cornell University contains equal parts peat moss and perlite or vermiculite. A mix used at the University of California is half peat and half sand. Both these mixes sometimes have fertilizer added to them, but seeds do not need fertilizer to germinate. Organic gardeners will do better to mist with dilute solutions of seaweed or fish emulsion as soon as the little plants show their first true leaves, when the nutrients will be useful to them. One cubic foot of either of these mixes will fill two standard flats (each 22 by 12 by 2½ inches) with some to spare.

If you want to start your seeds in soil, try a mix of equal parts pasteurized soil, sand, and peat moss. If you like the texture of commercial planting mixes but want to avoid the fertilizers while still providing nutrients for seedlings, you can try a mix of equal parts shredded sphagnum, peat, and pasteurized soil. Press the mixture through a sieve to get a fine texture.

Excellent drainage is critical for sprouting seeds and young seedlings. Lingering water fills up air spaces between soil particles; less oxygen is available to plant roots, and damping-off is more likely to strike. To improve drainage, you can put a layer of coarse sphagnum moss on the bottom of the flat before adding the planting mix. If you are planting seeds in pots, you can use gravel or pebbles from a freshwater stream instead of the sphagnum.

If you are using a soilless mix, fill flats or pots to within ½ inch of the top with the planting mix. If the planting mix contains soil, fill the container to within 1 inch of the top, then add a ½-inch layer of sterile material—vermiculite, perlite, or sphagnum. That allows seeds to germinate in the sterile layer and send their roots down into a source of nourishment. The ½-inch space at the top of the container allows for easy watering.

 *Planting Seeds*

You can plant seeds directly in the garden where the plants are to grow, in a *cold frame* (a boxlike structure with a removable glass top, which affords protection for plants from cold weather), in an outdoor nursery bed for later transplanting to the garden, or indoors under natural or electric light. No matter where you start your seeds, be sure to give them a finely textured growing medium and careful attention as they germinate and begin to grow.

PLANTING OUTDOORS

Many vegetables and most hardy annuals can be seeded directly into garden beds or rows. Plants that do not transplant well (nasturtiums, morning-glories, wildflowers, beans, peas, and root crops are examples) grow best when sown where they are to grow. Biennials, perennials, shrubs, and trees are often started in a cold frame or outdoor nursery bed. Biennials and perennials that cannot be made to bloom from seed in a single season are moved to the garden in their second year, when they will flower; many shrubs and trees grow slowly and will not be large enough for a spot in the garden for several seasons.

A nursery bed in a corner of the garden or a cold frame is a good idea for slow-growing or delicate plants, because the little seedlings will not have to compete for root space, moisture, and nutrients with bigger, sturdier plants in the main garden. Because the area is confined, it will also be easier to keep it clear of weeds, whose vigorous growth can quickly overwhelm young seedlings.

In addition to fine soil free of stones, a nursery bed will benefit from the addition of screened compost or fine peat moss. If your soil is heavy and full of clay, work in a 1-inch layer of sand, too. Make sure the nursery bed is big enough to allow you to transplant seedlings and keep them growing until they are big enough to go into the main garden.

Direct-seeding is not a good idea for seeds that are hard to germinate, or for seeds that must be planted when outdoor conditions are not hospitable. For example, this is true in the case of *tender annuals* (annuals that are harmed or killed by freezing temperatures) or vegetables that need a long, warm growing season. These must be started by northern gardeners while outdoor temperatures are still cold if they are to bloom or produce a crop before autumn brings the return of cold weather. Seeds that have complex dormancy needs are also more difficult to manage outdoors; it is easier to provide alternating periods of warmth and cold indoors, as described under Pretreatments for Seeds on page 18.

For seeds sown outdoors, whether in the garden, cold frame, or nursery bed, the depth of planting is important. Vegetable and flower seeds can be sown in rows or broadcast in beds. For fine seeds such as those of lettuce or pansies, a fine soil is important to ensure that the seeds make good contact with the soil.

PREPARING THE OUTDOOR SEED BED

Before planting, dig the soil so it is loose and friable (crumbly) to a depth of at least 6 inches in a nursery bed or cold frame, and a foot or more deep in the main garden. Break up any large lumps and remove all but the smallest stones. Rake the soil well to create a smooth, finely textured bed. Any compost, manure, or rock powders should have been incorporated several weeks or months prior to planting (in autumn for spring planting; in summer for autumn planting) so the materials have a chance to begin breaking down and releasing their nutrients before seeds are planted.

Never plant in wet soil—working wet soil may cause it to compact, making growth difficult for delicate new roots and shoots. Also, if you put too much pressure on wet soil during planting, it can form a hard surface crust when it dries and seedlings will not be able to break through.

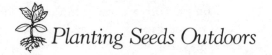 *Planting Seeds Outdoors*

The best way to sow fine seeds is to mix the packet of seeds with 1 cup of fine sand or coffee grounds to make them easier to handle. Sprinkle the mixture evenly over the prepared garden bed. Then sprinkle a very thin layer of fine soil on top of the seeds and mist the bed lightly to settle the seeds into the soil. It can be tricky to keep fine seeds from drying out since they're so close to the soil surface. Frequent sprinkling—perhaps even once a day—may be necessary. Water fine seeds very carefully—a sprinkling can with a rose attachment or a Haws-type watering can is a helpful tool. Check the soil every day to make sure it is moist.

To plant larger seeds, the easiest method is to make a furrow. Use the edge of a hoe blade for the largest seeds—corn, beans,

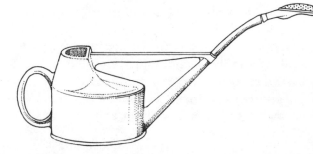

A Haws-type watering can provides a gentle flow of water that minimizes disturbance to seeds and delicate seedlings.

peas, pumpkins, squash—and use the handle of the hoe to make smaller rows. Plant large seeds two to three times as deep as their diameter. In heavy clay soils that hold lots of moisture, plant not quite to the recommended depth; in light, sandy soils that dry out quickly, plant slightly deeper than the recommended depth.

Planting depths for seeds can be found in Part 2 of this book and on the backs of commercial seed packets.

Gently tap the seeds out of their packet one at a time as you move along the row. Try to get the seeds evenly distributed and well spaced so you will have less thinning to do later. Cover the seeds with soil and firm the surface gently by patting with your hand or pressing lightly with the back of a shovel.

If you prefer to broadcast the seeds instead of planting in rows, rake some soil off the bed, scatter the seeds evenly over the bed, then cover them with the reserved soil to the correct depth.

Large seeds of corn and vegetables in the Cucurbita Family (cucumbers, melons, squash, and pumpkins) can also be planted in hills. Make mounds about 6 inches high and 3 to 4 feet apart. Plant five to seven seeds about 3 inches apart in the top of each mound. After the seedlings are up, thin to the strongest three or four plants in each hill. If you leave all the plants, you will encourage root competition that will weaken them and reduce your harvest.

Whether you are planting in rows, hills, or beds, remember to label the seeded areas immediately so you remember what's planted where—it's amazingly easy to forget where you put things, even in a small garden.

Many directly planted seeds will germinate in a few days, although some take as long as 2 to 3 weeks. Some gardeners like to plant slow-to-sprout seeds with others that germinate quickly; the fast plants will come up quickly and clearly mark the row so you won't disturb the slow-moving seeds as you go about your gardening chores.

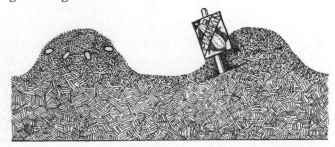

Plant corn and members of the squash family in hills. Each mound can hold five to seven seeds spaced approximately 3 inches apart.

Fluid Seed-Sowing Systems

A relatively new process for sowing seeds enables gardeners to presprout the seeds before planting and get earlier flowers or vegetables. Developed in England and introduced to the United States market by Thompson and Morgan in 1979, the system involves mixing the germinated seeds into a clear gel. All the necessary supplies are sold along with the gel.

Place flower or vegetable seeds in a shallow dish, moisten them, and put them in a warm place. Check daily to make sure they don't dry out and to look for signs of germination.

When the seeds sprout, mix them with the gel, put the mixture into an applicator, and squeeze the mixture into the garden row or container. If you place the seeds at the correct spacing distance you won't need to thin them later. Cover the seeds with soil to the correct depth. The gel will soak into the soil. You can also use fluid seed-sowing systems indoors, but their greatest benefits seem to be in outdoor gardens.

Presprouting seeds can give a head start to hardy annuals and such vegetables as peas and lettuce, which are seeded outdoors in early spring when harsh weather conditions may slow germination. The method is also said to eliminate transplant shock because the seedlings are not indoors long enough to become accustomed to the warm environment.

You can also sow seeds in gel without presprouting them. This is a handy method for sowing fine seeds that are difficult to handle, and is actually a way to make your own equivalent of a seed tape. You can make a homemade gel from unflavored gelatin. Combine a packet of gelatin with 2 cups of warm water and stir until the gelatin is completely dissolved. Pour the gelatin into a squeezable plastic bottle (ketchup or mustard dispensers work well). Allow the mixture to sit until the gelatin begins to set. Mix in the seeds and squeeze the soft-set gelatin/seed mixture along a prepared garden row or in rows in a prepared flat.

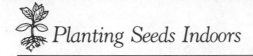

Planting Seeds Indoors

Starting seeds indoors offers more control over their environment as well as a greater choice of plants for the gardener. For gardeners in northern climates, an early start indoors makes it possible to grow many more tender and long-season flowers and vegetables than would be possible within the limitations imposed by the outdoor growing season. Gardeners in warm climates can start seeds for autumn and winter flowers and vegetables indoors instead of subjecting them to the fierce sun and intense heat of summer weather. Generally speaking, tender annuals such as impatiens and petunias, warm-season vegetables like tomatoes, eggplant, and celery, and perennial flowers are the plants most often started indoors. Shrubs and some trees can also be started indoors, as can vegetables in the cabbage family and others that take well to transplanting.

To sow seeds indoors, prepare containers or flats full of a planting mix as described earlier. Be sure the mix is moist, but not sopping wet, at planting time. To sow small seeds like those of begonias or coleus, mix the seeds with fine sand for easier handling, as described under Planting Seeds Outdoors on page 32. Scatter the seeds evenly over the surface of the planting mix. Rub some dried sphagnum moss through a window screen or sieve and

Mixing fine seeds with sand makes them easier to sow. Mist them gently after planting to moisten the seeds without dislodging them.

sift a layer of it about ⅛ inch deep on top of the seeds. Another way to plant fine seeds, if you have a great amount of time and patience, is to dump out the seeds on a piece of paper, pick them up individually with a tweezers, and place two seeds in each compartment of a prepared, divided flat. To water planted flats, either mist with water to settle the seeds into the medium or water from the bottom. To bottom-water, set the flat in a pan of water until the sphagnum is moist to the touch. Remove the container from the water and let any excess water drain off. Then, to hold in moisture, enclose the flat in clear plastic or cover it with a piece of glass. Do not place the closed flat in a sunny window or it will get too hot inside the cover.

To sow slightly larger seeds, such as those of tomatoes, gently firm the surface of the planting mix with a piece of wood or your hands. Broadcast the seeds on top, or make rows with a pencil or the edge of a ruler. Cover the seeds to the proper depth with more of the planting mix or with sifted sphagnum moss or sand. Water from below.

You can scatter large seeds over the soil surface or plant them in rows, ¼ to ⅜ inch deep.

In all cases try not to sow too thickly. Crowded plants are more prone to damping-off, and their roots are harder to separate at transplanting time.

If you want to give an early start to plants that do not transplant well, such as nasturtiums, beans, or squash, try planting three or four seeds in a 4- or 5-inch plastic pot. When it's time to put the plants in the garden, unpot them carefully, disturbing the root ball as little as possible, and plant them all as a single unit.

Label all containers with the contents and date of planting as soon as the seeds are sown. Whether the seeds are planted indoors or outdoors, it is important that the planting mix be kept constantly moist until they germinate. Test the soil daily with a fingertip to make sure it is moist. Outdoors, plunge your finger an inch or two into the soil. If the soil is dry, water carefully so the seeds are not dislodged. Indoors, test the surface of the soil; when it feels dry, water the containers from the bottom.

Seeds that are very sensitive to disturbance can be planted in double pots so they need never be watered directly. Plant the seeds in a moist medium in an unglazed clay pot, then place that pot inside a larger pot that has been lined with damp sphagnum moss. Keep the sphagnum moss constantly moist. The inner pot will

Planting seeds in double clay pots with moist sphagnum moss between them ensures even, constant moisture for seeds that should not be disturbed after planting.

absorb moisture through its walls, and the planting mix should remain moist at all times.

Seeds being germinated indoors generally do fine at normal room temperature—temperatures between 65 and 80° F are good for most seeds. Special temperature needs for particular seeds are noted in Part 2 of this book.

LIGHT

Most seeds germinate in the dark, covered with soil. But tiny seeds (such as those of begonias, lettuce, and coleus) sometimes need light to germinate, because they don't contain enough nutrients to let the plants grow very far to reach light. These seeds are not covered with soil at all. Instead, they are scattered over the soil surface and either pressed in very lightly or misted to bring them in contact with the soil. To make sure these seeds get plenty of light, you can place their containers about 3 inches below fluorescent lights.

Containers of seeds that do not need light to germinate, or that prefer darkness (such as parsley seeds), can be placed on top of fluorescent fixtures, where they will receive bottom heat from the ballasts in the fixtures. You can also place the containers in a closet or cover the tops with newspaper. Don't forget to check periodically for signs of germination.

If you want to hasten the germination process, you can try putting seed containers 6 inches under fluorescent lights and leaving the lights on 24 hours a day until shoots break through the soil.

Commercial seed packets usually note the planting depth for the seeds, but it helps to be aware of whether the seeds you are planting need light to germinate. The light needs of seedlings are discussed below.

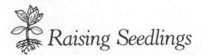

Raising Seedlings

Whether you start them indoors or outdoors, seedlings need special care to help them develop into sturdy, healthy plants. You will need to pay close attention to the amount of light, warmth, air, moisture, humidity, and fertilizer the young plants receive in order to get them off to a good start.

Whether seeds germinate in light or darkness, as soon as the shoots break through the soil surface, the plants need plenty of bright light to grow sturdy and stocky. Seedlings growing outdoors will get that light from the sun. Indoor seedlings can thrive either in the natural light coming through a window or under electric light provided by fluorescent or incandescent fixtures.

It is important that seedlings receive plenty of light without a lot of extra heat. Seedlings started outdoors in a cold frame would cook on clear, sunny days when temperatures rise inside the frame. If you are growing seedlings in a cold frame, be sure to open the lid partway on very sunny days in late winter and early spring, to allow the hot air to escape. You can also buy thermostatically controlled venting systems that automatically open the cold frame when temperatures exceed the thermostat setting. Later in spring, when the weather is warmer, you will need to remove the lid entirely. And if you start seeds outdoors in summer, you may need to provide shade for newly emerged seedlings for their first few days above ground, until they become used to the intense sunlight and warm air.

Indoors, a bright east-facing windowsill makes a good place to start small numbers of seeds. Most windowsills aren't wide enough to hold a flat, but they can accommodate pots and other small containers. A southern windowsill receives more light than an eastern sill, but it also gets hotter—perhaps uncomfortably warm for seedlings. Gardeners living in northern areas may do best to grow their seedlings in southern windows; gardeners in southern regions would do better to use eastern windows. To increase the amount of light available to plants on a windowsill you can line the sill and nearby wall surface with aluminum foil to reflect light back onto the plants. White walls and windowsills also reflect light.

Seedlings growing on windowsills receive most of their light from the direction of the window and tend to grow toward the light. To keep plants growing straight, the containers need to be given a quarter-turn each day so all parts of the plants get plenty of light.

Electric lights are another excellent source of illumination for indoor seedlings, and because plants are placed directly under them, the light strikes the plants more evenly than light from a window. Electric lights also allow you more flexibility in terms of where you grow your seedlings; you can raise the plants in a basement or seldom-used room where they won't be in your way.

Fluorescent lamps are generally better for seedlings than incandescent bulbs or plant spotlights because they give off less heat. Seedlings need to be very close to the lamps, and the heat from incandescent bulbs can damage them.

Plants respond best to light at opposite ends of the spectrum. Blue light encourages bushiness and regulates plants' respiratory functions. Red light is important for growth and flowering. To supply the broadest spectrum of light with fluorescent lamps, use either daylight tubes or a combination of cool white and warm white (in a two-tube fixture, use one cool white and one warm white tube). You can also use "grow light" tubes, which have a greater concentration of light in the red and blue wavelengths. These lights give off a pinkish-purplish glow and distort the color of leaves and flowers to the viewer's eye. But the lights work well, and since you are not growing seedlings for display, the color distortion is insignificant. These tubes are, however, more expensive than conventional fluorescent tubes.

When seeds have germinated, place the seedlings so the tops of the plants are about 4 inches below the lights and leave the lights on for 12 to 16 hours a day. Connecting the lights to a timer will turn them on and off automatically for you. As the plants grow, you will need to raise the lights accordingly. One way to do this is to suspend the fixtures on pulleys or chains that can be shortened a

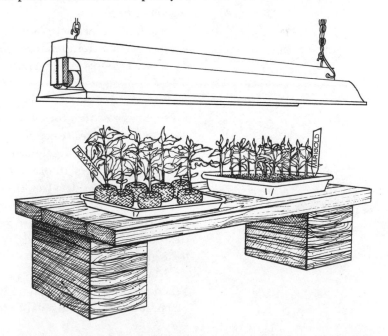

When starting seedlings indoors under lights, suspend the fixtures on chains or elevate the plants on stacks of books or wood blocks so that you can adjust the height of the lamps as the plants begin to grow taller.

link at a time. Or you can start out with the seedling containers elevated on books or blocks of wood that can be removed one at a time as the plants grow taller. As plants grow, they can be moved farther from the lights, with the tops of the plants 6 to 10 inches below the lights.

No matter what type of light you use, check your seedlings often to make sure they are getting enough of it. Plants receiving insufficient light develop stems that are spindly and elongated, and the few leaves they have are usually small and stunted.

TEMPERATURE

The best temperature for seedling growth is determined by their hardiness as mature plants. Seedlings of plants that grow best in cool weather—hardy annuals such as larkspur and calendula and cool-season vegetables like cabbage and broccoli, for example—will develop best in cool temperatures. These plants are good candidates for starting outdoors in a cold frame. It's a good idea to open the lid of the cold frame on warm, sunny days to give these seedlings plenty of fresh air, which will help them develop into stocky, compact plants. If you start seeds of cool-weather plants indoors, try to find a cool spot for them, where the temperature is between 50 and 65° F. If these seedlings grow where the temperature is too warm, they may be weak and spindly, with soft, succulent stems.

Seedlings of tender plants like wax begonias and eggplant can tolerate warmer temperatures. Indoor room temperatures of 60 to 75° F are fine for these seedlings.

AIR

Fresh air is essential for all seedlings, whether they prefer cool or warm temperatures. Keep the plants out of drafts, but make sure the air can circulate freely around and among them. Still, damp air encourages the growth of the fungi that cause damping-off and may also cause mildew (see Problems with Seedlings on page 50). Good air circulation promotes efficient transpiration of moisture from leaves, allowing them to readily release excess water vapor that builds up inside the cells as the plants manufacture food to fuel their growth.

Make sure your seedlings have enough space between them. When plants grow large enough so the leaves of neighboring plants touch, it is time to transplant and give the plants more room.

Indoors, if the air in the room where you are growing seedlings has little movement, you can use a small fan to keep it circulating. Do not aim the fan directly at the plants, but place it where it will stir the air in their vicinity. Outdoors, vent the cold frame on sunny days by opening the lid slightly to let in fresh air.

WATER AND HUMIDITY

Seedlings need regular, thorough watering, but they must not be allowed to stand in continuously wet soil. Soggy soil will cause the delicate roots to rot. The key to success is to water thoroughly but let the soil dry out a bit between waterings. Watch your plants for cues.

Seedlings that are getting too much water respond by showing wilting and yellowing of their leaves. Eventually the yellow leaves will drop off. Sometimes the leaf tips will become brittle. In extreme cases, the base of the stem and the lower leaves may begin to rot.

Seedlings that are too dry will droop and wilt. Unless the wilting is severe, you can revive dry seedlings by moving the plants out of direct sun and misting them lightly. Don't wait until your plants wilt before you water them; this kind of stress slows growth and results in weaker plants.

You can water seedlings either from the bottom or top. To bottom-water, set the pots or flats in the sink or a large container in a couple of inches of room-temperature water. Cold water will shock the plants, and hot water can damage them. When the soil surface feels moist, remove the containers from the water, allow any excess water to drain off, and return the plants to their place on the windowsill or in the garden. Capillary matting systems (in which plant containers rest on mats that draw water from a reservoir) provide even, automatic bottom-watering. They are available in some catalogs, sometimes as part of seed-starting kits. To water seedlings from the top, use a watering can and pour gently so you do not dislodge the little plants. Give enough water so that excess drains out of the drainage holes in the bottom of the containers. Pour off any water still standing in the drainage trays after 15 minutes.

Many gardeners worry that chlorine in their tap water may harm seedlings. In most cases the chlorine will not adversely affect plants, but it is easy enough to remove. Letting tap water stand in an open container for 24 hours before you use it will give the chlorine a chance to escape into the air—and it will bring the water to room temperature.

Although chlorine is generally not a problem, fluorine and ion-exchange water softeners can cause trouble for little seedlings. Ion-exchange water softeners substitute molecules of sodium for the calcium that is naturally present in hard water. Plants use calcium in building their cell walls; when they try to use the sodium instead, growth is hindered. You may find that you cannot use your tap water for seedlings if it contains fluorine or softeners. In simpler times gardeners could collect rainwater to give their indoor plants. But if you live in an area with polluted air or acid rain problems, you would probably be better off buying spring water for your seedlings.

HUMIDITY CHAMBERS FOR STARTING SEEDS

If the air inside your house is very dry and you want to increase the humidity around seedlings without the bother of misting them, as well as increase the length of time between waterings, you can enclose flats and pots in clear plastic sheets. Place the plastic over a framework of wire hoops to keep it from coming in contact with plant leaves. Make the hoops square instead of rounded so the top of the plastic lies flat. Then condensation that collects will drip down onto the plants and soil instead of running down the sides of the plastic into the edges of the flat. Place the plastic over the flat after you have planted the seeds in the moistened medium. Tuck the edges of the plastic under the flat. You may not have to water again for 2 or more weeks.

A simple humidity chamber, like the one shown here, increases the length of time seedlings can go between waterings, making them less trouble to care for.

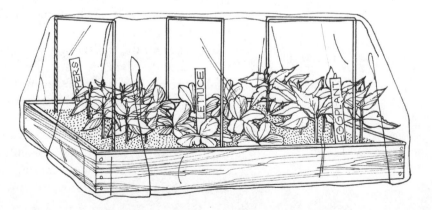

Instead of rigging up your own humidity chamber you might decide to invest in one of the various miniature greenhouses and seed-starting kits that are available commercially. They consist of a box or tray to hold soil or pots, which is covered with a domed or peaked lid of clear plastic. Some of the units provide bottom heat as well.

All these devices can be used for rooting cuttings as well as for starting seeds. While they do increase humidity and decrease watering frequency, it can be tricky to balance humidity and light—the increased humidity levels require a corresponding increase in light levels for good growth. In addition, a combination of high humidity and lots of light may cause a bloom of green algae to appear on the soil surface—an indication that better air circulation is needed. The algae will not harm seedlings, but the lack of sufficient air will cause problems. You really should remove the cover periodically to allow air to circulate around the plants, which will of course let the moisture escape.

FERTILIZERS

When seedlings produce their first true leaves, the nutrient stores in the seed have been exhausted and they must get their nourishment from the soil. If your seedlings are growing in a soilless medium you will have to feed them yourself. A solution of fish emulsion or seaweed concentrate, diluted to half the recommended strength, makes a good fertilizer for seedlings. Although both these products are organic, they are manufactured under conditions that ensure that they contain no disease-causing organisms. You can also use dilute manure tea or compost tea, but bear in mind that these materials are not sterile and could harbor damping-off fungi or other pathogens.

If your seedlings are growing in a soilless medium, fertilize them once a week. If the growing medium contains soil, you can feed the seedlings every other week.

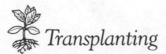 *Transplanting*

Seedlings grown in flats may need to be transplanted once or twice into bigger containers before it's time to put them out in the garden. The techniques of transplanting are the same whether the plants are indoors or outdoors. Plants going into the garden, however, must be *hardened-off* (gradually accustomed to outdoor conditions) prior to transplanting and will be placed at the spacing distance they will need as mature plants.

The first transplanting can take place when the plants have produced one or two sets of true leaves. Transfer the plants to new flats, spacing them 2 inches apart, or move them into individual peat pots or other containers. At this stage seedlings need to have soil included in their growing medium; one good mix is equal parts of soil, sand, and peat moss.

It is essential to handle small seedlings with great care, for their roots and stems are very fragile. Use a teaspoon to lift small batches of seedlings from the flat or pot and set them on a countertop or other clean work surface. Carefully separate the plants, disturbing the roots as little as possible. Try to leave as much of the original growing medium as you can around the roots of each plant. To lift a single seedling from the flat, carefully slip the end of a wooden plant label or popsicle stick under its roots, while gently holding the leaves between the thumb and forefinger of your other hand. Do not pick up the plant by its stem—you could easily snap the stem or injure the growing point. If you damage one of the leaves, the plant will still be able to continue growing. In the new container, place each plant into a hole that is large enough to hold all the roots and press the soil gently around the stem.

When transplanting young seedlings, lift them carefully by their leaves and support the roots from below with a plant label or Popsicle stick.

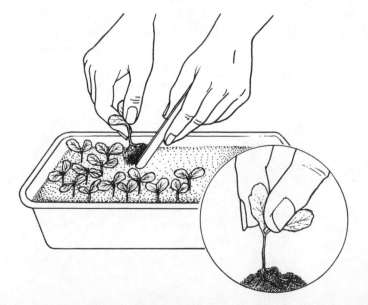

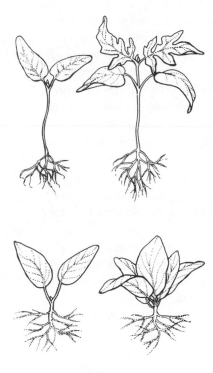

Seedlings grow in two different forms: Either the leaves cluster in a rosette around a central growing point at the soil level (lettuce and petunias have this habit), or the plant develops an upright, branched stem, with the growing point at the top (tomatoes are a good example of this form). Plant rosette-forming seedlings so the soil level is at the same place on the stem that it was in the original container; otherwise you may bury the growing point. Seedlings with upright stems can be buried to the base of the first leaves, and additional roots will grow from the buried stem. Water the plants to help them settle into the soil and ensure good contact between soil and roots.

When the plants' leaves touch one another, which may happen in just a couple of weeks, the seedlings should be transplanted again—into individual containers or, if weather permits, out to the garden. At this stage the seedlings will have developed more extensive root systems. Undivided flats of seedlings will need to be "blocked" a few days before transplanting to separate the roots. With a sharp knife cut down through the soil in lengthwise and crosswise rows, the same way you would cut a pan of brownies, so that each plant is in the center of a square of soil. The severed roots will heal in a few days, and each plant can then be lifted from the flat in its own block of soil.

After transplanting, give the plants bright light but no direct sun for a few days. If you are transplanting out to the garden, cover the row or bed with a shading cover. You can purchase covers of spun polyester from seed companies and garden supply firms, or you can make your own from fine-mesh nylon netting or a sheer,

Transplant seedlings with upright stems (top) by burying the stem to the base of the bottom leaves. Additional roots will form along the buried portion of the stem. Transplant seedlings with a rosette form (bottom) to the same depth they were growing previously.

Seedlings in undivided flats transplant better if they are blocked a few days before transplanting. Cut through the soil lengthwise and crosswise with a sharp knife to give each seedling its own block of soil.

translucent fabric. If necessary, elevate the cover on hoops of bent wire or short stakes to keep it from weighing down the tender plants. Peg down the corners to keep the cover from blowing off. Alternatively, cover the plants with cones of translucent paper.

If you are growing newly transplanted seedlings indoors on a windowsill, pull them back from the window or put sheer curtains between the plants and the glass to keep the sun off them. Plants growing under fluorescent lights should be placed about 6 inches below the lamps.

Give indoor seedlings temperatures between 60 and 65° F. For both indoor and outdoor plants, keep the soil moist, but do not overwater. Indoors, you may want to mist the plants once a day if the air in your home is very dry.

After a few days, when the seedlings start to grow again, remove the shading material. Give the plants plenty of sunshine and maintain good air circulation. Plants growing indoors can be fed once a week with a liquid organic fertilizer diluted to one-quarter or one-half strength until it is time to move them out to the garden.

Transplanting Preferences of Vegetables

These vegetables do not transplant well and should be direct-seeded.

Beans	Okra
Corn	Peas

The following vegetables transplant reasonably well as long as their roots are not disturbed. Plant in peat pots when starting indoors.

Beets	Pumpkins	Swiss chard
Carrots	Spinach	Turnips
Cucumbers	Summer squash	Winter squash

The following vegetables transplant easily.

Asparagus (when dormant)	Cauliflower	Kohlrabi
	Celery	Lettuce
Broccoli	Collards	Onions
Brussels sprouts	Eggplant	Peppers
Cabbage	Kale	Tomatoes

Transplanting Preferences of Annuals

The following annuals are difficult to transplant and should be direct-seeded or started in peat pots.

Baby's breath (*Gypsophila*)

Bachelor's buttons (*Centaurea*)

Butterfly flower (*Schizanthus*)

China aster (*Callistephus*)

Larkspur (*Consolida*)

Love-in-a-mist (*Nigella*)

Mignonette (*Reseda*)

Nasturtium (*Tropaeolum*)

Rose moss (*Portulaca*)

Shirley poppy (*Rhoeas*)

Stock (*Matthiola*)

Sweet pea (*Lathyrus*)

Zinnia, tall varieties

These annuals transplant well and can be started indoors.

Ageratum

Begonia

Calendula

Cosmos

Four o'clock (*Mirabilis*)

Geranium (*Pelargonium*)

Impatiens

Lobelia

Marigold (*Tagetes*)

Nicotiana

Petunia

Phlox

Salvia

Snapdragon (*Antirrhinum*)

Spider flower (*Cleome*)

Sweet alyssum (*Lobularia*)

Verbena

This group of annuals may self-sow.

Bachelor's buttons (*Centaurea*)

Calendula

Candytuft (*Iberis*)

Cosmos

Four o'clock (*Mirabilis*)

Larkspur (*Consolida*)

Mealycup sage (*Salvia farinacea*)

Morning-glory (*Ipomoea*)

Snapdragon (*Antirrhinum*)

Spider flower (*Cleome*)

Sweet alyssum (*Lobularia*)

SPECIAL TIPS FOR TRANSPLANTING OUT

As the time approaches for moving seedlings out to the garden, be sure the soil is properly prepared. Soil preparation for seedlings is the same as that for seeds: they need a light, loose, crumbly soil that is finely textured and well supplied with nutrients. As always, avoid working garden soil that is wet, or you run the risk of compacting it.

Seedlings started indoors will suffer serious shock if you transplant them to the garden without allowing them to gradually adjust to the harsher outdoor environment. Seedlings that suffer transplant shock will at best be set back in their growth; at worst, they may be killed. The key to maintaining strong, healthy seedlings is to give them a period of transition between indoors and outdoors that is known as hardening-off.

To harden-off seedlings, move them in their containers to a shady spot outdoors. Leave them outside for just a couple of hours the first day and gradually increase the length of time over a period of a week to 10 days. Bring the plants back indoors at night until the last night, when you can leave them outdoors overnight. You can also harden-off seedlings in a cold frame, opening the cover for a longer time each day. Put the plants in a sheltered spot on cold, rainy days—on a covered porch, for instance, or under the branches of evergreen shrubs, or next to the house below an overhanging roof. If you are using a cold frame, leave the cover closed during bad weather.

During the hardening-off period, don't forget to keep watering the plants as they need it.

When the hardening-off period is over, take some time to assess weather conditions before transplanting the seedlings. If a late cold spell has brought harsher than normal weather, wait another week or two before you move the plants permanently to the garden. Phenological indicators are a better guide to the weather than are calendar dates. For example, New England gardeners know that after lilacs are in full bloom, a damaging frost is not likely to occur.

About a week before you expect to transplant, feed the seedlings with fish emulsion or seaweed concentrate diluted to half the recommended strength to help them fend off transplant shock.

Late in the afternoon on the day before you plan to transplant, water the seedlings and the garden area that will receive them. An overcast day is best for transplanting. If you are transplanting when daytime temperatures are already quite warm, avoid planting at midday and instead do the work in the morning or late afternoon.

Have the planting holes ready before you remove the seedlings from their pots. Space the holes at the distance the plants will need when they reach their mature size. Spacing distances for individual plants can be found in Part 2. The hole should be big enough to accommodate the plant's root ball and deep enough to keep the plant growing at the same depth it was growing in the container. If the seedlings are elongated and spindly, it would be better to plant them deeper than they were before, so the lanky stems don't blow over in the wind.

Lift plants carefully from their containers as described on page 44, keeping as much soil intact around the roots as you can. If the plants are in peat pots, tear the sides before planting to make sure the roots can easily escape their confines. Make sure the tops of peat pots are completely buried so they don't act as wicks and draw the moisture from the walls of the pots.

Watch the plants for the first several days to make sure they are getting the right amount of light and moisture. Healthy seedlings send out new roots quickly and will establish themselves in well-prepared garden soil in a few days.

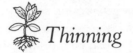

Thinning

Seedlings that were sown in undivided flats or directly in the garden will probably need thinning, unless you have an extremely steady hand and great patience when sowing seeds. Many of us are tempted not to thin seedlings—it seems somehow cruel to uproot the tiny plants, it is difficult to move them, and often there is no extra garden space available in which to plant them. But crowded plants do not grow well; they stay smaller and produce fewer flowers or less of a crop because they are competing with each other for space, moisture, and nutrients. It is especially important to give plants ample space if you live where summer weather is hot and humid or damp and foggy. Plants are prone to mildew and fungus diseases in such climates. For the good of your plants, you must be hardhearted and thin them.

Thin the seedlings early—as soon as they are big enough to grasp between your thumb and forefinger. If the plants are very crowded, use a cuticle scissors to snip off the stems at ground level—that way you will not disturb the roots of the plants you leave in the ground. Otherwise, just gently pull up the unwanted plants—a pair of tweezers is a handy tool for this job. If pulling up the plants loosens the soil, pat it back into place.

If you are growing salad crops, you can thin them twice—once when they are tiny, then again a little later. The second batch of thinnings can make a tasty, tender addition to a salad.

When seedlings are very crowded, you can use tweezers to thin them or clip them off at soil level with cuticle scissors.

Problems with Seedlings

The world can be a cruel place for youngsters, and seedlings will have to be strong to withstand the adversities they will encounter in the garden. Your goal is to raise seedlings that are compact and bushy, with stout, sturdy stems and good root systems. Still, there are a number of problems that seedlings may face, and an awareness of those difficulties will help you to prevent them.

Seedlings grown indoors may be beset by various problems caused by their environment and handling. The most common cultural pitfall is insufficient light. Seedlings that do not get enough light grow spindly and lanky, with their leaves spaced far apart. Their soft stems stretch toward the light in an effort to get closer to the source. The plants look pale and sickly. Seedlings receiving enough light are stocky and firm, with a good green color.

Temperatures that are too warm will also weaken seedlings.

Overwatering can be a problem too. Seedlings growing in a medium that is constantly wet are prone to root rot and to damping-off (discussed below).

Gardeners tend to be an overanxious lot during the winter, and many of us start our seeds indoors too soon. Plants that spend too long a time indoors will be large at transplanting time, accustomed to indoor conditions, and will have a hard time adjusting to life in the garden. Although none of us can control the weather, calculating planting dates carefully will better the chances that your seedlings will be at the optimum size for transplanting out at the proper time. If you find that your seedlings are getting too big before it's time to plant them in the garden, move them to a cold frame for their last few weeks of protected growth.

Another danger to seedlings is planting them out before they have been properly hardened-off. The recommended procedure is described under Special Tips for Transplanting Out, on page 47. It is essential to give seedlings enough time to adjust gradually to outdoor conditions before you plant them out. If you rush them into the garden they may be killed by severe weather, and they will certainly undergo transplant shock, which will shut down growth until the plants can adapt to their new home.

Seedlings growing outdoors are threatened by cutworms— small, dark-colored larvae that chew through the stems of young seedlings and cut them off at ground level. If you come out to the

Seedlings receiving too little light will be lanky with small, widely spaced leaves. The elongated stems will appear to grow toward the light source.

garden one morning and notice several of your little seedlings neatly mowed down, with no decayed area visible on the stem, you probably have cutworms. Cutworms burrow into the soil during the day, and if you poke a piece of stiff wire into the soil around the base of the toppled plants, you may be able to pull the culprits from their hiding places. In any case, you can protect the rest of your little seedlings by placing simple cardboard collars around the base of the plants. Make sure the collars are about 2 or 3 inches high and extend a couple of inches below the soil surface. You can make collars from strips of cardboard taped or stapled together, or by cutting off the tops and bottoms of cardboard milk cartons and cutting the cartons into two or three separate bands.

DAMPING-OFF

The worst scourge of young seedlings is a fungus disease known as damping-off. The symptoms are unmistakable: the stem develops a dark rot right at the soil line and falls over. The rest of the plant—leaves and roots—usually appears perfectly healthy. Sometimes the plants die while still standing, but more often they topple over. Seeds can also be attacked by damping-off before they have a chance to sprout; they simply rot.

Damping-off is a blanket term for a disease that can actually be caused by any one or a combination of a number of fungi. The culprit may be *Botrytis*, *Rhizoctonia*, *Pythium*, or *Phytophthora*. These fungi and their spores are ubiquitous in the environment—they drift in the air, hide in soil, float in water, and sit on the surface of seeds and plants. And they are always ready to attack little seedlings. Dampness, warmth, and still air all foster the growth of these fungi; you must carefully monitor the environment around your seedlings to avoid these conditions. Damping-off spreads rapidly when it strikes—it can overrun an entire flat of seedlings overnight.

The only treatment for damping-off is to prevent the disease in the first place. Luckily, there are several measures you can take to keep the fungi at bay: (1) You can plant your seeds in a sterile soilless medium. Sphagnum moss is especially helpful—it appears to inhibit the growth of the fungi. Sprinkling a thin layer of sieved sphagnum moss over the top of your planted seeds may help protect the plants when they emerge. (2) If you include soil or sand in the growing medium, be sure to pasteurize it first. (3) When you are planting seeds or working around seedlings, be sure that your

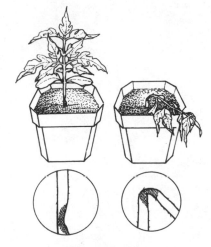

Damping-off appears as a dark rot that girdles the stem right above the soil line of otherwise-healthy seedlings. The plants collapse when their stems become too weak to support them.

hands, tools, containers, and work area are clean. Scrub with soapy water any containers that have been used before. Soak unglazed clay pots for half an hour in a disinfectant solution of one part liquid chlorine bleach to nine parts water. (4) You may want to surface-sterilize your seeds by soaking them in the same kind of bleach solution for 1 or 2 minutes. Drain the seeds on paper towels, then plant them immediately. Do not store the seeds after sterilizing them—the bleach solution will partially soften the seed coat, which may invite disease problems if the seeds are stored for any length of time. Seeds that are very sensitive to fungus and rot, such as cactus seed, are sometimes germinated in polyester fiber (like pillow stuffing) instead of conventional media.

CHAPTER TWO

Vegetative Methods of Propagation

Plants that grow slowly, plants that are difficult to grow from seeds, plants that do not usually produce seeds when cultivated outside their native habitat, and plants whose seeds will not produce new plants exactly like the parents are usually propagated by vegetative, or asexual, means. In vegetative propagation, a part of a mature plant is induced to form roots and shoots and grow into a new plant. Because the new plant carries exactly the same genes as its parent, it will grow into an exact copy of the parent. Vegetative methods of propagation include various types of cuttings, layering, budding, grafting, and different forms of division.

 ## Cuttings

A cutting can be defined as a piece of a parent plant that is made to form roots after it is cut from the parent. Cuttings, which can be taken from stems, leaves, and roots, have a number of advantages. They produce new plants faster than seeds, they are generally relatively easy to work with, and they are inexpensive. Many plants can be propagated from cuttings—perennials, shrubs, trees, annuals, and houseplants can all be grown this way.

Annuals to grow from cuttings include wax begonia (*Begonia*), geranium (*Pelargonium*), and *Impatiens*. Perennials that can be propagated from cuttings include rock cress (*Aubrieta*), basket-of-gold (*Aurinia*), bellflower (*Campanula*), *Chrysanthemum*, garden pink (*Dianthus*), forget-me-not (*Myosotis*), blue phlox (*Phlox divaricata*), mountain pink (*Phlox subulata*), and *Veronica*. Ground covers such as bugleweed (*Ajuga*), ivy (*Hedera*), and *Pachysandra* are often propagated from cuttings. Shrubs to grow from cuttings include *Abelia*, barberry (*Berberis*), boxwood (*Buxus*), *Camellia*, *Daphne*, *Deutzia*, *Euonymous*, holly (*Ilex*), crape myrtle (*Lagerstroemia*), privet (*Ligustrum*), and *Rhododendron*. Trees that can be grown from cuttings include redbud (*Cercis*), dogwood (*Cornus*), and *Franklinia*.

Stem cuttings are sections of a plant's stem. *Softwood* or *green cuttings* are taken from young, green stems while the plant is actively growing. Softwood cuttings are sometimes called slips because they are often side shoots that can be pulled or slipped from the stem without the use of a knife.

Hardwood cuttings are taken from stems when the plant is dormant and the season's growth has matured (hardened).

Single-eye cuttings consist of a single bud or eye with just a part of the stem attached.

Leaf cuttings are individual leaves, sometimes with their petiole (stem) attached.

Root cuttings are portions of roots.

TOOLS AND SUPPLIES FOR TAKING AND ROOTING CUTTINGS

You won't need many tools to take cuttings from your plants. Young green shoots and fleshy roots can be cut with a sharp grafting knife. (A grafting knife is similar to a penknife, but has a very sharp blade that is beveled on one side, and a sturdier, longer handle.) Woody stems and tough, fibrous roots can be severed with pruning shears. Cuttings can be rooted in flats or pots. You can make a classic container called a Forsyth pot for rooting a few cuttings at a time. To make a Forsyth pot you will need two unglazed clay flowerpots, one that is about 2½ to 3 inches in diameter, and the other a wide, shallow pot (called a bulb pan) that is 6 or 7 inches in diameter. Plug the drainage hole in the small pot

You can make your own Forsyth pot for rooting cuttings by placing a small, unglazed clay pot inside a bulb pan and filling the space between them with rooting medium. Be sure to plug the drainage hole in the small pot so that it will hold water.

but leave open the hole in the larger pot. Set the small pot inside the large pot and fill the space between them with rooting medium. Plant the cuttings in the medium, close to the walls of the small pot. Keep the small pot filled with water as the cuttings root. This will keep the growing medium evenly moist as the water seeps slowly through the walls of the small pot. To check whether the cuttings have rooted, give the small pot a twist to firm the growing medium around it, then lift it out and look for roots on the cuttings.

Commercial growers use elaborate automatic mist systems to propagate cuttings. Most home gardeners don't root enough cuttings to make such a system worth the expense, but some woody cuttings do root much more easily and quickly under mist. There are a number of types of mist systems to consider if you are seriously interested in rooting large numbers of woody cuttings. Some devices blow a fine mist into the air in greenhouses or specially enclosed chambers. Other systems spray mist or fog over the cuttings themselves. These systems can be used indoors or outdoors, and can be hooked up to automatic timers. You will probably need to run the system only during the day.

Choose a mist system that will operate on regular household water pressure. A strainer installed in the water line will help keep the mist nozzles from clogging.

Here are a few additional pointers: When the cuttings are first planted they will need the most misting. Your system will need to be operating for the longest, most frequent periods during the day. As roots form you will be able to gradually decrease the misting until it's time to plant the cuttings indoors.

Because mist keeps the leaves continuously wet, you can root cuttings in bright light, making them root faster. Many plants can even be rooted in a sunny spot outdoors. If you install a mist system outdoors, put up some sort of shield around the area to keep the wind from blowing away the mist.

A handier propagation aid for home growers is a simple propagation box made of wood. Enclosing cuttings in a box helps keep humidity levels high. Build a rectangular box long enough to accommodate your containers. The depth of the box will also depend upon the type of containers you will use to root your cuttings. The box should be deep enough to mount fluorescent tubes above the containers. A propagation box for flats of cuttings will not need to be as deep as a box that will hold pots. Attach two self-mounting 40-watt fluorescent tubes to the inside of the lid of the box. The tubes should be about a foot above the surface of the rooting medium. Hinge the lid of the box so you can get at the cuttings easily. Plant the cuttings in their containers, put them in the box, close the lid, and leave the lights on for 12 hours a day. Be sure the box is located where the temperature is at least 65° F, and remember to keep the cuttings moist. If you already have a setup in place for growing plants under lights, you can use a humidity chamber like the one described on page 42 for rooting cuttings.

There are also propagation boxes on the market that supply bottom heat for cuttings and come with vented plastic covers to retain moisture.

ROOTING MEDIA FOR CUTTINGS

Hardwood cuttings and root cuttings are usually planted in a nursery bed or a corner of the garden. However, softwood and leaf cuttings can be rooted in flats or pots indoors or in a cold frame. Softwood and leaf cuttings root best in a light, airy medium. Some good mixtures are equal parts of sand and peat moss, equal parts of vermiculite and perlite, and equal parts of peat and perlite. You can also put a ¼-inch layer of sand on top of the medium.

Many growers like to dip the ends of hardwood cuttings in liquid or powdered rooting hormones, which can help hard-to-root woody cuttings develop roots more quickly. To use these products, remove a small amount of the material from the package and dip the bottom of the cutting into it before inserting the cutting into the growing medium. Never dip cuttings into the package—if the cutting carries any disease organisms you will contaminate both the hormone product and all subsequent cuttings you dip into it.

Softwood Cuttings

Softwood cuttings are the easiest to work with and are most often used. In most cases, the best time to take softwood cuttings is when the plant is about halfway through the current growing season and the stems you are cutting are neither too young and soft nor too old and woody. Softwood cuttings are usually taken from greenhouse and bedding plants and summer- and fall-blooming perennials in spring; and from spring-blooming perennials, shrubs, and trees from June to August. You can take cuttings in early fall from

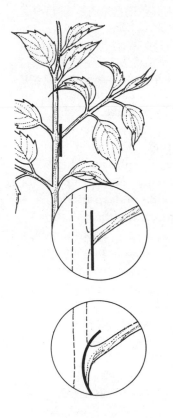

In most cases, softwood cuttings should be severed flush with the main stem (top). They should not be taken with a heel (bottom).

summer annuals and grow the plants indoors for winter flowers. Stems used as softwood cuttings should be firm but flexible—you should be able to bend them without crushing or snapping them. If the stem crushes when it is bent, it is too young to make a good cutting. If the stem snaps sharply in two, it is too old. As in all gardening matters, there are exceptions to this rule. Azalea and lilac cuttings root best when they are very young and soft; hydrangea and weigela cuttings root best when the stems are nearly mature and they are taken late in the season.

When choosing stems to use as softwood cuttings, look for shoots that are healthy and in good condition, but do not take the biggest, most vigorous ones. The best stems to use are young side shoots of medium vigor. Using a sharp knife, cut off each shoot cleanly at its base. The cuttings may be anywhere from 2 to 6 inches long. Do not take along a "heel" from the main stem; for most plants a heel is unnecessary, and cutting into the main stem leaves a wound that can become a site for disease or pest invasion. Plants whose cuttings do root best when a heel is included are noted in Part 2. Some plants produce the best shoots for cuttings along particular parts of their stems; these plants are also specified in Part 2.

If the plant has no small side shoots suitable for softwood cuttings, you can take cuttings from the tips of longer shoots. Roots spring most readily from stem sections directly below a leaf or pair of leaves. This point of leaf attachment is called a *node. Tip cuttings* will root best if the cut is made ¼ to ½ inch below a node. The traditional rule of thumb was that tip cuttings should be made directly below a leaf, right at a node, but this is no longer believed true. Some hardy shrubs root best when cut at a node (boxwood, cotoneaster, and pyracantha are examples), but for most other plants it does not appear to be important. Special needs of particular plants are given in Part 2.

ROOTING SOFTWOOD CUTTINGS

Moisture is absolutely essential for softwood cuttings; they must never be allowed to wilt or dry out. Place the cuttings in a moist rooting medium as you cut them. If you are taking a lot of cuttings, you can wrap them in a damp cloth or put them in a plastic bag until you finish cutting and are ready to put them in the medium. It might be tempting to take a bucket of water to the garden with you and drop the cuttings into it, but it's not a good idea. Too much water is as bad for cuttings as too little. Soaking them in water will prevent the cut surfaces from healing (oxygen is needed for this) and the cuttings may rot.

Softwood cuttings root best in a light, sterile, soilless medium. You can also put a ¼-inch layer of pure sand (builder's sand, not beach sand) on top of the medium. Some cuttings root best in pure sand; this information is given for individual plants in Part 2.

When you are ready to plant the cuttings, make sure the surface of the growing medium is smooth and even. Remove the leaves from the bottom third of each cutting. Do not make holes in the medium for the cuttings, but press them gently into the medium to ensure that they make good contact and no air spaces are left between stems and medium. Place them deep enough so they stand upright but never deeper than half their length. One-quarter to one-third their length is generally a good planting depth. Place the cuttings far enough apart so the leaves of neighboring cuttings do not quite touch one another. When all the cuttings are planted, water thoroughly to settle them into the medium.

During the period when softwood cuttings are rooting, *never* let them dry out. Keep the medium moist but not soggy and maintain a high level of humidity around the cuttings. Professional growers root cuttings in mist chambers, but for home gardeners with small numbers of cuttings, misting can be sufficient. In hot weather you will probably need to mist your cuttings several times a day.

You can also enclose the containers in clear plastic to keep the humidity high. If you do use plastic, remove it periodically to give

Before placing softwood cuttings in a flat of rooting medium, remove the leaves from the bottoms of the stems. Set the cuttings far enough apart so that their leaves do not quite touch one another.

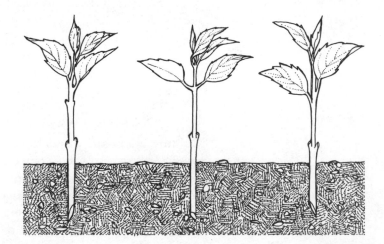

the cuttings some fresh air, make sure the plastic is elevated on sticks or wire hoops so it doesn't come in contact with the plants, and keep the containers out of direct sun or you will cook the cuttings. Fluorescent fixtures are a good source of light—the lamps should be about 8 or 9 inches above the tops of the cuttings. Use daylight tubes or a combination of cool white and warm white, and leave the lights on for 12 hours a day.

Bottom heat is also helpful for softwood cuttings. You can purchase a commercial propagation frame, or set flats of cuttings on a heating mat or on top of a water heater.

If you are rooting the cuttings outdoors in the garden or cold frame, shade them with netting or cheesecloth for the first week to 10 days. Gradually remove the shade when the cuttings have had time to establish themselves. Cuttings of broad-leaved evergreens will root in partial shade, but most others do better in a sunny spot.

Cuttings of woody plants that were started in spring will in many cases be ready to move into the garden by fall. Slow-rooting cuttings and those taken later in the season can spend the winter in a cold frame and go into the garden the following spring. Plant the cuttings 6 to 12 inches apart in the garden. When the plants get crowded, transplant them to their permanent locations.

 *Hardwood Cuttings*

Hardwood cuttings are easier to work with than softwood cuttings. They are tougher and need not be handled with such painstaking care. Hardwood cuttings can be stored easily before planting. Many hardy deciduous shrubs and vines, some ornamental trees, evergreen ground covers, and some fruits can be propagated from hardwood cuttings.

Hardwood cuttings are taken in fall, when the current season's growth has matured and the plant has dropped its leaves and begun its winter dormancy. October and November are generally the best months for taking hardwood cuttings.

Collect mature shoots of the current year's growth. The best stems to use are the ends of branches or new canes that have grown from the base of the plant. Do not make cuttings from late-season growth or from weak, spindly canes or branches. After collecting

Plants to Propagate from Cuttings

The following flowers can all be propagated from stem cuttings, unless otherwise noted.

Artemisia

Baby's-breath, perennial (*Gypsophila paniculata*)

Basket-of-gold (*Aurinia*)

Blanket flower (*Gaillardia*)

Bleeding heart (*Dicentra*), root cuttings

Butterfly weed (*Asclepias*)

Campanula

Candytuft, perennial (*Iberis sempervirens*)

Chrysanthemum

Coral bells (*Heuchera*), leaf cuttings

Delphinium

False rockcress (*Aubrieta*)

Globe thistle (*Echinops*), root cuttings

Lavender (*Lavandula*)

Phlox, garden (*Phlox paniculata*), root cuttings

Pinks, garden (*Dianthus*)

Poppy, Oriental (*Papaver*), root cuttings

Purple coneflower (*Echinacea*), root cuttings

Rock cress (*Arabis*)

Speedwell, spike (*Veronica spicata*)

Sundrops (*Oenothera*)

The following trees and shrubs can be propagated from softwood cuttings.

Abelia

Barberry (*Berberis*)

Beauty bush (*Kolkwitzia*)

Blueberry (*Vaccinium*)

Broom (*Cytisus*)

Butterfly bush (*Buddleia*)

Camellia

Cherry, flowering (*Prunus*)

Clematis

Cotoneaster

Crab apple, some species (*Malus*)

Crape myrtle (*Lagerstroemia*)

Deutzia

Dogwood (*Cornus*)

Forsythia

Fothergilla

Gardenia

Hibiscus

Honeysuckle (*Lonicera*)

Lilac (*Syringa*)

Magnolia

Maidenhair tree (*Ginkgo*)

Maple (*Acer*)

Olive, Russian and autumn (*Eleagnus*)

the shoots, cut them into pieces 6 to 10 inches long, making the cuts either straight across or on an angle. If the shoots are hollow or have a spongy, pithy center, make the bottom cut just below a node. If possible, make the top cut about ¼ inch above a *bud*.

Tie the cuttings in small bundles with fine wire or cord. Tap the

Pachysandra

Periwinkle (*Vinca*)

Privet (*Ligustrum*)

Rhododendron, deciduous types

Rose (*Rosa*)

Spiraea

Summersweet (*Clethra*)

Sweet gum (*Liquidambar*)

Sweetshrub (*Calycanthus*)

Sycamore (*Platanus*)

Weigela

Willow (*Salix*)

Wintercreeper (*Euonymus fortunei*)

Winter hazel (*Corylopsis*)

Wisteria

These trees and shrubs can be propagated from hardwood cuttings.

Alder (*Alnus*)

Beauty bush (*Kolkwitzia*)

Currant (*Ribes*)

Deutzia

Forsythia

Honeysuckle (*Lonicera*)

Hydrangea

Mock orange (*Philadelphus*)

Olive, Russian (*Eleagnus*)

Privet (*Ligustrum*)

Rose (*Rosa*), some climbing and rambling types

Rose-of-Sharon (*Hibiscus syriacus*)

Spiraea

Weigela

Willow (*Salix*)

The following evergreens can also be started from cuttings.

Azalea (*Rhododendron*), evergreen

Arborvitae *(Thuja)*

Barberry (*Berberis*)

Boxwood (*Buxus*)

Camellia

False cypress (*Chamaecyparis*)

Fir (*Abies*)

Firethorn (*Pyracantha*)

Hemlock (*Tsuga*)

Holly (Ilex)

Juniper (*Juniperus*)

Mountain laurel (*Kalmia*)

Pieris

Pine (*Pinus*)

Rhododendron, evergreen

Wintercreeper (*Euonymus fortunei*)

Yew (*Taxus*)

bottom of each bundle on a tabletop or other flat surface to even the ends of the stems. Label each bundle. Store the cuttings over winter in a trench 1 foot deep, in the garden or a cold frame. Stand the bundles of cuttings upright in the trench and fill the trench with sand. The cuttings should be completely covered with sand,

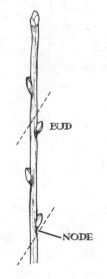

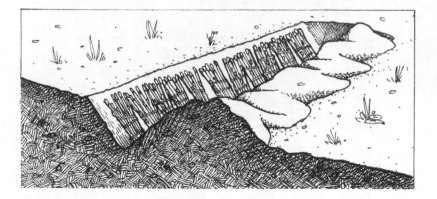

The best hardwood cuttings are made from sturdy shoots of this year's growth. Cut them into pieces 6 to 10 inches long. Tie the cuttings in bundles and store them over winter in a trench filled with sand.

but their tops should not be more than an inch below the surface. Leave the cuttings in the trench until spring to let them form *callus*. Callus is a thick tissue that forms to cover an injured part of a plant and is a good site for roots to grow from.

Plant the cuttings in spring, outdoors as soon as the soil can be worked or in a greenhouse. Outdoors, prepare a nursery bed with loose, porous, well-drained soil. Amend ordinary garden soil with peat moss and sand or vermiculite to lighten its texture. In the greenhouse, a sterile mix made of peat and vermiculite makes a good rooting medium for hardwood cuttings. Plant the cuttings in full sun, buried to the top bud or pair of buds. Water thoroughly to settle the soil around the cuttings and ensure good contact. You can space the cuttings 4 to 6 inches apart and move them after a year, or set them 9 inches apart and leave them in place for 2 or 3 years. Plant in rows 2 feet apart. Hardwood cuttings usually root in about 3 months. During this time, water whenever the soil dries out. To check whether cuttings have rooted, pull gently upward on them. If you meet resistance, the cuttings have probably formed roots.

STEM CUTTINGS FROM EVERGREENS

Evergreen trees and shrubs are also propagated by stem cuttings. Some evergreen shrubs can be grown from softwood cuttings taken in spring or summer, but most are grown from hardwood cuttings taken in fall. Conifer cuttings are best taken in early spring or midsummer. The terminology used to describe evergreen cuttings is confusing. Rather than defining what is meant by firmwood and ripewood, semihardwood, evergreen hardwood, and intermediate, we'll discuss evergreens as a plant group. The terminology is not important for home gardeners as long as you know how to treat the cuttings.

BROADLEAVED EVERGREENS

Take cuttings in October or November from your healthiest azaleas, boxwood, rhododendrons, and other broadleaved evergreen shrubs. Gardeners in warm climates can wait until December or even January. The best candidates are mature shoots at the tips of branches. The shoots should be approximately 3 to 5 inches long for standard size plants; they will be shorter on dwarf varieties. Cut just below a node if possible; however, it is not absolutely essential. Try to make all the cuttings the same length as you take them from the plant; it is not a good idea to cut them again to even them up. Cuttings are stored in a vertical position until planting time, so that chemicals that cause roots to form will begin to move to the base of the cutting. Making a second cut can interfere with the movement of the rooting chemicals. You can cut the stems either straight across or on an angle.

Remove the lower leaves and any flower buds. If the plant has very large leaves, you can cut off the tips (to as much as half the length of the leaf) to save space in the planting area. Dip the cuttings in rooting hormone if you are using one, and insert them into a moist rooting medium. You can root the cuttings in flats or pots in a cold frame or *hotbed* (a cold frame with heating cables under the soil) outdoors, or indoors enclosed in a plastic tent or propagation box. If the cuttings are indoors, make sure they get plenty of light. Try to give them bottom heat and give them air temperatures between 60 and 70° F. Keep the rooting medium evenly moist but not soggy.

When the cuttings have rooted, transplant them into individual pots or flats with more space and continue to keep the growing medium moist. Cuttings started indoors should be ready to plant out in a nursery bed after the last frost in spring; cuttings started in a cold frame will probably not be ready for the garden until the following spring.

CONIFER CUTTINGS

There is some disagreement in horticultural circles as to the best time to take cuttings from conifers. Some growers recommend taking the cuttings from mature wood in late fall, after one or two hard frosts. Other growers say that fall cuttings root too slowly and suggest taking them either in March or April, before the plants begin to grow, or in midsummer, when the season's growth has been completed but has not yet had a chance to harden. Experiment to see which approach works best for you.

Cut 3- to 6-inch shoots of the current season's growth. Make all the cuttings the same length so you will not have to recut them before planting. Cuttings taken from upright shoots will tend to grow into upright plants; cuttings taken from side shoots will tend to develop into bushy, spreading plants. This variation is especially evident in yews. Some growers recommend taking a heel with side-shoot cuttings.

Remove the foliage from the bottom third of the cuttings and plant them in a rooting medium. From this point on, treat them like softwood cuttings.

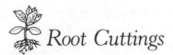 ## Root Cuttings

Root cuttings are a good means of propagation for a number of *herbaceous perennials* (plants whose root systems live on for years, but whose topgrowth dies back to the ground in winter), trees, shrubs, and woody vines. It is especially good for plants that send out suckers from their roots: blackberries and raspberries (*Rubus* spp.), garden phlox (*Phlox paniculata*), Oriental poppies (*Papaver orientale*), *Plumbago* species, *Wisteria* species, trumpet creeper (*Campsis radicans*), and sumac (*Rhus* spp.) are some examples. Root cuttings are also a good way to reproduce some trees and shrubs that do not root easily from cuttings, such as *Acanthopanax*, Kentucky coffee tree (*Gymnocladus dioica*), locust (*Robinia* spp.), and pagoda tree (*Sophora japonica*). You cannot, however, use root cuttings for plants that are grafted, because the new plants will be like the rootstock rather than the topgrowth.

You can take root cuttings at different times of the year. The easiest method is to dig up the parent plant in fall, when the leaves have fallen and the plant is dormant. Most root cuttings work best when they are between 1 and 3 inches long, and ¼ to ½ inch in diameter. There are exceptions, but this is a good general rule of thumb. It is generally helpful to have some small, fibrous, lateral roots on the pieces used for cuttings. After taking the cuttings, replant the parent plant.

The creeping roots of some spreading herbaceous perennials can also be used for root cuttings. Dig up the plants when they are resting after their flowering and active growing periods are over. For spring-blooming plants this occurs in midsummer; for summer-blooming plants the time is late summer or early fall; for autumn bloomers the roots are dug in late fall. Cut the roots into pieces about 2 inches long. Replant the parent plants after removing the roots you want.

You can also dig into the root ball of plants in active growth; carefully sever some roots and replace the soil without causing major disturbance to the parent plants.

There is some disagreement as to whether root cuttings should be planted vertically or horizontally. Some growers prefer to set the cuttings horizontally, while others claim that vertical planting produces plants with a better shape. Thin, bendable roots are easier to plant horizontally. In any case, plant the cuttings in the same medium you would use for stem cuttings, with 3 to 4 inches of medium under the bottom of the cutting and about ½ inch of medium above the tops. Keep the medium moist but not soggy. You can plant cuttings taken in fall in a cold frame, indoors under lights, or in a greenhouse. Or you can store them over the winter and plant them outdoors the following spring. Store the cuttings in boxes of moist sand in the cold frame or in an unheated but frost-free cellar. Cuttings taken in spring or summer can be planted outdoors in loose, crumbly soil. Set the cuttings far enough apart so the young plants will have space to grow to transplanting size.

 *Layering*

Layering is a technique for rooting branches of woody plants while they are still attached to the parent plant. A layer is not severed from the mother plant until it has formed roots. Layering is used to propagate plants that do not come true from seed (that is, those whose seeds do not produce new plants identical to the parent plant), that are difficult to root as cuttings, or that cannot be easily grafted or budded. It is a good method for home gardeners to use because it is easy, requires no special tools or equipment, and is generally a reliable means of getting new plants. Raspberries are commonly propagated by layering. Other plants that respond to layering include garden pinks (*Dianthus*), periwinkle (*Vinca*), flowering quince (*Chaenomeles*), *Cotoneaster*, witch hazel (*Hamamelis*), *Rhododendron*, *Spiraea*, and lilac (*Syringa*).

In order for layering to succeed, the soil in which the branches are rooted must be loose and light so it can be packed around the stems without compacting, and it must be rich in organic matter to promote the growth of strong, healthy roots. The soil must be well drained and well aerated yet be able to retain moisture. The soil must be constantly moist, but not soggy, while the roots are forming.

Because you will be layering established plants, you cannot simply dig up all the soil and enrich it. Instead, carefully dig several inches of the topsoil from around the roots of the mother plant, taking care to disturb the roots as little as possible. Mix the soil with sand, peat moss, and compost, then replace it around the roots of the parent and in the area in which you will be rooting the branches.

Healthy one-year-old shoots work best for layering. If the parent plant is in good shape and you have pruned it regularly, you will have plenty of shoots to use. But if you want to layer an old plant that has been neglected, you will first have to prune it back and feed it with compost or composted manure to stimulate the growth of new shoots.

Simple, compound, and serpentine layering (which are known collectively as true layering) are usually done in early spring, as soon as the soil can be worked and while the plant is still dormant. Tip layering and mound or stool layering are done with the current season's shoots later in spring, when the new shoots are several inches long. Air layering is usually done in late spring or early summer. Continuous layering is also done in spring.

SIMPLE LAYERING

Simple layering produces one new plant from each layered stem and works well for shrubs that have a lot of low, flexible branches. Make a slit in the ground about 6 inches deep by inserting the tip of a spade and pulling the handle back and forth a few times. The distance between the slit and the mother plant depends on the length of the branch you want to layer. You will need to bury the stem about 5 or 6 inches (not less than 3 inches) from its tip.

Bend the branch down to the ground, as flat as possible. To

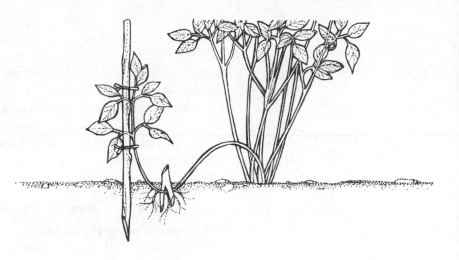

To perform simple layering, pin down a shoot and bury it at one point along its length.

keep the shoot from snapping off the plant at its base, bend it in the opposite direction from the way it grows and twist it slightly as you bend. Place the stem in the slit and anchor it with U-shaped pieces of heavy wire or with forked twigs or a stone of sufficient weight. Bend the tip of the shoot upward so 3 to 6 inches of it will extend above the soil surface. Cover the buried part of the stem with the improved soil mix and step on it with your foot to pack the soil around the stem.

To hasten the rooting process, you can first remove a strip of bark about 1 inch wide from the entire circumference of the stem at the point where it will be buried. Girdling the stem in this way encourages the formation of callus tissue. Or, instead of girdling the stem, you can wound it by cutting diagonally about halfway through the underside of the stem. If the stem is very stiff, insert a wooden matchstick into the cut to hold it open. If the stem breaks easily, you can make it more flexible by cutting into the upper side of the stem and twisting it before pegging it down. Some gardeners like to put a little rooting hormone powder on the injured part of the stem to encourage rooting.

The speed at which the layers will grow roots depends on the type of plant, the age of the shoot being layered, and environmental conditions during the growing season. Many plants suitable for layering will have rooted by early fall and can then be severed from the mother plant. You can tell if the layer has rooted by pulling on it gently—roots will resist your pull. In climates where winters are severe, it is best to leave the new plants where they are until spring, when you can dig them with a ball of soil around their roots and transplant them to a nursery bed. In milder climates, dig and transplant the new plants. Keep them shaded and well-watered during warm autumn weather.

Some plants, such as magnolias, witch hazel, and rhododendrons, azaleas, and other evergreens root slowly and will have to remain attached to their parents for as long as 2 or 3 years. Azaleas and rhododendrons must be handled differently from other plants in simple layering; see Part 2 for details.

CONTINUOUS LAYERING

Continuous layering is one way to produce several new plants from each layered shoot. It is sometimes used on ash-leaved maples (*Acer negundo*), river maples (*A. saccharinum*), and some *Viburnum* species. It is also used for fruit trees including apples, cherries, and plums. To perform continuous layering, make a narrow trench 6 inches deep in the soil, beginning close to the mother plant. Lay the entire length of the shoot (except for the tip) flat in the trench and peg it down. Do not fill the slit with soil until the buds on the stem have grown 4 to 5 inches long. Then, as the shoots grow, gradually fill the slit with soil. You can facilitate rooting by making a shallow cut on the bottom side of the layered stem at each node. The following spring or fall, after roots form, sever and transplant the new plants.

In continuous layering, the entire shoot except for the tip is buried, and several new plants are produced along the stem.

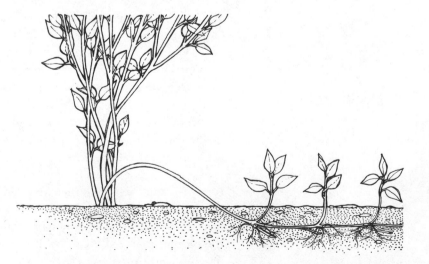

To perform serpentine or compound layering, bury a shoot at several points but not along its entire length. Bury alternate nodes with one below ground and the next above ground.

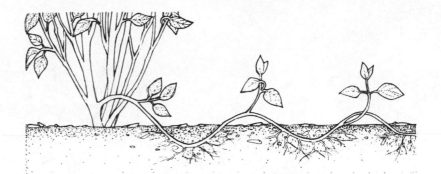

SERPENTINE OR COMPOUND LAYERING

In serpentine layering, the stem is buried at several points but not along its entire length. This method is a good way to propagate woody vines such as clematis, climbing honeysuckles, grapes, ivies, and wisteria. Prepare a long, narrow trench as you would for continuous layering, but instead of burying the entire stem, bend the stem in a series of curves and bury every other node, alternating along the length of the stem.

TIP LAYERING

Tip layering can be used to reproduce plants that root easily at the tips of their branches, such as forsythia, blackberries, and black raspberries. Just peg the tips of the branches to the ground and cover them with soil.

MOUND OR STOOL LAYERING

This type of layering is primarily used on low, bushy shrubs that produce a lot of shoots close to the base of the plant. Evergreen azaleas and, to a lesser degree, deciduous azaleas (*Rhododendron* spp.), Japanese quince (*Chaenomeles speciosa*), flowering almond (*Prunus glandulosa*), dwarf Russian almond (*P. tenella*), alpine currant (*Ribes alpinum*), and *Spiraea* × *bumalda* can all be propagated this way. So can Siberian dogwood (*Cornus alba* 'Sibirica'), dwarf horse chestnut (*Aesculus parviflora*), silver linden (*Tilia tomentosa*), gooseberries (*Ribes* spp.), and hybrid magnolias (*Magnolia* cultivars).

In mound layering, the shoots are not laid in a trench but are instead allowed to grow vertically. It is best to use shoots of the current season. As they grow, mound soil around them in two or

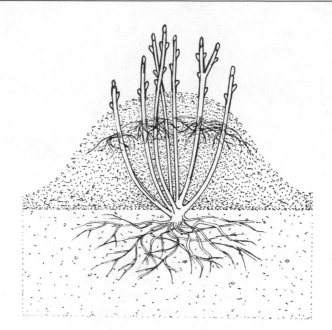

For mound layering, add soil around shoots of the current season as they grow. Roots form inside the soil mound.

three stages as they get taller. When the shoots are 4 inches high, mound about 3 inches of rich, crumbly soil around them. When the shoots have grown another 3 to 4 inches, add 3 more inches of soil to the mound. Keep the soil moist throughout the growing season. The following spring, when the shoots have formed roots, sever them from the parent and transplant them to a nursery bed.

If you want to use year-old shoots for mound layering, first remove a ring of bark from the base of each shoot to induce the formation of callus. Heap soil around the shoots, and pack it around and between them. Do this in early spring while the plant is still dormant, instead of during the growing season as you would for new shoots. From this point, handle year-old shoots undergoing mound layering just as you would treat simple layers.

A variation of mound layering used for larger shrubs, such as large-fruited blueberries, is called *stumping*. In stumping, you cut the old shoots off the stem at ground level, then mound a moist mixture of sand and peat moss on top of the stump to a depth of about 4 inches. You can nail together a simple frame of boards to place around the mound to hold it in place. Shoots will grow from the old stump and will form roots within the mound. Keep the sand-peat mixture moist until fall, when the new shoots have rooted, then cut off and transplant the young plants.

AIR LAYERING

Air layering, also called pot layering or Chinese layering, is most familiar to indoor gardeners who use it to rejuvenate elderly house plants whose woody stems have grown tall and lost their lower leaves over time. Rubber plants, ficus, and crotons are some likely candidates for indoor air layering. But air layering also works on some outdoor shrubs. Flowering dogwood (*Cornus florida*), winter hazel (*Corylopsis* spp.), smokebush (*Cotinus coggyria*), *Cotoneaster* species, holly (*Ilex* spp.), crab apples (*Malus* spp.), *Tamarisk* species, some *Rhododendron* and *Viburnum* species, *Wisteria* species, and Japanese zelkova (*Zelkova serrata*) all respond to air layering.

To air-layer a shrub, remove a ring of bark ½ to ¾ inch wide from the branch to be rooted. Scrape off the *cambium tissue* (the thin layer of soft green, white, or reddish tissue directly under the bark, lying between the bark and the wood) to expose the wood. You can sprinkle just a bit of rooting hormone powder on the exposed edges of the bark on the upper side of the stripped area. Wrap moist (not wet) sphagnum moss around the wound and wrap that securely with polyethylene plastic. Be sure the plastic you use is polyethylene, which holds in moisture but is permeable to air.

Tightly seal the top and bottom of the plastic with tape to make sure no rainwater can get in. The sphagnum must stay moist until roots have formed, but if it gets too wet the rooting process will be hampered.

The roots should have formed by late fall. At that time, cut the new plants from the parent and plant them in pots or in a cold frame.

In air layering, a strip of the bark and cambium tissue is removed (left), the wound is wrapped in damp sphagnum moss (center), and the moss is wrapped with polyethylene and sealed top and bottom with tape (right).

Plants That Respond to Layering

The following plants can be propagated by some form of layering.

Apple (*Malus*)

Azalea (*Rhododendron*),
   evergreen types

Blackberry (*Rubus*)

Cherry (*Prunus*)

Clematis

Gooseberry (*Ribes*)

Grape (*Vitis*)

Hydrangea

Ivy (*Hedera*)

Magnolia

Pinks, garden (*Dianthus*)

Quince, flowering (*Chaenomeles*)

Raspberry (*Rubus*)

Wisteria

Grafting

Grafting and budding join growing parts of two plants together so that they unite to produce a single new plant. For grafting, choose a piece of a plant stem containing buds or a single bud from a variety with the fruit, flowers, foliage, or form you want. Unite it with another plant, which will provide the root system on which the plant will grow.

The process is essentially the same for both grafting and budding, except that budding involves a thin slice of stem containing a single bud, while grafting involves a piece of stem that contains more than one bud. (See pages 77–80 for more detailed information on budding.) Grafting and budding offer a way to propagate woody plants that do not come true from seed, that do not produce seeds in most gardens, that are too big or inflexible for layering, or whose cuttings would be difficult or slow to root. Grafting can also be used to create plants that are hardy in climates where they could not otherwise survive, or that have beautiful flowers or full-size fruit on a dwarf plant. Grafting is widely employed on roses, fruit trees, some flowering and shade trees, some ornamental shrubs, tree peonies, and evergreens. Evergreens are very difficult to graft; home gardeners will have better luck working with deciduous trees and shrubs.

The stem piece of the graft is called a *scion*. Scions are generally one-year-old shoots ⅛ to ¼ inch in diameter and 4 to 6 inches long, with several buds. The root piece upon which the scion is grafted is called a *stock* or *understock*. The stock may be a seedling, a rooted cutting, a piece of a root, or even a mature tree. Grafting onto a mature tree is called topworking; since it does not involve planting it will not be discussed here. Understocks are often one or two years old, and the same diameter or slightly larger than the scion. Size and age of stocks varies with the type of plant. The stock plants can be growing in containers or in the garden, and in some cases may even be bare-rooted.

The scion and stock are united by placing the cambium tissues of both pieces together. The tissues intertwine and grow together. The scion and stock must be close botanical relatives in order to be grafted. A few plant families have a great deal of compatibility (the Rose Family is one example) and plants from different genera can be successfully grafted. But for the most part the graft partners must belong to the same genus.

In addition to compatible plants, several other elements are important for a successful graft. For one thing, the cambium tissue of scion and stock must be well matched and make good contact with one another in order for the cells to join. Clean, sharp tools and straight cuts will make the matching process easier. To ensure good contact between the scion and stock, at least one side of the scion's cut surface is aligned with one cut side of the stock. Sometimes two or even more sides are matched up. All you need for the graft to work is for one cell of the scion to join with one cell of the stock. Some growers place the scion at an angle instead of parallel to the stock, so the cambium layers cross. The position of the scion is not important as long as the cambiums make good contact. Various alignments are described in the sections on specific types of grafts, under Types of Grafts on page 74.

When the two pieces are matched, the graft has to be securely tied to keep the joint tight. Rubber band ties sold for this purpose are easy to work with. You can stretch them as you wind them around the graft to get a nice tight wrap. Another advantage is that the rubber may disintegrate before it gets too tight for the growing tree and constricts the graft union. You can also use string or grafting tape to bind the union.

The other essential for a good graft is constant moisture. If the tissues of either the scion or stock dry out they will not fuse together. When you cut the scions, refrigerate them in bags of damp sphagnum moss if you can't use them right away. After the graft is bound, seal it with grafting wax or wrap it in plastic to maintain adequate moisture in the tissues. You will know in a few weeks if the graft has "taken." If the scion bud starts to swell, you have succeeded.

When the graft has completely healed (it takes one to several months), remove the wrap and gently cut away the bindings before they constrict the plant's growth.

Most grafting is done in early spring while the plants are still dormant. But the scion can be held in cool storage (as long as you keep it moist) to maintain it in a dormant state, then grafted later in the season when the stock is actively growing. It is most important that the scion be dormant both when it is cut and when it is grafted.

The best time to collect scion wood is in late fall or early winter. Choose vigorous shoots, a foot or more long, of the previous season's growth. If necessary, you can also use shoots that are two or three years old. Tie the stems in bundles, pack them in damp sawdust or peat moss, and store them in a damp place where the temperature will be around 40° F over the winter.

Wrapping the bundles in plastic will help hold in moisture. Check periodically throughout the winter to make sure the sawdust or peat moss is still moist.

When you are ready to perform the graft in spring, cut off 2 to 3 inches from the bottom and top of the scion—the best buds are found on the middle of the stem.

Plants that can be used as grafting stocks are not widely available to home gardeners. Commercial nurseries can supply some stocks, particularly dwarfing understocks for fruit trees, but in most cases you will have to grow your own stocks from either seeds or cuttings.

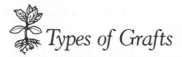 *Types of Grafts*

There are numerous types of grafts, and they are of varying degrees of practicality as far as home gardeners are concerned. Some of the more widely used grafts are described on the following pages.

To make a splice graft, cut both understock and scion at a smooth angle; match the cut surfaces and tie the graft together. After tying, seal the graft with grafting wax or compound, or wrap it in plastic.

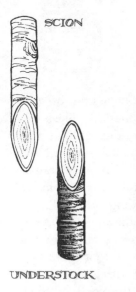

SCION

UNDERSTOCK

SPLICE GRAFT

This simple graft is a relatively quick method for deciduous plants that are less than ½ inch thick. In the nursery trade, splice grafting is usually performed on stocks that are growing in containers. Slice the understock with a smooth, slanting cut that is three to four times as long as the diameter of the stock. Cut the scion the same way. Line up the exposed cambium layers of scion and stock and tie them securely in place with rubber ties or cord. One drawback to this kind of graft for inexperienced practitioners is that, because the cuts are smooth and only made on one side, the two pieces may slip while you're trying to tie them and the cambium tissues may not make good contact. Be sure you keep the scion and stock correctly aligned. When the graft is bound in place, seal it with grafting wax or compound, or wrap it with plastic.

CLEFT AND WEDGE GRAFTS

Cleft grafting is usually used on large deciduous trees or on smaller understocks growing in containers or nursery beds. A variation of it is used to graft grapes onto more vigorous or disease-resistant rootstocks (see Grapes in Part 2). A cleft graft can also be used to graft a scion onto a root cutting. Cleft grafts are usually made in early spring, when the buds on the rootstock begin to swell, but while the scion is still dormant. To make a cleft graft, split the stock and cut the bottom of the scion into a wedge shape. Insert the scion into the split in the stock so that the cambium tissues line up or cross on one or both sides. The pieces should fit together tightly, so you may not need to bind them. However, if you are in any doubt, tie the graft. Seal the union with grafting wax or compound, or use plastic. Be sure to cover all the cut surfaces with the sealant, and completely fill the cleft.

A wedge graft is similar to a cleft graft, except the stock has a wedge-shaped cut to receive the wedge-shaped end of the scion. Both scion and stock should be approximately the same size, and the graft will have to be tied in place. Wedge grafts are most often done on herbaceous plants or those with soft wood.

WHIP AND TONGUE GRAFT

This type of graft is used on small branches, on grapes, and for root grafting nursery stock. Seedling stocks can be growing in containers or bare-rooted. This graft is called a whip graft because

For a cleft graft, cut the scion in a wedge shape that fits snugly into a cleft cut into the under-stock. If a cleft graft does not fit together tightly, tie it. All cleft grafts should be sealed. Swelling buds on the scion indicate a successful graft.

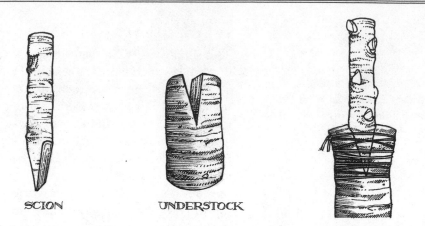

SCION   UNDERSTOCK

it is often used on young trees (whips), and a tongue graft because of the way it is cut. A whip and tongue graft is basically like a splice graft with a notch cut into it; it has more edges than a splice or cleft graft, and the pieces are more difficult to cut, but a whip and tongue graft exposes more cambium tissue than other grafts, the scion fits neatly into the stock, and the union is easy to bind. This type of graft is generally made in early spring.

To make a whip and tongue graft, first cut the stock and scion as you would for a splice graft, then split each piece vertically. The angled cut on the top of the stock should be about four times as long as the stock's diameter. If you are working with a tree, cut the vertical tongue with a knife instead of splitting the wood; splitting

A whip and tongue graft is like a splice graft with a notch cut into both stock and scion. This type of graft exposes more cam-bium tissue than splice or cleft grafts. Tie the graft when the pieces are in place.

SCION

STOCK

will leave rough edges that can interfere with the contact between the cambium areas. Make the vertical cut or split to about a third of the way down from the cut end of the stock. Cut the base of the scion in the same way, and fit the scion and stock together so the cambium areas are aligned on at least one side. Then bind and seal the graft.

Budding

Buds are embryonic stems or leaves that appear as small projections along the plant stem. They are most frequently found at the point where a mature leaf joins the stem. Budding is a form of grafting in which a single bud instead of a scion is grafted onto the rootstock. Budding is generally performed on roses, fruit trees, and some shade trees. Stone fruits in particular (cherries, peaches, plums) take better to budding than grafting because it is difficult to split their wood to make grafts. Budding is an efficient means of propagation for commercial growers because a single plant can produce many offspring. It works best on young trees five years old or less, and on branches no more than ½ inch in diameter.

Budding can be done when mature buds are available and the bark slips or peels easily from the wood of the stock. Generally this means late summer—late July or August—after the plants have made their current season's growth but before the new wood hardens for winter. Budded plants are more vigorous when they receive a dormant period shortly after the budding is performed.

Stocks used in budding are seedlings in their second season of growth or older. The bark of the stock, like that of the scion, must be loosened so the bud can be inserted.

Buds are taken from the current year's growth. Use firm, woody stems about the diameter of a pencil. The buds in the leaf axils should look firm and mature. Cut a piece of the stem 10 or more inches long (called a *budstick*) and remove the blades of the leaves. Keep a portion of each *petiole* (leaf stem) attached to the budstick to serve as handles when you are working with the buds. If you cannot complete the budding right away, you can wrap the budsticks in plastic and store them in the refrigerator for a few days until you're ready to use them.

When you are ready to use the budstick, cut off and discard 2

When selecting a stem to use as a budstick, look for a firm, woody stem, about as thick as a pencil, with well-developed buds in the leaf axils. When the budstick is cut, remove the leaf blades but leave part of each petiole attached to the budstick.

or 3 inches from the top and bottom. You will harvest buds to use in budding from the budstick. You will find the best buds toward the middle of the stick; look for the plumpest, firmest ones. When you have trimmed the budstick, keep it wrapped in damp burlap while you work—it must never be allowed to dry out.

SHIELD OR T-BUDDING

Shield or T-budding is the type most often used. Begin by making a T-shaped cut in the bark of the stock where you will insert the bud. A knife with a straight blade will work best. Rock the knife blade back and forth to make the horizontal cut, then, starting about 1 inch below the horizontal cut, carefully draw the knife upward through the bark to make the vertical cut. Make the cut deep enough to go all the way through the bark, but do not cut into the cambium. Loosen the bark around the cuts by twisting the blade underneath it.

Cut the bud from the budstick with a piece of bark in the shape of a shield. Cut from below the bud, drawing the knife upward. Use a shallow, slightly angled cut to remove the bud—do not cut horizontally or too deeply. Cut all the way through the bark, not so shallowly that the soft cambium tissue will be damaged, but not so deeply that you cut into the wood beneath it. A properly cut bud includes only the bark and cambium layer. An exception can be made in the case of fruit trees, where it is acceptable to take a thin strip of wood with the bud.

When you have cut the shield, pick it up carefully by the petiole with your thumb and forefinger, lift it from the stick, and insert it under the edges of the T-shaped cut in the stock. Push down on the shield until the heel of the bud is resting against the crosswise cut and the shield fits tightly in the T. Tie above and below the bud with raffia, plastic, or rubber "budding strips." Rubber budding strips are 2 feet long and ⅜ inch wide. If you use raffia, cut it into pieces about 20 inches long and soak it in water to make it pliable before use.

To tie the bud in place, first bring the strip over the top of the shield, then start at the bottom of the vertical cut and wind smoothly upward. Cover the entire cut and all of the shield except for the bud itself. Wind tightly to hold the bud in place and make an airtight wrap.

You do not need to seal with wax or plastic as you would other kinds of grafts. You will need to remove raffia or plastic strips after

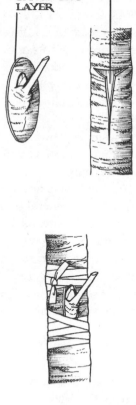

CAMBIUM LAYER

To make a shield bud, insert the shield-shaped bud from the scion (top left) in a T-shaped cut in the stock (top right). Tie the union securely in place.

2 to 4 weeks to avoid constricting growth and girdling the stem. Rubber strips can stay in place until they rot.

After the bud has been in place for a few weeks, examine the petiole on the bud. If it shrivels and falls off, the budding has been successful. If the petiole shrivels but stays attached to the bud, the operation has failed.

The final step in the budding process is to remove the top of the stock when the new bud begins to grow. The bud will stay dormant until the following spring. Do not cut off the top of the stock until early in that season, when the bud begins to swell. For shrubs, cut the stock right above the T. For trees, cut about 6 inches above the bud; the remaining piece of the stock can be used as a stake to support the growing bud during its first season of growth. Cut off the 6-inch stub right above the graft union in late summer. Then remove any suckers that may be produced from the rootstock.

REVERSE T-BUDDING

Reverse T-budding, or up-budding, is like shield budding except that the T-shaped cut in the stock is made upside down. The procedure is the same, except when inserting the bud into the cut you will have to push upward on it instead of downward. For some trees that have large buds (some pears, for example), a vertical cross-shaped cut works better than a T. Instead of making the horizontal cut at the top or bottom of the vertical cut, you make it in the middle.

JUNE BUDDING

June budding is a type of shield budding that is used in warm climates where the growing season is long and plants don't go completely dormant. In June budding you force the bud to start growing in the same season you graft it onto the stock, thus saving a year in the process.

The budding is performed like regular shield budding. Then, 5 to 10 days after the bud has been grafted, you must bend or partially break the top of the stock in order to force the bud to begin growing. Do not completely sever the top until the shoot growing from the bud produces enough leaves to nourish the whole plant. When it does, cut off the top of the stock right above the bud.

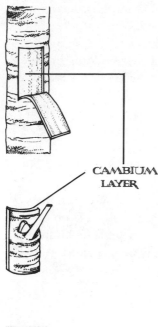

CAMBIUM
LAYER

For plate budding, cut the bud with a rectangular piece of bark (center) and fit it into a corresponding rectangular cut in the stock (top). Bring up the flap of bark on the stock to cover the bottom of the bud piece. H-budding (bottom) is similar to plate budding, except two flaps of bark are cut on the stock.

June budding works especially well on plants whose rootstocks grow quickly, such as peaches and plums.

PLATE BUDDING

Plate budding is not used as widely as shield budding. To make a plate bud, cut three sides of a rectangle into the bark of the stock to form a flap, and bend it down. Cut the bud with a matching rectangle of bark instead of a shield, and match the cambium around the bud to the exposed area on the stock. Bring the flap of bark on the stock back up over the bark attached to the bud (do not cover the bud) and tie securely. From this point on handle the graft the same as a shield bud.

H-BUDDING

H-budding can be used for trees whose thick bark would be difficult to bend for a plate bud. To make an H-bud, you cut a double rectangle in the bark, with one flap attached at the top and the other at the bottom. Cut the bud with a rectangular shield, match the cambium to the exposed area on the stock, and close both flaps over the shield. Tie in place and handle like a shield bud.

PATCH BUDDING

Patch budding is also used for trees with thick bark, such as mangoes, pecans, and other nut trees. It is the same as plate budding except no flap of bark is left on the stock—the rectangular area is simply exposed. Patch budding is usually performed in early spring with dormant buds from the previous season, but it can also be done in summer with buds from the current season.

 *Division*

Division is a quick, easy way to propagate plants that multiply themselves by means of rhizomes, suckers, or underground growths or offsets. Most herbaceous perennials form growth buds, or eyes, that can be separated from the plant to grow into new plants. *Astilbe*, daylily (*Hemerocallis*), *Chrysanthemum*, *Hosta*, *Iris*, beebalm (*Monarda*), and peony (*Paeonia*) are just a few of the perennials that respond to division. Many bulbs and some shrubs, such as honeysuckle, mock orange, and *Spiraea*, can be divided as well. To divide an established plant, you cut or break apart the plant crown, or a clump of suckers, or a bulb, corm, or tuber that has developed offsets or become a collection of individual pieces. The plant segments will grow into new plants identical to their parent.

The traditional rule of thumb in terms of timing has been to divide spring-blooming plants in early fall, summer-blooming plants in late fall, and autumn-blooming plants in early spring. Most perennials are reasonably tolerant of division at different times of year, as long as you don't disturb them during the coldest and hottest weather.

DIVIDING PERENNIALS

Almost all perennials can be divided; in fact, most of them need it periodically to rejuvenate the plants and keep them producing lots of flowers. The frequency of division varies from plant to plant (see Part 2 for specifics), but most perennials will show you when they need to be divided. Signs to watch for are crowding of the plants and blossoms that are fewer in number and poorer in quality than those the plant has produced in previous seasons. Some plants, such as chrysanthemums, need to be divided every year or two to remain vigorous and free-flowering. Others, such as astilbe and daylilies, need dividing every 3 or 4 years. Still other plants, including bleeding heart and Oriental poppies, don't like to be disturbed and should be divided only when the plants look weak and flower quality declines.

The ease with which a perennial can be divided depends upon the type of root system it has. The first step in dividing most plants is to cut back the stems to ground level. Then remove the topsoil from around the plant, insert a spading fork or shovel at an angle under the root ball, and carefully lift the plant from the soil. Try to leave intact as many of the roots as you can.

If the plant has a cluster of *crowns* (the point at which stems and roots join), pull or cut the clump apart with a knife to split it into sections that each contain several *eyes* (growth points, where new shoots will form). If the plant forms a large mass of crowns, push two spading forks into the clump back to back. Push and pull the handles back and forth to pry the clump apart. Plants that form thick, tight clumps (phlox is one example) may have to be chopped apart with a hatchet or sharp spade. The roots of low-growing evergreen plants, such as *Phlox subulata* and primroses, can be pulled apart with your fingers.

To divide perennials with a large, dense mass of crowns, push two spading forks into the clump and lever them back and forth to pry the crowns and roots apart.

Some perennials, like daylilies and peonies, have fleshy roots, each of which has several eyes. To get new plants, you can pull or cut apart the roots so that each piece contains two or more eyes, and plant the pieces.

Irises and some other perennials have fleshy rhizomes that branch underground or at the soil surface. Each eye on the rhizome contains a growth bud. You can pull the clumps of stems apart so that each stem contains an underground bud, then replant the divisions.

As you divide the clumps of roots and stems of all these kinds of perennials, remove and discard the old, tough roots at the center of the plant, and replant the younger, more vigorous roots from the outer parts of the clump.

An alternative way to divide perennials that form numerous crowns, like hostas, or those that do not like to be disturbed, is to dig up and remove some of the outer crowns while leaving the main plant in place.

Replant the divisions right away so they do not have a chance to dry out. Most plants should be replanted at the same depth they were growing before (exceptions are noted in Part 2). If you are dividing plants in fall, make sure 4 to 6 weeks remain before you expect the first hard frost, so the divisions will have time to send out new roots and establish themselves before cold weather sets in. Be sure the transplants get plenty of water while they are rooting.

In northern gardens, many newly divided perennials benefit from a winter mulch to hold in the cold. After the soil freezes late in fall, lay down a covering of loose mulch—salt hay, shredded leaves, and evergreen branches are all effective. Shallow-rooted plants, such as chrysanthemums and shasta daisies, find a winter mulch especially helpful. The mulch keeps the soil from thawing during spells of mild winter weather and then refreezing. Thawing and refreezing causes the soil to heave and buckle, and perennial roots may be pushed out of the ground and exposed to killing cold.

DIVIDING BULBS

There are several ways to divide bulbs, depending on whether they are true bulbs, corms, or tubers.

Many true bulbs, such as tulips and narcissus, produce offsets, or bulblets, which will grow into new plants. A few years after it is planted, the bulb will have produced a number of these bulblets around the outside. The bulblets compete with the main bulb and

To divide true bulbs like narcissus, pull off the small offsets that form around the outside of the parent bulb and plant them.

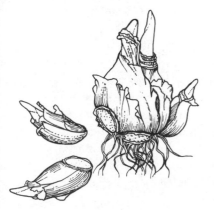

To get new plants from scaly bulbs like those of lilies, remove and plant the outer scales from mature bulbs.

Corms produce little cormels around the base. To divide corms, separate all the cormels and plant them; discard the old corm.

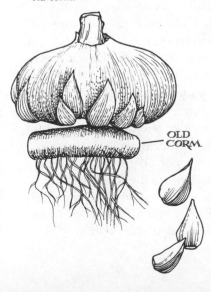

OLD CORM

each other for water and nutrients; they grow slowly and may produce nothing but leaves if you leave them attached to the main bulb. When you notice that a bulb planting in your garden has become crowded and produces fewer flowers, it's time to divide. When the leaves have died back in summer, dig up the bulbs, separate the offsets from the parent, and replant them all right away in loose, deeply dug soil that is rich in organic matter. If you prefer, you can let the offsets dry for a day in an airy, shady place, then store them until you are ready to plant other new bulbs in fall.

You can also divide this type of true bulb by cutting the bulb lengthwise into four or eight pieces. Put the pieces in a plastic bag full of moist vermiculite and seal the top of the bag to retain moisture. Put the bag in a warm (70° F), bright place, but keep it out of direct sun. Check the bag often to make sure the vermiculite stays moist and to look for signs of growth. When small bulblets and roots have formed, in 1 to 3 months, plant them in pots in a mixture of equal parts of soil, compost, and perlite. Hardy bulbs need 3 months of cold weather before they will start to grow. Store the pots outdoors in a protected place or in a cold frame.

Another type of true bulb, called a scaly bulb, produces structures called scales, which resemble the cloves of a garlic bulb. Many lilies have this type of bulb. To get new plants, dig the bulbs in fall and pull off the outer scales. Place them with the bottom end down in a container of moist vermiculite or equal parts peat moss and sand. The scales will grow little bulblets that can be planted to produce new plants. Some lilies produce bulbils on underground parts of the stem, or along the stem in the axils of the leaves. All these offsets can be planted. It takes anywhere from 1 to 4 years for the plants grown from such offsets to reach flowering size, depending on the species.

Plants that grow from corms rather than true bulbs (gladiolus and crocus are two examples) are handled slightly differently. The corm dies each year and the plant produces a new one to take its place. Little cormels are also produced around the base of the corm. Dig the corms of tender plants like gladiolus in fall; dig hardy corms like crocus after the plants have bloomed and the leaves have died back. Separate the new corm from the old, withered one, and detach the little cormels. Discard the old corm and immediately replant the new one and the cormels if the plant is hardy, or save them to plant in spring if the plant is tender.

You can also divide corms by cutting them into pieces, each

Plants That Respond to Division

The following plants can all be divided. This list includes perennials, bulbs, ground covers, ornamental grasses, and shrubs.

Artemisia	Daffodil, narcissus (*Narcissus*)
Aster	*Dahlia*
Astilbe	Daylily (*Hemerocallis*)
Barberry (*Berberis*)	*Delphinium*
Basket-of-gold (*Aurinia*)	*Deutzia*
Beebalm (*Monarda*)	*Euonymus*
Bergenia	False dragonhead (*Physostegia*)
Black-eyed Susan (*Rudbeckia*)	False rockcress (*Aubrieta*)
Blanket flower (*Gaillardia*)	Foxglove (*Digitalis*)
Bleeding heart (*Dicentra*)	Gayfeather (*Liatris*)
Blueberry (*Vaccinium*)	*Geranium*
Campanula	*Hibiscus*
Candytuft, perennial (*Iberis*)	Honeysuckle (*Lonicera*)
Chrysanthemum	*Hosta*
Columbine (*Aquilegia*)	Hyacinth (*Hyacinthus*)
Coral bells (*Heuchera*)	*Hydrangea*
Coreopsis	*Iris*
Crocus	Lamb's ear (*Stachys*)

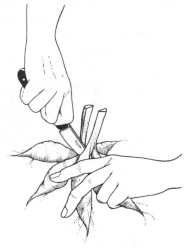

To divide tuberous-rooted plants like dahlias, cut apart the root clump so that each section has an eye and part of the old stem attached. Replant the divisions in the spring.

with an eye, and planting them in the manner described earlier for true bulbs that have been cut in pieces.

Tuberous roots such as those of dahlias are another type of bulbous structure that can be divided. These roots produce eyes at the base of the stem, where the stem and roots meet. To divide them, cut apart the root clumps so that each piece contains an eye and part of the old stem. The roots of tender plants like dahlias must be dug and stored indoors over winter in regions that experience freezing temperatures in winter. If you live in one of these zones, it is best to store the roots intact and divide them when you are ready to replant the next spring. After digging the fat roots, let them dry out for a few days in a cool, dark, ventilated but frost-free place (a cellar, for example). Remove the topgrowth, shake off the dry soil, and let the bulbs dry for another couple of days. Then pack the roots in boxes of dry sand, peat moss, or tissue paper, and store them in a cool, dark, dry, airy place with a

Lilac (*Syringa*)

Lily-of-the-valley (*Convallaria*)

Lilyturf (*Liriope*)

Lupine (*Lupinus*)

Magic Lily (*Lycoris*)

Maltese cross (*Lychnis*)

Mock orange (*Philadelphus*)

Mountain bluet (*Centaurea montana*)

Pachysandra

Pampas grass (*Cortaderia*)

Phlox, garden (*Phlox paniculata*)

Pincushion flower (*Scabiosa*)

Pinks, garden (*Dianthus*)

Primrose, polyanthus (*Primula × polyantha*)

Purple coneflower (*Echinacea*)

Raspberry, blackberry (*Rubus*)

Ribbon grass (*Phalaris*)

Rock cress (*Arabis*)

Sea pink (*Armeria*)

Sneezeweed (*Helenium*)

Snowdrop (*Galanthus*)

Snow-in-summer (*Cerastium*)

Speedwell (*Veronica*)

Spiderwort (*Tradescantia*)

Spiraea

Squill, Siberian (*Scilla siberica*)

Stonecrop (*Sedum*)

Summersweet (*Clethra*)

Sundrops (*Oenothera*)

Sunflower (*Heliopsis*)

Sweet woodruff (*Galium*)

Tulip (*Tulipa*)

Violet, viola (*Viola*)

Yarrow (*Achillea*)

temperature no lower than 50° F. Always make sure the surfaces of the roots are dry before storing, or they may rot or develop mildew.

DIVIDING SHRUBS

Some shrubs, such as mock-orange (*Philadelphus* spp.) and *Spiraea* species, form crowns or clumps or spread by means of underground shoots, and can be divided like perennials. In most climates the best time to divide shrubs is in early spring while the plants are still dormant. Where winters are mild you should divide in autumn.

If it is not too large, dig the mature shrub, cut the clump into sections, and replant immediately. If the shrub has sent out suckers or stems that have rooted, you can use a spade to sever them from the main plant without digging the plant, then dig and replant the severed young plants. Or you can carefully dig out the youngsters and detach them from the parent with pruning shears or a saw. In all cases, replant the divisions right away.

CHAPTER THREE

Plants from the Nursery

Plants are sold by garden centers and nurseries in three forms: in containers, bare-rooted, or balled-and-burlapped. Annuals for bedding, herbs, and vegetables are usually sold in flats, six-packs, or small individual pots. Herbaceous perennials usually come in pots. Bulbs are sold loose or in mesh bags. Trees and shrubs may be container-grown, bare-rooted, or balled-and-burlapped. This chapter provides some guidelines for choosing the healthiest specimens, and for planting and caring for the different types of plants.

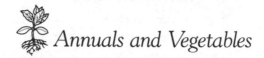

Annuals and Vegetables

The best way to get top-quality bedding plants and vegetables is to buy from a reputable local nursery or garden center. If you are new to gardening or to your area, ask gardening friends where they buy their plants. Find out which local firms have been in business for a long time. Visit the garden centers to look over the plants; observe the conditions in which they are kept and ask questions of the staff. Plants in good condition, neat and clean surroundings, and a knowledgeable staff are indicators of a well-run establishment.

It is usually wise to avoid buying plants in supermarkets and discount stores—their main business is not horticultural, and they often have plants of poor quality. Also, the sales staff probably has no training in caring for plants before they're sold; it's not uncommon to see seedlings and potted plants wilting on the hot sidewalk in front of supermarkets and bargain stores because no one has thought to water or shade them. Plants kept in such conditions are subject to a great deal of stress, and chances are they were not top quality to begin with. They may be cheaper than nursery plants, but they may be no bargain because they may not perform well in your garden.

When choosing annual bedding plants, vegetables, or herbs at the garden center, look for plants that are stocky, compact, and bushy. Don't buy the largest plants—they will suffer more shock when you transplant them, and their growth will be set back. It may be tempting to buy vegetables already fruiting or annuals already in bloom, but these plants may end up producing most of their crop or flowers *later* than smaller plants that make a quicker and easier transition into your garden.

Stay away from spindly, gangly plants that may not have gotten enough light, and avoid buying top-heavy plants that have grown too big for their containers. Instead, look for plants with a healthy green color (not pale or yellowed); firm, straight stems; large leaves that are close together on the stem; and a generally healthy, sturdy appearance. Check for signs of pests and disease (look especially in the leaf axils and on the undersides of leaves). Shake the plants gently to see if whiteflies are present. Scrape away some of the surface soil from seedlings in the cabbage family to check for club root; if the roots look soft and yellowish, don't buy the plants.

If you have a choice between seedlings in individual containers, divided flats, or market packs, choose them over undivided flats crowded with plants. Plants in their own containers will have larger root systems that will suffer less disturbance during transplanting than seedlings whose roots will have to be blocked or disentangled.

Turn over the individual pots to see if roots are growing through the drainage hole. If you see lots of roots there, the plant is root-bound and too large for its container. Make another selection.

The techniques for planting bedding plants are discussed on page 47 under Special Tips for Transplanting Out. Most nursery plants will already be hardened-off when you buy them ready for the garden. However, many nurseries have plants—especially tender ones—for sale a bit in advance of planting time. The plants are displayed outdoors at the nursery during the day and moved back indoors at night. If you are buying impatiens or tomatoes or other tender plants early in the season, inquire at the nursery whether the plants are fully accustomed to outdoor conditions.

If you cannot put newly purchased plants in the garden right away, place them in a protected location out of direct sun and sheltered from strong winds until you can plant them. Check the soil in the flats or pots daily, and when it feels dry below the surface, water thoroughly.

Annuals are usually planted in groups or drifts in flower gardens, or in rows in vegetable plots and cutting gardens.

There are several planting systems you can choose from for vegetables, including conventional single rows, wide rows, and intensive beds. The traditional method is the single row. To plant in single rows, space plants at the distance recommended on the plant label or in Part 2. Single rows have a generous amount of space between them to allow the gardener easy access to the plants to weed, water, and harvest. But single rows make the least efficient use of garden space. If row planting appeals to you and your soil is

The tomatoes in the rear of this garden illustrate the traditional single-row method of planting. Wide-row planting is shown with the lettuce plants in front. Wide rows make more efficient use of garden space.

BED ROW

SQUARE~CENTER

EQUIDISTANT

Intensive planting includes the use of bed rows (top), square-center spacing (center), and equidistant spacing (bottom).

in good shape, you may want to try planting in double or wide rows—two or three rows spaced the same distance apart as plants within the row, with standard between-row spacings separating the wide rows to allow access for weeding and watering.

The most efficient systems for planting vegetables involve intensive spacing—the plants are much closer together than in conventional rows. In intensive spacing, the leaves of neighboring plants just barely touch when the plants are mature. This system is feasible only in beds that are accessible from all sides and small enough so that you can reach into the center without stepping into the bed. For most of us, a comfortable width is 4 feet. The soil in intensive beds must be of superior quality to support so many plants. It must be deeply dug, loose, crumbly, rich in organic matter, well supplied with nutrients, and well drained but still able to hold moisture. The beds can be raised or at the same level as the surrounding soil.

Three planting schemes are available for intensive beds. In the bed-row system, plants are set in rows spaced closely together.

Another system, called square-center spacing, divides the bed into a grid, with plants spaced the same distance apart on four sides. In equidistant spacing, rows of plants are staggered, with the plants equidistant from one another in all directions. Staggering the rows allows you to fit the maximum number of plants in the bed.

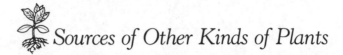 *Sources of Other Kinds of Plants*

Perennials, shrubs, trees, and bulbs can all be purchased both locally and by mail. There are advantages and disadvantages to both sources.

In local nurseries and garden centers you can see what you are buying. The plants are usually container-grown or balled-and-burlapped, so they can be held for a short time before planting if you are busy. The drawback is that garden centers cannot offer as great a selection of plants and colors as a mail-order firm. You won't find rare varieties at the garden center, but you will, as a rule, find plants that grow well in your area. Some local nurseries put out catalogs; if yours does, get a copy and study it while you are planning your garden, before you buy plants.

Nurseries have the largest selection of plants in spring, but it's a good idea to visit at other times of year, too, to see what's there and which plants may be in bloom or showing their autumn foliage. These visits can help you plan additions to your garden and yard for future seasons. Also, more and more gardeners are discovering the advantages of planting in fall. Hardy bulbs have always been planted in fall, as are many shrubs and trees. Gardeners in many parts of the country can plant some types of perennials in fall, as well as sow seeds of hardy annuals for bloom the following spring. In the warmest climate zones, most planting is done in autumn and winter.

If you are unsure of the environmental needs of a plant you are considering buying, ask the staff. They should be helpful and informative; if they are not, take your business elsewhere.

Some local nurseries offer assistance in planning your garden and for a fee will help you design your landscape and select plants. Sometimes these services are extremely helpful, and sometimes they are primarily a way to sell more plants.

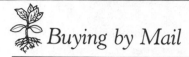 *Buying by Mail*

The mail-order nursery business is healthy and growing in the United States; sales of perennials, trees, and shrubs have increased markedly in recent years. Even venerable seed houses like Burpee have added many nursery plants to their catalogs. Mail-order nurseries offer a wide selection of plants, many of which (most trees and shrubs, for example) are shipped bare-rooted and must be planted as soon as they arrive. Some plants are shipped in containers—usually herbaceous perennials. If in doubt about in what form your plants will arrive, ask the nursery.

Gardeners all tend to have their favorite mail-order suppliers. If you are unsure which companies are reliable, the best way to find out is to read their catalogs. Splashy color photographs are not necessarily the best indicator of a reputable firm. Read the plant descriptions—the plant's botanical name should be given, along with an informative (but not hyperbolic) description; the climate zones or regions where the plant will grow; and special environmental needs, such as a tolerance or preference for shade. Beware of catalogs full of "wonder plants" and "miracle flowers"—if the plants sound too good to be true, they probably are. Some catalog companies are actually growers of the plants they sell; others are middlemen selling stock grown elsewhere. It is usually best to buy directly from a grower—growers take great pride in what they sell, and they are generally willing to give cultural advice and answer questions. When reading mail-order catalogs, in addition to reading the plant descriptions, look for information on whether or not the company grows the plants they sell. Will they send complete cultural information with every plant they ship? Will they replace plants that die in their first season?

Before ordering, study the catalog to familiarize yourself with the company's shipping policies, dates, method of shipment, and return policy.

Most nurseries try to ship at or near the right planting date for your area, but if you specify a shipping date, many nurseries will oblige. Specifying a shipping date can be especially helpful if you are ordering plants from a specialty supplier in a different part of the country.

If your plants arrive in poor condition, report it to the supplier. Most companies will give you replacement plants or a refund if the plants were damaged during shipping and not as a result of careless treatment after you received them. See the sections on Container-Grown Plants on page 94 and Bare-Rooted Plants on page 97 for information on how to care for plants from mail-order sources if you cannot plant them right away.

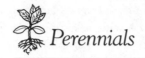 *Perennials*

Garden centers have the largest selection of perennial plants in spring. Buy them as early in the season as you can to get the widest choice and the healthiest plants, and also to give the plants the longest possible growing season in your garden.

Mail-order nurseries generally ship plants in the season when they are best planted—spring or fall. In many cases plants shipped in early spring are dug at the nursery the previous fall before the ground freezes, then held over the winter in refrigerated storage. When you receive perennials by mail, unpack them right away. If you cannot plant them immediately, put them in a cold frame or other sheltered place and do not let them dry out. Order early to get the best selection.

Whether you buy plants at the garden center or receive them by mail, examine them carefully. Container plants should be compact, healthy, sturdy, and actively growing. Avoid plants with spindly stems, pale or yellowed leaves, damaged leaves, and distorted or misshapen leaves and flowers. Look for signs of pests and disease. If you can't plant right away, keep the plants watered—small pots dry out quickly. Perennials purchased through mail-order companies may be shipped while they are dormant. In this case you will receive roots or crowns of the dormant plants. Perennial roots and crowns should be firm, with no evidence of mold or fungus and no soft spots.

 Bulbs

You can buy bulbs by mail or at local garden centers. Buying by mail affords a wider choice and also allows you to buy extra-large exhibition grade bulbs or bulbs that are precooled for forcing indoors. But at the garden center you can pick out the bulbs yourself. In either case, here's what to look for.

The bulbs should be firm all over, not soft or shriveled (with a few notable exceptions, like winter aconite and anemones, which will be shriveled and should be soaked before planting). The bulbs should have no soft spots, no discolorations or mold. The *basal plate* (the flat base from which roots grow), on bulbs that have one, should be firm to the touch. You should see no insect damage.

If you are buying locally, select large, solid bulbs. They should feel weighty—if they are very light they are probably dried out. Avoid buying bulbs that have sprouted. Shoots mean that the bulb has started to grow a top before it has had a chance to grow roots to support and nourish the plant.

If you buy from a mail-order firm, examine the bulbs carefully when you get them. It is not uncommon for a shipment of bulbs to contain one or two that are dry or damaged, but if any more than that are less than top quality, complain to the supplier and request replacements. Avoid buying bulbs on sale—the bulbs may be from last season and not of good quality.

Hardy spring bulbs are sold and planted in fall. Gardeners in the coldest climates (Zones 3 and 4) should plant in September; in Zones 5 and 6, plant in September or October; farther south, you can plant in November. Tender summer bulbs are sold and planted in spring, after the danger of frost is past. Autumn-flowering bulbs are shipped in late summer—August and September—and should be planted immediately to bloom a couple of months later.

In all cases be sure to order early; if the bulbs arrive too soon for planting, store them in a cool, dry place until it's time to plant. Be sure to buy enough bulbs to put on a good show in your garden. Small bulbs especially (crocuses, grape hyacinths, squills) are inexpensive, so treat yourself and buy lots of them.

PLANTING BULBS

Bulbs grow best in a loose, deeply dug soil that is rich in organic matter. Dig plenty of compost into the bed, and enrich it with bone meal every year. Add approximately ½ to 1 cup of bone meal per square yard of bed.

For the most effective display, plant the bulbs in clusters or groups. Large bulbs such as daffodils and tulips need only three or five to make a group; small bulbs such as crocuses look better when planted in groups of eleven or thirteen. Plant odd numbers, not

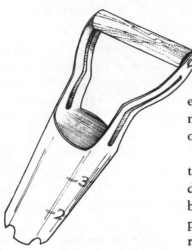

A bulb planter makes it simple to plant bulbs at the proper depth.
Long-handled models are also available.

even numbers, for a more natural look. If you want to create a naturalistic effect over a large area, scatter handfuls of bulbs on top of the soil and plant them where they fall.

The depth of planting varies with the size of the bulb. A rule of thumb is to plant bulbs two and one-half times deeper than the diameter of the bulb; specific depths are given in Part 2. Special bulb-planting devices make it easy to dig the holes—you simply push the tool into the soil to the correct depth, and when you remove it the soil comes along.

 ## Container-Grown Plants

Many nurseries now grow, ship, and sell plants in containers. Container-grown plants are becoming increasingly popular for a number of reasons. The plants can be planted in gardens at any time during the growing season—they can be planted while in active growth or even in bloom. Transferring plants from containers to the garden imposes very little damage on roots, so the plants suffer minimal transplant shock. In addition, if you are too busy or the weather is not suitable to plant the plants as soon as you buy them at the garden center or receive them in the mail, you can leave the plants in their containers for several days or even a few weeks before you put them in the ground. Just make sure to put them in a sheltered spot and keep them well watered while you are holding them.

Nurseries grow the plants in black plastic tubs, composition or pressed cardboard pots, or metal containers. One thing to keep in mind is that sometimes plants are field-grown and then dug and potted up to be sold. These plants are not established in their containers and must be handled more carefully than true container-grown plants. They should be treated like bare-rooted plants and planted immediately. Ask at the nursery when you buy plants if they were grown in their containers.

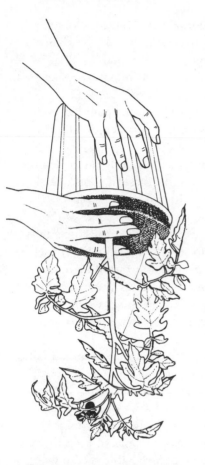

When removing a nursery plant from its pot, support the stem and soil ball with one hand as you tip the pot upside down with your other hand.

PLANTING CONTAINER-GROWN PLANTS

Most containers should be removed at planting time. You may even want to take plants out of biodegradable pressed-cardboard containers to make sure they have not developed a condition called "container habit" (discussed below). Metal containers can be hard to remove, so have the nursery cut the container before you take the plant home.

The best way to remove a plant from its container is to turn the container upside down, supporting the plant by placing your hand over the top of the soil. Tap the bottom of the pot with the handle of a trowel, and the plant should slide out easily with its root ball intact. For large plants in big containers you will need an assistant. Turn the pot on its side, and have your assistant support the top of the plant while you tap the bottom and, if necessary, the sides, of the container. If the plant does not slip readily out of the container, you will have to cut the container away from the root ball. Never tug on the plant's stem or leaves to pull it from the container—you can easily damage the plant and set back its growth.

When the plant is out of the pot, examine its root system carefully. The roots of container-grown plants are accustomed to a small space and to receiving regular watering. In the garden, however, the roots will have to travel down through the soil to find adequate supplies of moisture and nutrients to support the plant.

In the container, the roots coil around and around the inside of the pot. If the plant has been in the container a long time, the roots may have filled it completely, and some of the roots may have become twisted around each other. Some of the larger roots, with no place else to go, may have broken through the soil surface and wrapped around the trunk or stem. Eventually they could strangle the plant.

When you move the plant into the garden, the roots may be reluctant to stretch out into the garden soil. After all, they are accustomed to being in a light, loose potting medium. Instead of striking out into the denser garden soil surrounding the root ball, the roots may keep coiling around and around, as if they were still growing in the pot. This condition is known as *container habit*. A plant with container habit will survive as long as it receives regular water. But when the soil freezes or dries out to the depth of the bottom of the root ball, the plant will die because it has sent no roots out into the surrounding soil.

You can help plants to break the container habit. First of all, when you dig the planting hole make it substantially larger than the plant's root ball (8 to 12 inches larger for perennials or 18 to 24 inches larger for trees and shrubs). To help roots make an easier transition between the potting medium and the garden soil, improve the soil texture by mixing the soil from the planting hole with an equal amount of compost, peat moss, vermiculite, perlite, or sand.

Remove the plant from its container and carefully untangle and spread out the roots. If the root ball is a tight mass of roots, take a sharp knife and cut through it vertically in two or three places. Try to ease the root ball apart. In extreme cases, pry out some of the longer, tougher roots with a large screwdriver and break them away from the ball to encourage the plant to send out new roots. If the plant has a long *taproot* (a large main root that grows straight down and deep into the soil), straighten it out as much as you can before planting. Also look at the roots on top of the soil ball, where they attach to the stem or trunk. If you see any roots wrapped around the trunk or other roots, cut them off.

As you work around the roots, you may find that some soil falls out of the root ball and leaves a hole or opening among the roots. Fill any such cavities with some of your improved soil mix before you put the plant in the garden hole. All this work on the roots must be done quickly, before the roots start to dry out. It might be a good idea to mist the roots with water as you work to keep them moist. Plants that have not developed container habit need only have the root ball gently squeezed a few times to loosen the roots before you set them in the planting hole.

Set the plant in the hole so that it will be at the same depth as it was growing in the container. Spread the roots gently down and outward to encourage them to grow into the soil. Fill in around the roots with soil, working it carefully around them with your fingers. When the hole is half filled with soil, fill it with water to settle the soil around the roots and to eliminate air pockets. When the water has drained away, fill the rest of the hole with soil and firm it around the stem or trunk. Then water again. Check to make sure no nursery tags remain on the plant; if you find any, remove them. A nursery tag left on a branch or trunk can constrict the limb as the plant grows and may eventually cut into the bark and open a pathway for disease or pests to attack.

When planting container-grown plants whose roots have become potbound, you may need to make several vertical cuts in the root ball with a sharp knife before you can ease the roots apart.

Bare-Rooted Plants

Bare-rooted plants are dug from nursery beds, and the soil is washed or shaken from their roots before the plants are shipped. The plants are shipped (and planted) while they are dormant. Nurseries ship plants in this form because without soil they are lighter and thus less expensive to ship. Deciduous trees and shrubs and small evergreens are often shipped in this form, as are roses and some herbaceous perennials. Nut trees, and some fruit and shade trees, which have long taproots, are also shipped bare-rooted because they would be difficult to ball-and-burlap.

Bare-rooted plants are sold with their roots wrapped in damp sphagnum moss or excelsior to keep them moist, and are packaged in plastic, cardboard, or waxed paper containers. Sometimes the plants are sold with their roots in a loose packing medium.

Examine the plants carefully when they arrive from the mail-order supplier or before you buy them at the garden center or nursery. The plants are supposed to be dormant, and should not be putting out new shoots. If the plants do have new shoots more than a couple of inches long, don't buy them. The existing canes or branches should be firm and appear healthy. If they are shriveled and dry, return or do not purchase the plant.

Whether you receive your bare-rooted plants by mail or buy them at a garden center, you will need to plant them as soon as possible after you get them. The plants must be dormant at the time of planting. In most parts of Zones 7 and 8, autumn is the best time to plant; in the South, Southwest, and southern California (Zones 9 and 10), you can plant in winter. In northern gardens, the best time to plant is in very early spring, as soon as the soil can be worked.

It is absolutely vital that the plants' roots are never allowed to dry out. As soon as the plants arrive, or as soon as you get them home, open the package, put the plants in water deep enough to cover all the roots, and let them soak overnight. Plant them the next day if you possibly can. Keep the roots in water, or wrap them in plastic or wet cloths, until you actually put the plant in the hole. If you must hold the plants longer than a day or two, *heel* them into a shallow trench (setting them on an angle and covering the roots loosely with soil).

If you cannot plant bare-rooted stock within a day or two of receiving it, heel the plants into a shallow trench, lean them at an angle, and loosely cover the roots and most of the stems with soil.

PLANTING BARE-ROOTED PLANTS

Dig the planting hole 8 to 12 inches wider than the root spread and deep enough so the plant is positioned at the same depth as it was growing at the nursery. The soil line may be visible on the stem; if you cannot see a soil line, look for the point where the roots join the stem. This point should, in most cases, be 1 to 2 inches below the soil surface. When the hole is dug, put a shovelful of compost in the bottom and mix it into the soil in the bottom of the hole.

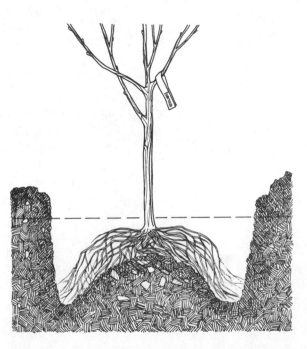

To plant a bare-rooted plant, set the plant in the hole on top of a mound of soil and spread the roots down and over the mound (left). When the hole is half-filled with soil, water to eliminate air pockets between roots and soil (center). When the hole is completely filled with soil, rock the plant gently back and forth to settle it (right); then water again.

Remove the plant from the bucket of water. Inspect the roots carefully to check for damage. If you find any bruised or broken ones, take a sharp pair of pruning shears and cut off the roots right above the damaged parts.

Check the topgrowth as well, and cut off any weak or damaged stems. For additional details on pruning, see Pruning at Planting Time on page 103 and the entries on individual plants in Part 2.

A traditional way to help keep roots moist during and after planting is to make a slurry of fine, silty soil and water, and dip the roots into it before putting the plant in the ground. The soil particles coat the fine root hairs that are especially quick to dry out, and keep them moist during planting.

Position the plant in the hole and carefully spread the roots out and downward, the way they normally grow. You may find it easier to make a mound of soil in the bottom of the hole and spread the roots over it and down the sides. Straighten the roots so they do not double over or crowd one another.

Fill the hole about halfway with soil, then fill the hole with water to settle the soil around the roots and to eliminate air pockets. When the water has drained through the hole, fill the remainder of the hole with soil, rock the plant gently to settle it,

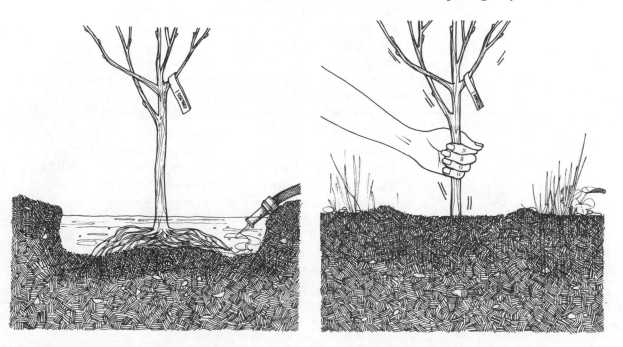

and water again. If your soil tends to be dry, construct an earth ridge just inside the circumference of the planting hole to hold water. Make sure the plant receives plenty of regular moisture as it establishes itself in its new home. If the weather is dry you will have to water. Check for any nursery tags that may remain on the plant and remove them.

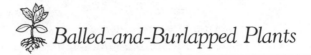

Balled-and-Burlapped Plants

Some trees and shrubs are sold with their roots in a ball of soil, wrapped in burlap. Balling-and-burlapping is used for deciduous trees and shrubs whose relatively shallow, many-branched root systems can be easily contained within a ball of soil. It is also used for azaleas, rhododendrons, and other broad-leaved evergreens, which never go totally dormant, as well as for live Christmas trees and other needled evergreens. Balling-and-burlapping allows plants to be moved with minimal disturbance to their roots.

Nurseries usually grow these plants in fields and dig them along with their soil ball. Often the plants' roots are pruned while the plant is being grown in the field to produce a compact, sturdy root system that will hold the soil ball well.

You can plant balled-and-burlapped plants whenever the soil is workable, but spring and fall are the best times. Moisture is critical for the roots to establish themselves in the garden, and summer heat and drought can severely stress the plants.

If you are buying a balled-and-burlapped plant at the nursery, check the soil ball carefully. Some nurseries sell plants with an artificial soil ball made by compressing peat moss or another lightweight material around the roots and wrapping the ball in burlap. These plants are not truly balled-and-burlapped; they are actually bare-rooted and you should handle them as such.

Balled-and-burlapped plants are heavy—a 10-inch soil ball (appropriate for a plant 18 to 24 inches tall) weighs 30 pounds; the 15-inch soil ball needed for 4- to 5-foot plants weighs 75 pounds. The diameter of the root ball is generally about one-quarter to one-third the plant's height. Transporting and planting balled-and-burlapped stock is usually a two-person operation. At the very least you will probably need a dolly to move the plants.

When you are moving a balled-and-burlapped plant, carry it with your hands under the soil ball, to keep the ball from breaking open. Carrying the plant by its stem or branches can break up the soil ball and damage the roots.

It's best to plant balled-and-burlapped plants as soon as you get them home from the nursery. If you can't plant right away, set the plants in a shady spot, cover the soil balls with a loose mulch, and keep the soil moist until you can get the plants into the ground.

Dig the planting hole 18 to 24 inches wider and deeper than the size of the soil ball. Mix a shovelful or two of compost with the soil from the hole before planting. Put some of this soil in the bottom of the hole and work it in well; make sure the soil in the bottom of the hole is nice and loose.

Carefully lift the plant and lower it into the hole. Remember to bend from your knees instead of your waist when you (and your assistant, if you need one) are picking up the plant, and keep your back straight as you lift the plant. Bending over to pick up a heavy object is a good way to injure your back.

The burlap wrapping, if it is true burlap (made of cotton or jute), will decay underground, so it is not necessary to remove it at planting time. You should, however, cut off any ropes that are binding the soil ball together, loosen the burlap around the soil ball,

When planting a balled-and-burlapped plant, be sure to roll back the burlap so that it will be completely underground when the hole is filled with soil.

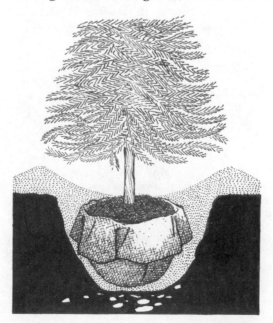

and roll it back so it will be completely underground when the planting hole is filled with soil. If the "burlap" is actually polypropylene, you will need to remove it entirely.

Lower the plant carefully into the hole, working slowly so you don't crack the soil ball. The top of the soil ball should be level with, or in some cases slightly above, the surrounding soil level. In very loose soil it is good to set the plant slightly higher to allow for settling, and in heavy soils you should plant high to promote good drainage. When the plant is in the hole, carefully fill in around the soil ball with the compost-enriched soil you prepared. Don't pack the soil too tightly—you want to avoid compacting it. Follow the same procedure described earlier for bare-rooted plants: fill the hole halfway with soil, then fill it with water. When the water drains away, fill the rest of the hole with soil, then water again to settle it around the plant.

If your garden soil tends toward dryness, make a shallow depression in the soil just inside the circumference of the planting hole to catch and hold water. Make sure this saucer is smaller than the diameter of the root ball to be sure that the captured water soaks down into the root ball and not alongside it. To avoid constricting future growth remove any nursery tags still remaining on the plant.

Balled-and-burlapped plants also benefit from pruning after you plant them, as described in the following section.

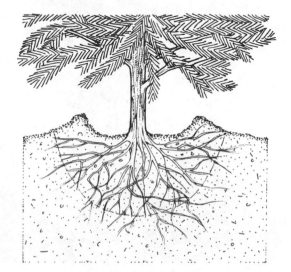

If the soil tends to be dry, make a depression around the base of new plants to catch and hold water, ensuring as much moisture as possible for the roots.

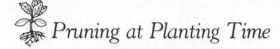

Pruning at Planting Time

Woody plants need to be pruned when they are planted to compensate for the loss of some roots during transplanting and to put less of a strain on the remaining roots so they can establish themselves in the soil more quickly. Container-grown plants need the least amount of pruning at planting time. Plants with a rounded growth habit, such as dwarf boxwood, can simply be sheared back to improve their shape. For taller plants with an open-centered habit, such as mock orange, prune away weak, spindly branches to open up the plant's shape. You can cut back the topgrowth by as much as one-third in order to get the plants off to a good start.

Bare-rooted trees require a little more attention than container-grown trees. At planting time prune broken or crushed roots as described on page 99. Leave healthy roots just as they are. Prune broken or damaged branches, any branch that crosses over another branch, and any branch that grows vertically (at an angle of 45 degrees or less) from the trunk of the tree. Leave all other healthy branches alone.

It is important to remove any branches emerging at an angle of less than 45 degrees from the trunk of a fruit tree. The branches left on a fruit tree at this stage of growth become the scaffold branches—the primary structure—that will have to support the weight of the fruit in future years. Branches that emerge from the trunk at an angle of 45 degrees or more are stronger than branches

UNPRUNED FRUIT TREE

OVERHEAD VIEW PRUNED TREE

When planting fruit trees, remove branches emerging from the trunk at an angle of less than 45 degrees (left), and be sure the scaffold branches (right, shown in top view) are distributed evenly around the trunk.

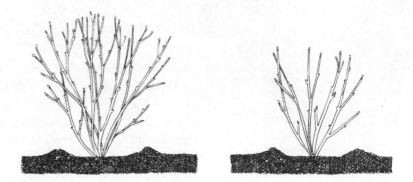

When planting bare-rooted woody shrubs, prune away spindly or damaged branches as well as branches that cross over other branches.

growing more vertically. The scaffold branches should be evenly distributed around the trunk. Fruit trees growing in a central leader form (such as apples) should have the leader cut back to a length of about 3 feet; trees with an open-centered habit (such as peaches and apricots) should have the central leader removed in its entirety.

Bare-rooted trees and shrubs with more than one main stem can be thinned at planting time. Cut back any weak or damaged stems all the way to ground level. Cut back the remaining stems by one-half to bring the topgrowth into balance with the root system, some of which was lost when the plant was dug and prepared for shipment at the nursery. If you are planting bush fruits, such as blueberries, remove any fruit buds you find on the bush—the plants should not be allowed to bear fruit during their first season in the garden.

Balled-and-burlapped trees and shrubs have more of their root system intact than bare-rooted plants, so you do not need to prune their topgrowth as severely. For trees with a central leader, do not prune the leader, but cut back the rest of the branches by one-third. Cut back the branches of multistemmed trees and shrubs by one-third. Also, remove any weak, damaged, or crossed branches. Shear back lightly the branches of needled evergreens. See Part 2 for specific pruning needs of individual plants.

Caring for Newly Transplanted Plants

Water is the most important requirement for new transplants. Regular, even moisture is essential for new roots to establish themselves in the soil. If the weather is hot and your garden receives less than an inch of rain every week to 10 days, water your new plants twice a week. Be sure to water thoroughly, so the moisture soaks down to the bottom of the root ball. Just wetting the soil surface will encourage the plants to send out shallow roots that will be harmed quickly during spells of dry weather. You want instead to encourage your plants to send roots deep into the soil where they will be better able to withstand droughts.

Mulch is also helpful for new plants. A 3- to 4-inch layer of loose, organic mulch (such as salt hay, shredded bark, or compost) will help conserve soil moisture, maintain an even soil temperature, and keep down weeds during the plants' first year in the garden. If you are planting in early spring, wait until the soil warms up before laying the mulch. If you are planting in fall, you can apply the mulch right after planting.

SPECIAL CARE FOR TREES

Young trees need a bit more care after planting than do shrubs and herbaceous plants. It is a good idea to wrap the trunks of young trees with a special tree wrapping paper to prevent sunscald, reduce moisture loss, and help prevent borers from attacking. Begin where the lowest branch meets the trunk and wrap downward to the base in neat, overlapping spirals. You can bind the tree wrap with twine to reinforce it. The tree wrap can be left in place for up to 2 years.

Most trees with trunks more than an inch in diameter will also need to be staked or supported by guy wires to keep them upright and put less strain on the roots while they are establishing themselves. For trees 2 inches or less in diameter, drive an 8-foot stake into the ground next to the trunk. Fasten the tree to the stake with a loop of cloth, burlap or soft rope, or sturdy wire threaded through a piece of old garden hose. Never use wire alone, because it can cut into the bark as the tree grows. For trees 2 to 3 inches in diameter, use two or three stakes on opposite sides of the trunk. For bigger trees, you can attach guy wires to lag hooks in the trunk or thread them through pieces of hose and run them around the lower branches, then connect the wires to low stakes on opposite sides of the tree.

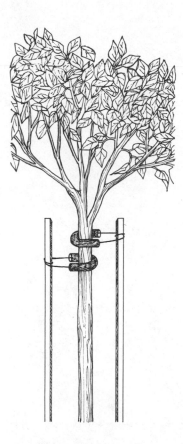

Fasten newly planted trees to stakes using pieces of heavy wire threaded through a piece of old garden hose.

Part 2

Planting
Guide

CHAPTER 4

How to Plant Your Favorite Plants

The following pages offer guidelines for planting and propagating more than 250 vegetables, herbs, fruits, nuts, annuals, perennials, trees, and shrubs.

Bear in mind that gardening is not a precise science, and that gardening procedures cannot be reduced to formulas. The information given in this book—as in any gardening book—represents an average set of conditions under which the plants grow best for most people. But plants are living things, and they perform differently in different gardens and varying weather conditions from year to year.

Experimenting with different plants in your garden over the years will teach you which propagation methods will work best for you. The heading *Propagation* appears in each of the plant entries that follows in this chapter. Under this heading, you will find listed the best ways to reproduce each plant. Other propagation methods may also be feasible, but those listed in this category are the easiest and most likely to succeed. They are presented in descending order of reliability for home gardeners—the method I think will work best for typical backyard conditions is given first.

A number of standard terms are used throughout this plant guide. Here's what they mean.

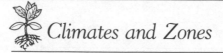

Climates and Zones

Climates and hardiness zones, like all other aspects of gardens, are not absolute. Local conditions and microclimates within geographic areas are very variable. For example, a garden in an exposed, windy site or at the bottom of a hill where cold air collects may have growing conditions equivalent to those of the next zone north. Conversely, a bed next to the south-facing wall of a house is more sheltered than the local norm; plants in such a location will bloom earlier than usual, and you may be able to grow some plants that are not ordinarily hardy in your zone.

Most plant entries in this book give information on individual plants in terms of USDA hardiness zones where possible and applicable. Climates are described using three general terms: *cool*, *temperate*, and *warm*. You can interpret cool climates to refer generally to Zones 3 to 5, temperate climates to indicate Zones 6 and 7, and warm climates to mean Zones 8 to 10. Zones 6 and 7 wind their way across the country and represent more or less average growing conditions, if indeed there is such a thing as an average condition. Zones 3 to 5 have a shorter, cooler growing season than Zones 6 and 7, and Zones 8 to 10 have a long frost-free growing season and mild winters.

Planting Times

When you read about planting times in this chapter, you will not see them given in terms of calendar dates. Instead they are indicated either in terms of number of weeks before or after the average date of the last expected spring frost or first fall frost.

Frost dates are most relevant for vegetables, herbs, and annuals. Your USDA County Extension Agent can give you the average dates of the last and first frost in your area.

Use these dates as a general guide, but remember that they represent an average and will vary from year to year according to weather conditions. Use common sense when planting. If you want to set out tomato plants, and your spring weather has been cooler than normal, wait an extra week or two before planting out.

One reliable way to judge planting conditions is through a close observation of the rhythms of nature, known as *phenology*.

Gardeners who use phenology establish planting times by observing the growth cycle of particular local plants or the activities of animals in the wild, such as the appearance of the first violets, the arrival of the first spring peepers in a pond, or the departure of resident purple martins in the fall. For example, one gardener's maxim advises that you plant tender crops when oak leaves are the size of a mouse's ear (about 1 inch long). Oak trees are the last to leaf out in spring, and when they do, danger of frost is almost certainly past. Watching your oak trees will probably give you a better clue as to when to plant than watching your calendar.

Herbaceous perennials, bulbs, and trees and shrubs (both ornamental and fruiting varieties) are planted either in spring or fall. Gardening tradition used to dictate that spring-blooming plants be planted in fall, and summer- and autumn-blooming plants in spring. But experience has shown that fall is a good time to plant not just spring-blooming plants, but also many trees and shrubs.

The issue of how to define spring and fall in various hardiness zones is trickier. Again, conditions vary from year to year and garden to garden. As a general rule of thumb, the bulk of spring planting takes place in February and March in Zones 8 to 10, in April in Zone 7, and in May in Zones 3 to 6 (later in the month as you go farther north). Most fall planting is done in September in Zones 3 and 4, in September or October in Zones 5 and 6, and in October or November in Zones 7 to 10. Gardeners in Zones 8 to 10 should dig most hardy spring bulbs after they bloom, store them in a cool place over summer, and replant in fall. Consult with your County Extension Agent and other gardeners in your neighborhood to get advice on the best times to plant.

 Soils

Garden soils are composed of four kinds of particles—sand, silt, clay, and humus. The best garden loams are made up of 10 percent humus, 20 to 30 percent clay, and 60 to 70 percent sand and silt. They are crumbly and finely textured. *Sandy loam* soils have a greater proportion of *sand* particles ($\frac{4}{50}$ to $\frac{1}{50}$ of an inch). Sand promotes drainage and the incorporation of air into soil. Sandy soils are very light in texture, drain very quickly, and tend to be dry and relatively low in nutrients. Adding compost or other forms of organic matter gives them more humus and improves their moisture-holding capacity. *Silt* particles are smaller than sand particles but larger than clay particles. *Clay loam* soils are predominantly *clay* particles, which are very tiny ($\frac{1}{500}$ to $\frac{1}{5000}$ of an inch). Clay promotes water retention and helps roots absorb water and trace elements from the soil. Clay particles pack tightly together, making those soils very dense and heavy. Soils high in clay drain slowly and may become waterlogged and compacted. Adding organic matter to clay soils lightens their texture and improves their drainage. *Humus* is a collection of particles of decayed plant matter. Humus acts as a food to beneficial microorganisms in the soil, improves drainage by increasing soil porosity, and returns nitrogen, potassium, phosphorous, and trace elements to the soil.

Drainage is an important characteristic to consider when planning any garden. Good drainage is essential for most plants; most popular garden plants don't grow well in soggy soil. Although water and the nutrients dissolved in it are necessary for roots, oxygen is also essential. Waterlogged soils do not allow roots to receive enough oxygen. On the other hand, soils that drain too quickly do not allow roots time to absorb enough water and dissolved nutrients to fuel plant growth. The ideal soil is one that holds moisture long enough that roots can absorb what they need, but not so long that they suffocate from lack of air. This is what is meant by moist but well-drained soil.

Fertility is determined by the amount of organic matter and nutrients a soil contains. Rich soils are high in both organic matter and nutrients—nitrogen, phosphorous, potassium—and contain trace elements (such as iron and boron). Plants that are heavy feeders grow best in rich soils.

In a fertile soil, nutrients and trace elements are available to plant roots in a chemical form that plants can use for growth, repair, and reproduction. The availability of nutrients and trace elements to plant roots is enhanced by healthy levels of soil microorganisms, by the activities of soil-dwelling creatures such as insects and worms, and by a soil pH that is neither too acid nor too alkaline. To sum up, a rich, fertile soil teems with microscopic and insect life; it contains an abundance of humus, which serves as a source of food for these denizens of the underground; and it has a texture that supports both the incorporation of air and the retention of enough water to help the plants take in nourishment.

Soils of average fertility are fine for most plants, and soils of less-than-average fertility are even preferred by some types of plants. For example, the flavor of some herbs is intensified when the plants grow in poor soil because poor soil causes the leaves to produce more of the volatile oils that give them their taste and scent.

Most plants are tolerant of a range of pH. Preferred pH ranges and special pH needs are given for individual plants wherever possible. A pH of 7.0 is considered neutral; numbers below 7.0 indicate acid soils, and numbers above 7.0 indicate alkaline soils. Many plants thrive in a slightly acid to neutral range of 6.0 to 7.0. The pH affects the availability of nutrients and trace elements to plant roots. When soil pH is too strongly acidic or alkaline, trace elements and nutrients assume forms that are not soluble in water. Changes in pH also affect the viability and activity of soil microorganisms. Your local USDA County Extension Agent can test the pH of your soil, and home testing kits are available at many garden centers. Few garden soils are so extremely acid or alkaline that they cannot support plant growth, and it is best to simply choose plants that will thrive in the conditions close to those you have to offer. It is foolish to try to adjust the pH to any great extent, although minor changes can be made. To raise the pH of a too-acid soil, you can add lime. Alkaline soils are usually found only in arid and semiarid regions of the United States. You can reduce the pH of alkaline soils by incorporating naturally acidic amendments, such as composted oak leaves or peat moss; you can also treat alkaline soils with epsom salts or sulfur.

A number of organic soil amendments are useful for adjusting pH, building better soil structure, and adding nutrients. Ground limestone, when incorporated into a heavy clay soil, improves the soil texture by causing the tiny particles to clump together, thus lightening the soil's dense texture. It is also used to raise the pH of very acid soils. Dolomitic lime is especially beneficial because it contains magnesium, which plants need and many soils lack.

Peat moss, a fluffy, dark brown substance, is partially decomposed plant remains. Peat moss is a good source of organic matter and can enhance the ability of light soils to hold water. It is generally acidic and a good soil amendment for acid-loving plants, such as azaleas. Although peat moss can absorb many times its weight in water, when it dries out it can form a hard crust and act as a wick, drawing moisture out of the soil. It is beneficial when incorporated into soil, but it does not make a good mulch.

Compost is the decayed remains of many different life-forms. Gardeners typically make compost by heaping together garden refuse, food scraps, soil, and some animal products, such as eggshells and manure. The nutrient value of compost depends on what went into it, but any properly made compost is excellent for improving soil structure and adding organic matter.

Animal *manures* add organic matter, nitrogen, phosphorous, and potassium, as well as trace elements, to soil. Composted manures are best—fresh manure, especially chicken, which is very high in nitrogen, may burn plant roots. Horse and cow manures are generally considered the best to use. Manure from pets (cats and dogs) should not be used.

Major sources of phosphorous are *bonemeal* and *rock phosphate*. Bonemeal is made from steamed, ground animal bones—a by-product of the meat packing industry. In addition to phosphoric acid, it also contains some nitrogen. Rock phosphate is powdered rock that supplies phosphorous slowly over an extended period of time. Its nutrient is more readily available if you till it into the soil along with compost or manure instead of using it as topdressing.

Good potassium sources include *greensand, granite dust,* and *wood ashes*. Greensand, a mineral compound of iron, potassium, and silica deposited eons ago in ancient seabeds, is not available everywhere. It is also a source of trace elements. Granite dust, which releases its potassium slowly, is a by-product of the building industry. It is best tilled into the soil like rock phosphate. Wood ashes supply potassium and smaller amounts of phosphate, the amounts of both being determined by the type of wood. The nutrients are very soluble, but wood ashes do raise soil pH rather significantly and should be used with care.

 Light

The amounts of sunlight plants need to grow are generally defined as full sun, partial shade, or shade. Full sun means that plants receive at least 6 hours of direct, unobstructed sun each day. Partial shade will give plants 2 to 6 hours of sun, with light shade during the rest of the day. Shade indicates 2 hours of sun—or light, dappled shade all day. Deep shade means that plants receive no direct sunlight at all; few plants can grow in such conditions.

Annuals

AGERATUM
A. houstonianum

WHERE TO PLANT: Full sun to partial shade (where summers are long and hot, Zones 7 and south, plant in light shade), in well-drained soil of average fertility but rich in organic matter, with a pH of 5.0 to 6.0.

WHEN TO PLANT: Start seeds indoors 8 weeks before the last expected frost (February or March) or in a cold frame in March. Seeds germinate in about a week at a soil temperature of 70 to 75° F. Set plants out in the garden after all danger of frost is past. Ageratum grows best in warm weather, but it is considered half-hardy.

SPACING: Space plants of dwarf varieties 6 to 9 inches apart; taller varieties 12 inches apart.

PLANTING DEPTH: Seeds need light to germinate; press them lightly into soil but do not cover with soil.

PROPAGATION: From seeds started indoors. Direct-seeding is not recommended because young seedlings have difficulty competing with weeds.

PLANTING TIPS: If planting nursery seedlings, pinch back the plants when you set them out to encourage bushy, compact growth.

Ageratum is a good plant for edgings, rock gardens, and containers.

ALCEA

A. *rosea*, Hollyhock

WHERE TO PLANT: Full sun, in deep, fertile, well-drained soil, with a pH between 6.0 and 7.0.

WHEN TO PLANT: Start seeds indoors 7 to 8 weeks before the average date of your last frost and set out plants a week or two after the last frost date. Seeds germinate in 1 to 2 weeks at a soil temperature of 70 to 85° F.

Soaking seeds in water overnight hastens germination.

Hollyhocks include both biennials and short-lived perennials, but some cultivars ('Pinafore' and 'Summer Carnival') will bloom the first year if given an early start indoors.

For flowers the second year, direct-seed in spring, 1 to 2 weeks after the last frost.

SPACING: Space plants 18 or more inches apart.

PLANTING DEPTH: Seeds germinate best with some light; barely cover them, and do not plant more than ¼ inch deep.

PROPAGATION: Seeds.

PLANTING TIPS: Hollyhocks grow tall and belong at the back of beds and borders. The plants often self-sow, and plants that bloom the first year will bloom again in their second summer.

Hollyhocks are susceptible to fungus diseases. It is best to destroy severely infected plants.

AMARANTHUS

A. *tricolor*, Joseph's coat, Summer poinsettia

WHERE TO PLANT: Full sun, in average, well-drained soil, with a pH of 6.0 to 7.0. This annual is grown primarily for its brilliantly colored leaves, including red, yellow, orange, and chocolate. Rich soil produces larger leaves, but of paler color. Heavy clay soil may encourage root rot.

WHEN TO PLANT: Start seeds indoors 6 weeks before the last expected frost; seeds germinate in 10 to 14 days at a soil temperature of around 75° F.

Set outdoors after all danger of frost is past. Where summers are long and warm (Zones 7 and south), direct-seed when the soil has warmed in spring. The plant is tender and seeds need warmth to germinate.

SPACING: Thin if necessary so plants stand 2 feet apart.

PLANTING DEPTH: Sow seeds ⅛ inch deep.

PROPAGATION: From seeds started indoors.

PLANTING TIPS: Amaranthus is easy to grow and attractive in the back of beds and borders.

Transplants poorly when large, especially when in bloom.

ANTIRRHINUM

A. majus, Snapdragon

WHERE TO PLANT: Full sun to partial shade, in light, moist but well-drained soil containing plenty of organic matter, and with a pH of 6.0 to 7.0. Snapdragons do not do well in heavy, slow-draining soils.

WHEN TO PLANT: In cool and temperate climates start seeds indoors about 12 weeks before the average date of your last frost. Germination takes 10 to 14 days in soil at 70° F. Move plants to a cold frame in spring when the weather moderates, and plant them in the garden when the danger of frost is past.

In warm climates (Zones 8 to 10), direct-sow in fall for winter flowers.

SPACING: Set plants 6 or more inches apart, depending on variety.

PLANTING DEPTH: Seeds need light to germinate; press them lightly into soil but do not cover with soil.

PROPAGATION: Seeds.

PLANTING TIPS: Snapdragons are perennial where winter temperatures do not drop below 10° F, and they may self-sow farther north. They are prone to fungus diseases (blight, botrytis, anthracnose, and snapdragon rust), so it is best to start with new seeds or plants each year. Be sure to buy disease-resistant seeds or plants resistant to rust; if they are not labeled as resistant, ask the supplier if they are.

(continued)

ANTIRRHINUM—*Continued*

PLANTING TIPS:
(continued)

A range of snapdragon cultivars is available in several flower forms and a host of sizes and colors. Plant tall cultivars in the back of the garden, smaller cultivars in beds, borders, or containers.

Snapdragons make excellent cut flowers.

ARCTOTIS

A. stoechadifolia, African daisy

WHERE TO PLANT: Full sun, in light, well-drained soil of average fertility, with a pH between 6.0 and 7.0. Arctotis tolerates drought but flowers best where nights are cool. It does best in coastal areas.

WHEN TO PLANT: Start seeds indoors 5 to 6 weeks before the average date of your last spring frost. Seeds germinate in approximately 1 to 2 weeks at a soil temperature of 60 to 70° F. Set out plants when the soil is warm and nighttime temperatures no longer drop below 50° F. Arctotis is a tender annual.

SPACING: Set plants 6 to 12 inches apart.

PLANTING DEPTH: Sow seeds ⅛ inch deep.

PROPAGATION: Seeds started indoors.

PLANTING TIPS: Arctotis is a lovely plant for beds and borders, and makes a good cut flower.

BEGONIA

B. × *semperflorens-cultorum*, Wax begonia

WHERE TO PLANT: Sun, partial shade, or shade (best in partial shade), in rich, moist but well-drained soil containing lots of organic matter and with a pH of 6.0 to 7.0.

WHEN TO PLANT: Start seeds indoors 10 or more weeks before the average date of your last spring frost—in January or February. Seeds germinate in about 15 days at a soil temperature of 70 to 80° F. Set plants started indoors or purchased from the nursery out in the garden after all danger of frost has passed and nighttime temperatures no longer drop below 50° F. Begonias are tender and cannot tolerate cold weather.

To start new plants for winter bloom indoors, take leaf or stem cuttings in late spring or summer.

SPACING: Set plants 6 to 8 inches apart in the garden. Young seedlings can be thinned to 1 to 2 inches apart when they develop their first true leaves.

PLANTING DEPTH: Seeds are very fine and need light to germinate. Scatter them over the surface of a very finely textured potting medium (see Recipes for Seed-Starting Media on page 29) and press them in gently but do not cover them.

PROPAGATION: Cuttings or seeds.

PLANTING TIPS: Begonias are nice edging plants for beds and borders, and also grow well in containers. Varieties with bronzy leaves can generally tolerate more sun than green-leaved varieties. Flowers come in shades of red and pink, as well as white.

BRACHYCOME

B. iberidifolia, Swan River daisy

WHERE TO PLANT: Full sun, in light, well-drained soil of average fertility, with a pH of 6.0 to 7.0.

WHEN TO PLANT: Start seeds indoors 5 to 6 weeks before the average date of your last spring frost or direct-seed after all danger of frost is past. Seeds germinate in 10 to 18 days at a soil temperature of 70° F. In mild climates, direct-sow in early spring.

Swan River daisy grows best in cool weather.

SPACING: Space plants 6 inches apart.

PLANTING DEPTH: Cover seeds lightly with soil.

PROPAGATION: Seeds.

PLANTING TIPS: Plants bloom about 80 days after seeds germinate. Brachycome forms handsome, low, colorful mounds and is useful as an edging in beds and borders. Brachycome blooms for only a few weeks before declining. For a longer display, sow seeds at 3-week intervals.

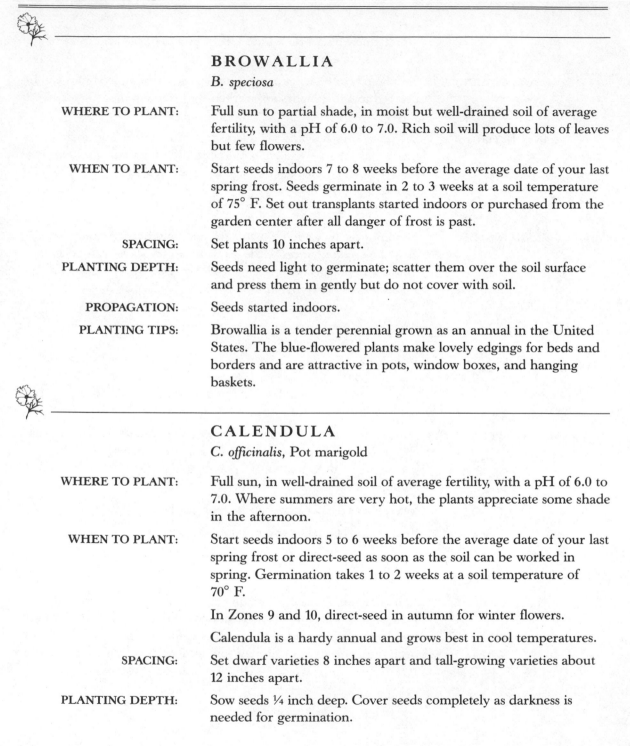

BROWALLIA
B. speciosa

WHERE TO PLANT:
Full sun to partial shade, in moist but well-drained soil of average fertility, with a pH of 6.0 to 7.0. Rich soil will produce lots of leaves but few flowers.

WHEN TO PLANT:
Start seeds indoors 7 to 8 weeks before the average date of your last spring frost. Seeds germinate in 2 to 3 weeks at a soil temperature of 75° F. Set out transplants started indoors or purchased from the garden center after all danger of frost is past.

SPACING:
Set plants 10 inches apart.

PLANTING DEPTH:
Seeds need light to germinate; scatter them over the soil surface and press them in gently but do not cover with soil.

PROPAGATION:
Seeds started indoors.

PLANTING TIPS:
Browallia is a tender perennial grown as an annual in the United States. The blue-flowered plants make lovely edgings for beds and borders and are attractive in pots, window boxes, and hanging baskets.

CALENDULA
C. officinalis, Pot marigold

WHERE TO PLANT:
Full sun, in well-drained soil of average fertility, with a pH of 6.0 to 7.0. Where summers are very hot, the plants appreciate some shade in the afternoon.

WHEN TO PLANT:
Start seeds indoors 5 to 6 weeks before the average date of your last spring frost or direct-seed as soon as the soil can be worked in spring. Germination takes 1 to 2 weeks at a soil temperature of 70° F.

In Zones 9 and 10, direct-seed in autumn for winter flowers.

Calendula is a hardy annual and grows best in cool temperatures.

SPACING:
Set dwarf varieties 8 inches apart and tall-growing varieties about 12 inches apart.

PLANTING DEPTH:
Sow seeds ¼ inch deep. Cover seeds completely as darkness is needed for germination.

PROPAGATION: Seeds.

PLANTING TIPS: Calendula is easy to grow; its sunny golden flowers are nice in beds and borders and good for cutting. Calendula grows well in containers.

Slugs are fond of calendulas, so if slugs are a problem in your garden, you may want to avoid this plant.

CALLISTEPHUS
C. chinensis, China aster

WHERE TO PLANT: Full sun is best, although partial shade is acceptable. Soil should be moist but well-drained, of average fertility, with a pH of 6.0 to 7.0.

WHEN TO PLANT: Start seeds indoors 5 to 6 weeks before the average date of your last spring frost. Seeds germinate in 10 to 14 days at a soil temperature of 70° F.

Direct-seed or set out transplants after all danger of frost is past.

SPACING: Set plants 10 to 15 inches apart.

PLANTING DEPTH: Sow seeds ⅛ inch deep.

PROPAGATION: Seeds started indoors.

PLANTING TIPS: China asters are highly susceptible to two diseases—aster yellows and fusarium wilt. To reduce the risk of fusarium wilt, do not plant asters in the same place 2 years in a row. When buying seed, look for disease-resistant varieties.

China asters are handsome in beds and borders or in pots, and make good cut flowers, although plants will not produce more flowers when blossoms are cut. To enjoy a prolonged bloom period, plant asters in 3-week successions until midsummer.

CATHARANUS
C. roseus, Madagascar periwinkle, Vinca

WHERE TO PLANT: Full sun to partial shade, in moist but well-drained soil of average fertility and containing lots of organic matter, with a pH of 6.0 to 7.0. The plants are adaptable and can tolerate heat and drought as well as moist, shady conditions.

CATHARANUS—*Continued*

WHEN TO PLANT:
In cool climates start seeds indoors 11 to 12 weeks before the average date of your last spring frost and set out plants a week or two after the last frost date. Seeds germinate in 2 to 3 weeks. Seeds germinate best at a soil temperature of 70 to 75° F.

In warm climates, direct-sow after danger of frost is past. Plants are perennial in Zones 9 and 10.

SPACING:
Set plants 12 inches apart.

PLANTING DEPTH:
Sow seeds ⅛ inch deep.

PROPAGATION:
Seeds.

PLANTING TIPS:
The trailing plants make excellent temporary ground covers, and can also be used as edgings or grown in hanging baskets. Flowers are pink or white.

CENTAUREA

C. cyanus, Bachelor's button, Cornflower

WHERE TO PLANT:
Full sun, in well-drained soil of average fertility, with a pH between 6.0 and 7.0.

WHEN TO PLANT:
In cool and temperate climates, direct-seed early in spring as soon as soil can be worked and when the danger of heavy frost is past. In warm climates (Zones 9 and 10), direct-sow in fall for winter flowers. Seeds germinate in about 10 days, and plants bloom 2 months after planting. Make successive sowings 2 to 3 weeks apart through summer in cool and temperate climates, or through fall in warm climates.

SPACING:
Thin seedlings to stand 6 to 12 inches apart.

PLANTING DEPTH:
Cover seeds ¼ inch deep with fine soil.

PROPAGATION:
Direct-seeding. Centaureas do not transplant well. Plants may self-sow.

PLANTING TIPS:
The plants are hardy annuals and grow best in cool weather.

Bachelor's buttons are lovely in beds and borders, and make good cut flowers. In addition to the traditional clear blue, they also come in red-violet, white, and shades of pink. They generally grow to 3 feet high. Some dwarf types are available that grow to just 15 inches high. Plants bloom most prolifically during cool, sunny weather.

CLARKIA
C. amoena

WHERE TO PLANT:	Full sun, in moist but well-drained soil of average fertility, with a pH of 6.0 to 7.0. Clarkia is a hardy annual native to the Rocky Mountains and grows best where summers are cool.
WHEN TO PLANT:	Direct-seed in spring, as soon as the soil can be worked. In warm climates (Zones 9 and 10), sow in fall for winter flowers. Seeds germinate quickly—in about 5 days—and plants bloom 3 months after planting.
SPACING:	Thin seedlings to stand 9 inches apart.
PLANTING DEPTH:	Barely cover seeds; they germinate best with some light.
PROPAGATION:	Direct-seeding. Clarkias do not transplant well. Plants may self-sow.
PLANTING TIPS:	The plants are attractive in beds and borders and look best planted in clumps or massed together in one portion of a cutting garden. They make lovely cut flowers.
	Clarkias will tolerate poor soil but do not perform well in hot, dry weather.

CLEOME
C. hasslerana, Spider flower

WHERE TO PLANT:	Best in full sun but will tolerate partial shade. The soil should be well drained and of average fertility, with a pH of 6.0 to 7.0.
WHEN TO PLANT:	Start seeds indoors 6 to 8 weeks before the average date of your last spring frost and set out plants 1 to 2 weeks after the last frost date. Seeds germinate in about 10 days at a soil temperature of 68 to 85° F. Or direct-seed around the date you expect the last spring frost. Cleomes grow and flower best in warm weather.
SPACING:	Space plants 12 to 36 inches apart.
PLANTING DEPTH:	Sow seeds ⅛ inch deep.
PROPAGATION:	Direct-seeding; spider flowers do not transplant well.
PLANTING TIPS:	Spider flowers are easy to grow and may self-sow prolifically. The plants grow quite tall and are striking in the back of the beds and borders.

(continued)

CLEOME—*Continued*

PLANTING TIPS:
(continued)

Plants are drought-tolerant.

Cultivars come in shades of pink or lavender plus white. Self-sown plants will usually revert to a single color—lavender.

CONSOLIDA
C. ambigua, Larkspur

WHERE TO PLANT: Full sun to partial shade, in rich, fertile, moist but well-drained soil containing plenty of organic matter and with a pH of 6.0 to 7.0.

WHEN TO PLANT: Direct-seed in early spring, as soon as soil can be worked, 2 or more weeks before the last expected frost. Or start seeds indoors in peat pots 6 to 7 weeks before the average date of the last spring frost. Germination takes 1 to 3 weeks at 65 to 75° F. Be sure to transplant with a minimum of disturbance to roots; larkspur does not transplant well.

In warm climates (Zones 9 and 10), sow in fall for flowers in winter or early spring.

Larkspurs are hardy annuals closely related to delphiniums. They grow best in cool weather.

SPACING: Set plants 10 to 12 inches apart, depending on the variety.

PLANTING DEPTH: Sow seeds ⅛ inch deep.

PROPAGATION: Direct-seeding, if your growing season is long enough. Plants may self-sow.

PLANTING TIPS: Larkspur is delightful in the back of beds and borders, and nice for cutting. Flowers are blue-violet, purple, pink, or white. Plants bloom about 100 days after planting.

Larkspur may also be sold under the name *Delphinium ajacis*.

COREOPSIS
C. tinctoria, Calliopsis

WHERE TO PLANT: Full sun, in well-drained soil of average fertility, with a pH of 6.0 to 7.0. Plants will tolerate poor soil.

WHEN TO PLANT:	Start seeds indoors 5 to 6 weeks before the average date of your last frost or direct-seed in early spring when the soil can be worked. Seeds germinate in 5 to 10 days at a soil temperature of 70 to 75° F.
	In warm climates (Zones 9 and 10), sow in late summer or fall for winter flowers.
SPACING:	Set plants 8 inches apart, but plants often bloom best when somewhat crowded.
PLANTING DEPTH:	Cover seeds lightly with soil.
PROPAGATION:	Seeds.
PLANTING TIPS:	The yellow flowers of annual coreopsis are charming in beds and borders, and nice for cutting.
	Cultivars are available in heights ranging from 8 to 36 inches. The tall types are suitable for naturalizing in meadows.

COSMOS
C. bipinnatus

WHERE TO PLANT:	Full sun in very well-drained soil of average fertility, with a pH between 6.0 to 7.0. Cosmos can tolerate drought and poor soil, but needs excellent drainage. Soil rich in nitrogen encourages weedy foliage and fewer, later flowers.
WHEN TO PLANT:	Direct-seed shortly after the average last frost date. Or start seeds indoors 4 weeks before the average date of your last spring frost. Seeds germinate in 1 to 2 weeks at a soil temperature of 68 to 86° F. Set out transplants shortly after the average last frost date.
SPACING:	Space plants about 12 inches apart, depending on the variety.
PLANTING DEPTH:	Cover seeds very lightly—no more than ⅛ inch deep—so some light can reach them.
PROPAGATION:	Direct-seeding.
PLANTING TIPS:	Cosmos is easy to grow, lovely in beds and borders, and good for cutting.
	This variety grows to about 4 feet and looks best at the back of the border.

CYNOGLOSSUM
C. amabile, Chinese forget-me-not

WHERE TO PLANT:
Full sun to partial shade, in well-drained soil of average fertility, with a pH of 6.0 to 7.0.

WHEN TO PLANT:
Start seeds indoors 7 weeks before the average frost-free date and set out transplants about 2 weeks before that date. Or direct-seed in early spring, as soon as the soil can be worked. Germination occurs in 5 to 10 days.

In warm climates, sow in fall for winter flowers.

SPACING:
Space plants 9 inches apart.

PLANTING DEPTH:
Seeds need darkness to germinate. Cover them lightly with soil.

PROPAGATION:
Seeds.

PLANTING TIPS:
Cynoglossum is a biennial that is easy to grow and blooms the first year from seed; plants often self-sow.

The plants are handsome massed in beds and borders. They do not make good cut flowers because they wilt almost immediately after cutting.

GAILLARDIA
G. pulchella, Blanketflower

WHERE TO PLANT:
Full sun, in light, well-drained soil of average fertility, with a pH of 6.0 to 7.0. Gaillardia does poorly in soggy soils.

WHEN TO PLANT:
Direct-seed after danger of frost is past. In areas where the frost-free growing season is short, start seeds indoors 4 to 5 weeks before the average date of your last spring frost and set out plants when all danger of frost is past. Seeds germinate in about 3 weeks and plants bloom in 3 months from seed.

In warm climates sow gaillardia in fall for winter flowers; the plant is a hardy annual and can tolerate cool temperatures.

SPACING:
Space plants 12 inches apart.

PLANTING DEPTH:
Sow seeds ⅛ inch deep.

PROPAGATION:
Seeds. Plants may self-sow.

PLANTING TIPS:
Gaillardia is easy to grow, attractive in beds and borders, and good for cutting. Because its growing habit is rangy and untidy, it looks best in an informal setting, such as a cottage garden. It is a native of the American plains, and as a result, tolerates drought well.

GOMPHRENA

G. globosa, Globe amaranth

WHERE TO PLANT:
Full sun, in well-drained soil of average fertility, with a pH of 6.0 to 7.0. Grows well in hot, dry places.

WHEN TO PLANT:
Start seeds indoors 6 to 8 weeks before the average date of your last spring frost and set out plants when all danger of frost is past. Or direct-seed when all danger of frost is past. Seeds germinate in about 2 weeks.

Plants grow best in warm weather.

SPACING:
Space plants 6 to 10 inches apart.

PLANTING DEPTH:
Plant seeds $1/16$ to $1/8$ inch deep. Barely cover seeds with soil.

PROPAGATION:
Seeds.

PLANTING TIPS:
Globe amaranth is easy to grow and handsome planted in masses in beds and borders. It holds its color well when dried. The round flower heads resemble clover and come in red-violet, white, and shades of pink. Plants range from 9 to 30 inches high. The shortest cultivars make easy-to-grow edgings for beds.

GYPSOPHILA

G. elegans, Annual baby's-breath

WHERE TO PLANT:
Full sun, in light, well-drained soil of average fertility, with a pH close to 7.0. In warm climates where summer sun is very intense, provide some afternoon shade. Gypsophila blooms best in a soil that is close to neutral pH. It does best in acid soil if lime has been added to raise the pH.

WHEN TO PLANT:
In cool and temperate climates, direct-seed in mid-spring, when danger of frost is past. In warm climates, sow in autumn for winter flowers. Baby's-breath is a hardy annual and grows best in cool temperatures.

GYPSOPHILA—*Continued*

SPACING: Space plants 12 to 18 inches apart.

PLANTING DEPTH: Sow seeds ¼ inch deep.

PROPAGATION: Direct-seeding. Plants may self-sow.

PLANTING TIPS: Annual baby's-breath is easy to grow, good for cutting, and attractive in beds and borders or rock gardens. The dainty sprays of tiny white flowers dry beautifully, too.

Since plants have a short bloom period, successive sowings 2 weeks apart during the spring will give a better supply of flowers.

HELICHRYSUM

H. bracteatum, Strawflower

WHERE TO PLANT: Full sun, in well-drained soil of average fertility, with a pH of 6.0 to 7.0. Strawflowers do not like wet soil.

WHEN TO PLANT: Start seeds indoors 5 to 6 weeks before the average date of the last spring frost and set out plants when all danger of frost is past. Seeds germinate in 2 to 3 weeks at a soil temperature of 70 to 75° F. You may also direct-seed when frost danger is past.

SPACING: Set plants or thin seedlings to 10 to 12 inches apart.

PLANTING DEPTH: Sow seeds ¹⁄₁₆ inch deep.

PROPAGATION: Seeds.

PLANTING TIPS: Strawflowers are beautiful for cutting. They also air-dry easily and are excellent for wreaths and dried arrangements. Plants grow tall, so put them at the back of beds and borders.

Plants may self-seed in light, sandy soils.

IBERIS

I. umbellata, Globe candytuft

WHERE TO PLANT: Full sun, in well-drained soil of average fertility, with a pH of 6.0 to 7.0.

WHEN TO PLANT: In cool climates, direct-seed in early spring as soon as the soil can be worked. In warm climates, sow in fall for winter flowers.

Seeds germinate in 1 to 2 weeks in soil at 70 to 85° F, and plants bloom about 2 months later.

SPACING:
Thin seedlings to 6 to 9 inches apart.

PLANTING DEPTH:
Sow seeds ⅛ inch deep.

PROPAGATION:
Direct-seeding.

PLANTING TIPS:
Globe candytuft is a hardy annual that self-sows in many gardens.

The plants are easy to grow, nice as edgings in beds and borders, and good for cutting. Flowers are lavender, purple, or white.

Blooming usually declines as hot weather comes on. For a second bloom period in fall, shear plants lightly in midsummer.

IMPATIENS
I. balsamina, Balsam
I. wallerana, Bedding impatiens

WHERE TO PLANT:
Plant balsam in full sun. Plant bedding impatiens in shade or partial shade. Both prefer moist but well-drained soil rich in organic matter, with a pH between 6.0 and 7.0.

WHEN TO PLANT:
Start seeds of *I. balsamina* indoors 7 to 8 weeks before the average date of your last spring frost and set out plants when all danger of frost is past. Or direct-seed when all danger of frost is past. Seeds germinate in 1 to 2 weeks at 70° F.

Start seeds of *I. wallerana* indoors 10 to 11 weeks before the last expected frost, and set out plants when frost danger is past. Or propagate from stem cuttings taken from mature plants in summer.

SPACING:
Space balsam 8 to 10 inches apart; bedding impatiens about 12 inches apart.

PLANTING DEPTH:
Seeds of both *I. balsamina* and *I. wallerana* germinate best when they get some light. Press them gently into soil but do not cover them with soil.

PROPAGATION:
Seeds or, for *I. wallerana*, stem cuttings. Stem cuttings of *I. wallerana* root readily in water.

PLANTING TIPS:
Balsam is a tall plant for the middle or back of beds and borders;

IMPATIENS—*Continued*

PLANTING TIPS:
(continued)

bedding impatiens is lovely massed in the front of the garden or planted in containers.

Balsam self-sows prolifically if grown in a well-mulched garden. It is easy to root out unwanted seedlings early in spring.

KOCHIA

K. scoparia, Summer cypress

WHERE TO PLANT:
Full sun, in very well-drained soil of average fertility, with a pH between 6.0 and 7.0. Good drainage is important for summer cypress, and a dry soil is better than a wet one.

WHEN TO PLANT:
In cool or temperate climates, sow seeds indoors in peat pots 6 to 7 weeks before the average date of your last spring frost and set out plants when all danger of frost is past. Kochia does not transplant well, so handle carefully to minimize root disturbance.

In areas with a longer growing season, direct-seed when all danger of frost is past. Seeds germinate in about 2 weeks at a soil temperature of 70 to 75° F.

SPACING:
Thin plants to stand 1½ to 2 feet apart.

PLANTING DEPTH:
Seeds need light to germinate. Scatter them over the soil surface and press in gently but do not cover with soil.

PROPAGATION:
Seeds.

PLANTING TIPS:
Summer cypress is a foliage plant that can be grown as a summer hedge or border. You can also grow it in large pots. Plants grow 2 to 3 feet high and spread up to 2 feet.

Kochia often self-sows and may become weedy. It grows best in warm weather.

LATHYRUS

L. odorata, Sweet pea

WHERE TO PLANT:
Full sun, in rich, deeply dug, moist but well-drained soil, with a pH of 6.0 to 7.0.

WHEN TO PLANT:
In northern climates where spring weather goes quickly from cold

to hot, sow seeds indoors in individual peat pots about 6 weeks before the last expected frost.

Soak seeds in water overnight or file the seed coat before planting. Seeds germinate best in a soil temperature of 55 to 65° F. Germination takes 10 to 14 days. Move plants outdoors after the danger of heavy frost is past; sweet peas can tolerate light frost. Transplant carefully to minimize root disturbance.

In areas where spring weather is cool, direct-seed in spring as soon as the soil can be worked.

In warm climates (Zones 9 and 10), sow in fall for flowers in winter and early spring.

Seeds germinate best in cool soil, and plants grow and flower best in cool weather.

SPACING: Set plants or sow seeds 6 inches apart.

PLANTING DEPTH: Plants seeds ¼ to ½ inch deep.

PROPAGATION: Seeds.

PLANTING TIPS: Train climbing sweet peas along trellises or strings to form a screen; grow bush varieties in beds and borders.

Sweet peas make wonderful cut flowers; their sweet fragrance is intoxicating, and flowers come in white and many shades of pink, purple, and violet.

LOBELIA

L. erinus, Edging lobelia

WHERE TO PLANT: Full sun to partial shade, in moist, fertile soil containing lots of organic matter, with a pH of 6.0 to 7.0. In cooler climates plant in full sun; in warm climates give lobelia some shade.

WHEN TO PLANT: Start seeds indoors 9 to 10 weeks before the average date of your last spring frost and set out plants when all danger of frost is past.

The seeds germinate slowly; plants bloom in a little over 3 months from seed. Lobelia is usually not direct-seeded.

SPACING: Set plants approximately 6 inches apart.

PLANTING DEPTH: Seeds germinate best with some light; press them lightly into soil, but do not cover them.

LOBELIA—*Continued*

PROPAGATION:	Seeds started indoors. Because it is difficult to get lobelia seeds to germinate, plants from a nursery are a good option.
PLANTING TIPS:	Lobelia is attractive as an edging plant in beds and borders, in rock gardens, and in hanging baskets and window boxes. Its small flowers are violet-blue or white.

LOBULARIA

L. maritima, Sweet alyssum

WHERE TO PLANT:	Full sun to partial shade, in well-drained soil of average fertility, with a pH of 6.0 to 7.0.
WHEN TO PLANT:	Direct-seed in spring as soon as the soil can be worked and danger of heavy frost is past.
SPACING:	Thin seedlings to stand 6 inches apart.
PLANTING DEPTH:	Do not cover seeds as light is necessary for germination.
PROPAGATION:	Direct-seeding. Plants often self-sow.
PLANTING TIPS:	Sweet alyssum is easy to grow and delightful as an edging for beds and borders, in rock gardens, and in containers. Its tiny flowers can be had in white, lavender, or purple.

MATTHIOLA

M. incana, Stock

WHERE TO PLANT:	Best in full sun, but can tolerate partial shade. Plant in fertile, moist but well-drained soil rich in organic matter, with a pH of 6.0 to 7.0.
WHEN TO PLANT:	Sow seeds indoors 5 to 6 weeks before the average date of your last spring frost and set out plants when all danger of frost is past.
	Seeds germinate in approximately 7 to 10 days at a soil temperature of 70° F.
	In climates where spring weather is cool, direct-seed around the last frost date. In Zones 9 and 10, sow seeds in early fall for late winter or early spring bloom.
SPACING:	Set plants 8 to 16 inches apart, depending on the variety.

PLANTING DEPTH:	Seeds germinate best in the presence of some light. Press them gently into the soil surface and barely cover with soil.
PROPAGATION:	Seeds started indoors.
PLANTING TIPS:	Stocks bloom in a little over 2 months from seed, and are lovely, fragrant additions to beds and borders.
	Plants are hardy annuals and generally grow best in cool climates.

MIRABILIS

M. jalapa, Four-o'clocks

WHERE TO PLANT:	Full sun is best, but plants will also tolerate partial shade. Give them well-drained soil of average fertility and rich in organic matter, with a pH of 6.0 to 7.0.
WHEN TO PLANT:	Direct-seed when all danger of frost is past. Or sow seeds indoors 5 to 6 weeks before the average date of your last spring frost and set out plants when danger of frost is past. Germination takes 7 to 12 days at a soil temperature of 70 to 85° F.
SPACING:	Thin plants to 14 inches apart.
PLANTING DEPTH:	Sow seeds ½ inch deep.
PROPAGATION:	Seeds. Plants may self-sow.
PLANTING TIPS:	Four-o'clocks are easy to grow and nice in beds and borders, where their flowers open in late afternoon.
	The plants form thin tubers that can be dug in fall, stored over winter, and replanted the following spring.

MYOSOTIS

M. sylvatica, Annual forget-me-not

| WHERE TO PLANT: | *M. sylvatica* is a biennial grown as a hardy annual. It grows in sun, partial shade, or shade, in moist but well-drained soil rich in organic matter, with a pH of 6.0 to 7.0. In areas where sun is intense, plants require some shade. |
| WHEN TO PLANT: | Some varieties of *M. sylvatica* will bloom the first year if seeds are started indoors early in the season. Start seeds indoors 6 to 8 weeks before the last frost date. Set out plants in early spring. Seeds |

MYOSOTIS—*Continued*

WHEN TO PLANT: *(continued)*	germinate in 1 to 2 weeks at a soil temperature of 55 to 65° F. Seeds sown outdoors in early spring may not bloom until early fall.
SPACING:	Set plants 6 inches apart.
PLANTING DEPTH:	Sow seeds ¼ inch deep. Cover the seeds with soil, because they require darkness for germination.
PROPAGATION:	Seeds sown indoors and direct-seeding.
PLANTING TIPS:	Forget-me-nots are beautiful additions to beds and borders or rock gardens.
	Forget-me-not reseeds itself readily.

NIGELLA

N. damascena, Love-in-a-mist

WHERE TO PLANT:	Full sun, in well-drained sandy or gravelly soil of average fertility, with a pH of 6.0 to 7.0. Nigella prefers a dry soil and a cool growing season.
WHEN TO PLANT:	Direct-seed in early spring, as soon as the soil can be worked and after danger of heavy frost is past.
	Or start seeds indoors in individual peat pots 4 weeks before the last frost date and plant out about a month later. Seeds germinate in 10 to 15 days at a soil temperature of 65 to 70° F.
SPACING:	Space plants 8 inches apart.
PLANTING DEPTH:	Cover seeds lightly with soil.
PROPAGATION:	Direct-seeding; nigella does not transplant well. If you start seeds indoors, transplant with care to minimize root disturbance.
PLANTING TIPS:	Love-in-a-mist is handsome planted in masses near the front of beds and borders.
	Plants self-sow freely. Nigella seedpods make excellent additions to dried arrangements and wreaths.

PAPAVER

P. rhoeas, Shirley poppy, Field poppy

WHERE TO PLANT:	Shirley poppies are hardy annuals that prefer full sun and well-drained soil of average fertility, with a pH of 6.0 to 7.0.

WHEN TO PLANT: For summer blooms, direct-seed in late fall for next year's flowers. You can also sow in early spring, as soon as the soil can be worked and the danger of heavy frost is past.

In warm climates (Zones 9 and 10), sow in fall for winter flowers.

Make succession plantings every 3 weeks until the middle of the growing season for extended bloom.

SPACING: Thin plants to stand 1½ feet apart.

PLANTING DEPTH: Press seeds gently into soil and cover only lightly.

PROPAGATION: Direct-seeding; poppies have a long taproot that makes transplanting very difficult.

PLANTING TIPS: Shirley poppies are easy to grow and lovely in beds and borders. They bloom from seed in about 2 months, in a range of warm, soft colors.

PELARGONIUM
P. × domesticum, Regal geranium
P. × hortorum, Zonal geranium
P. peltatum, Ivy-leaved geranium

WHERE TO PLANT: Geraniums are tender perennials grown as annuals in the United States. They prefer full sun and well-drained soil rich in organic matter, with a pH of 6.0 to 7.0. Regal geraniums can tolerate partial shade and need moister, richer soil than the other types.

WHEN TO PLANT: Start seeds indoors 9 to 10 weeks before the average date of your last expected spring frost. To improve germination, soak seeds on wet paper towels for a day or two before planting. Provide bottom heat (70 to 75° F) until seeds germinate. When the first true leaves appear, transplant to individual 2-inch pots. Transplant again to 4-inch pots when the plants outgrow the smaller pots. Move plants to the garden after all danger of frost is past.

Or take cuttings in late summer and grow plants indoors over winter to plant out in spring. Cuttings will root in a rooting medium or in water.

SPACING: Set plants 1 to 1½ feet apart.

PLANTING DEPTH: Sow seeds ¼ inch deep.

PELARGONIUM—*Continued*

PROPAGATION:
Some varieties grow quickly and easily from seed, but cuttings are the best method of propagation.

Make cuttings 4 inches long. Remove the bottom leaves, but keep at least three leaves on each cutting. Let the cuttings dry overnight, then place them in pots of moist rooting medium, in bright light but out of direct sun. Provide bottom heat and keep the medium moist until the cuttings root.

PLANTING TIPS:
Geraniums, especially the zonal types, are attractive in beds and borders. Regal geraniums are handsome pot plants, and ivy-leaved types are lovely in hanging baskets.

Regal and ivy-leaved geraniums need cooler nights and more moisture than zonals. The hot, humid summer weather of the Deep South may cause leaf burn.

PETUNIA
P. × hybrida

WHERE TO PLANT:
Full sun, in fertile, moist but well-drained soil rich in organic matter, with a pH between 6.0 and 7.0.

WHEN TO PLANT:
Start seeds indoors 10 to 12 weeks before the average date of your last expected spring frost and be sure to keep the growing medium moist. When plants develop three or four leaves, transplant to individual peat pots. Set out plants when all danger of frost is past.

Petunias may be direct-seeded after the last frost date, but plants started this way develop too slowly to bloom for the entire summer.

In warm climates (Zones 9 and 10), petunias can be planted in fall.

SPACING:
Space plants 8 to 10 inches apart, depending on the variety.

PLANTING DEPTH:
Press seeds lightly into soil. Do not cover seeds with soil as light is required for germination.

PROPAGATION:
Seeds started indoors or young plants from a garden center.

PLANTING TIPS:
Hundreds of petunia cultivars are available, with a wide range of flower forms and colors.

Grow them in beds and borders, or plant cascading varieties in hanging baskets.

PHLOX
P. drummondii, Annual phlox

WHERE TO PLANT: Full sun, in light, well-drained, sandy loam, with a pH of 6.0 to 7.0. Phlox will tolerate less fertile soils but will be smaller; it cannot tolerate poor drainage.

WHEN TO PLANT: Sow seeds indoors about 6 weeks before the average date of your last spring frost and set out plants when all danger of frost is past.

Or direct-seed when frost danger is past and as soon as soil can be worked. Seeds germinate best in cool soil—55 to 65° F. Germination takes 1 to 2 weeks.

SPACING: Set plants about 10 inches apart in rich soil, closer together in poorer soil (plants will be smaller in poor soil).

PLANTING DEPTH: Sow seeds ¼ inch deep; cover them completely as darkness is needed for germination.

PROPAGATION: Direct-sowing or sowing in peat pots.

PLANTING TIPS: Dwarf varieties of phlox are the most versatile for beds and borders, where they make lovely edgings and good cut flowers. They can also be planted in rock gardens.

Phlox resents transplanting. When starting seeds indoors, use peat pots. Transplant carefully to avoid root disturbance.

PORTULACA
P. grandiflora, Rose moss

WHERE TO PLANT: Full sun, in any well-drained soil, of average or even poor fertility, with a pH of 6.0 to 7.5. Portulaca is ideal for hot, dry climates and will grow and bloom in poor, dry soils where many other plants will falter.

WHEN TO PLANT: Start seeds indoors 6 to 7 weeks before the average date of your last spring frost and set out plants when all danger of frost is past. Seeds germinate in 10 to 15 days at a soil temperature of 70 to 85° F. Or direct-seed when all danger of frost is past.

SPACING: Set plants 10 to 12 inches apart.

PLANTING DEPTH: Seeds need light to germinate; press them lightly into soil but do not cover them.

PORTULACA—*Continued*

PROPAGATION: Seeds sown indoors. Plants self-sow readily.

PLANTING TIPS: Portulaca is easy to grow and versatile; plant it as an edging in beds and borders, in rock gardens, next to walls and along pavements, or in containers. The low, sprawling plants bloom in a host of brilliant, warm colors.

Seeds are very fine and may wash away if sown directly in the garden. For more reliable results, start seeds indoors.

RESEDA
R. odorata, Mignonette

WHERE TO PLANT: Full sun, in fertile, well-drained soil rich in organic matter and with a pH of 6.0 to 7.0. In climates where the summer sun is strong, plants appreciate some shade in the afternoon.

WHEN TO PLANT: Direct-seed in early spring as soon as the soil can be worked.

SPACING: Set plants 10 to 12 inches apart.

PLANTING DEPTH: Seeds need light to germinate; press them lightly into soil but do not cover.

PROPAGATION: Direct-seeding; mignonette does not transplant well.

PLANTING TIPS: Mignonette is grown for its heavenly fragrance; its flowers are greenish and not very attractive. Plant it among other, prettier flowers to lend its scent to beds and borders.

The plants grow best in cool climates.

RICINUS
R. communis, Castor bean

WHERE TO PLANT: Full sun, in very well-drained soil of average fertility, with a pH of 6.0 to 7.0. Excellent drainage is important; castor beans cannot tolerate soggy soil.

WHEN TO PLANT: Start seeds indoors 7 to 8 weeks before the average date of your last frost and set out plants when frost danger is past. Soak seeds in warm water for 24 hours before planting; they should germinate in 2 to 3 weeks.

In climates with a long growing season, you can direct-seed in spring when all danger of frost is past.

SPACING:	Set plants 3 to 4 feet apart—they grow up to 6 feet tall, and their leaves are huge.
PLANTING DEPTH:	Sow seeds ⅜ inch deep.
PROPAGATION:	Seeds.
PLANTING TIPS:	Plant castor beans for their immense tropical-looking foliage. The flowers of this tender annual are inconspicuous.

The seeds are borne in prickly pods and are quite poisonous; do not grow this plant if your household includes small children.

RUDBECKIA
R. hirta 'Gloriosa', Gloriosa daisy

WHERE TO PLANT:	Plants flourish in full sun to partial shade and in practically any well-drained soil. The ideal pH range is 6.0 to 7.0, but plants are tolerant of a wider range. They can withstand drought and hot sun, but perform best in rich, moist soil.
WHEN TO PLANT:	Start seeds indoors 6 to 7 weeks before the average date of your last spring frost and set out plants after danger of heavy frost is past. Seeds germinate in 5 to 10 days at 70 to 75° F.

Or direct-seed in early spring as soon as the soil can be worked and the danger of heavy frost is past.

SPACING:	Set plants about 12 inches apart.
PLANTING DEPTH:	Sow seeds ¼ inch deep.
PROPAGATION:	Seeds.
PLANTING TIPS:	Gloriosa daisies are actually short-lived perennials grown as annuals. They often reseed themselves.

These durable, adaptable plants are attractive in beds and borders and make good cut flowers. They are also nice in meadow gardens. The daisylike flowers are golden yellow with a flush of carmine red near the center.

SALPIGLOSSIS

S. sinuata, Painted tongue

WHERE TO PLANT:	Full sun, in fertile, well-drained soil rich in organic matter, with a pH of 7.0 to 8.0. You can amend acid soil with lime to achieve the desired pH.
WHEN TO PLANT:	Start seeds indoors 8 to 9 weeks before the average date of your last spring frost and set out plants when danger of frost is past. Or direct-seed when all danger of frost is past. Seeds germinate in 2 to 3 weeks at 70 to 75° F.
SPACING:	Set plants 12 inches apart.
PLANTING DEPTH:	When sowing indoors, do not cover seeds with soil but do cover the flats or pots with black plastic; the seeds are fine but need darkness to germinate. Outdoors, sow right on the surface of the soil.
PROPAGATION:	Seeds started indoors.
PLANTING TIPS:	Salpiglossis is showy in the middle to back of beds and borders, and good for cutting.
	Seeds are very fine, and those sown outdoors may wash away before germination.

SALVIA

S. farinacea, Mealycup sage
S. splendens, Scarlet sage

WHERE TO PLANT:	*S. farinacea* is a perennial to Zone 8 and is grown as an annual in Zones 3 through 7. *S. splendens* is a tender annual. Both prefer full sun to partial shade, well-drained soil of average fertility and rich in organic matter, and a pH between 6.0 and 7.0.
WHEN TO PLANT:	Start seeds of scarlet sage indoors 6 to 7 weeks before the average date of your last spring frost and set out plants when all danger of frost is past.
	Start seeds of mealycup sage indoors 8 to 10 weeks before the last expected frost and set out plants when all danger of frost is past and the weather is warm.
SPACING:	Space plants of both types about 12 to 18 inches apart.

PLANTING DEPTH:	Seeds need light to germinate; press them lightly into soil but do not cover them with soil.
PROPAGATION:	Seeds.
PLANTING TIPS:	Mealycup sage often self-sows. Plant it in beds and borders, where its spikes of violet-blue flowers are a beautiful contrast for yellow or pink flowers. This species is also good for cutting and drying.

Scarlet sage is a popular bedding plant; newer purple and creamy white cultivars are easier to integrate into color schemes than the traditional fiery red cultivars.

SCABIOSA
S. atropurpurea, Pincushion flower

WHERE TO PLANT:	Full sun, in loose, well-drained soil of average fertility and rich in organic matter, with a pH of 7.0 to 8.0. Scabiosa prefers an alkaline soil.
WHEN TO PLANT:	Start seeds indoors about 6 weeks before your last expected spring frost.
	Transplant into the garden when all danger of frost is past.
	Or direct-seed when all danger of frost is past. Seeds germinate in about 2 weeks.
	Plants grow best in cool weather.
SPACING:	Set plants 6 to 12 inches apart.
PLANTING DEPTH:	Sow seeds ¼ inch deep.
PROPAGATION:	Seeds.
PLANTING TIPS:	Mass pincushion flowers in beds and borders, or grow them in a cutting garden. The flowers attract bees.

SCHIZANTHUS
S. × wisetonensis, Butterfly flower

WHERE TO PLANT:	Full sun—or in warm climates (Zones 8 to 10), partial shade—in moist, fertile soil rich in organic matter, with a pH of 6.0 to 7.0. Schizanthus is native to the Andes mountains of Chile. It does not

SCHIZANTHUS—*Continued*

WHERE TO PLANT:
(continued)
thrive in areas with hot, dry summers but flourishes in areas where summers are cool, such as mountain and coastal areas of the North.

WHEN TO PLANT:
Start seeds indoors 9 to 10 weeks before the average date of your last spring frost. Germination takes 3 to 4 weeks at a soil temperature of 60 to 70° F. Make several successive sowings to prolong the blooming period.

Set out plants when all danger of frost is past. Handle seedlings carefully when transplanting because the stems break easily.

SPACING:
Set plants 12 inches apart.

PLANTING DEPTH:
Seeds are tiny and germinate best in darkness; do not cover them with soil, but instead cover flats or pots with black plastic until germination occurs.

PROPAGATION:
Seeds started indoors.

PLANTING TIPS:
Schizanthus is lovely in beds and borders.

TAGETES
T. erecta, American or African marigold
T. patula, French marigold

WHERE TO PLANT:
Full sun, in well-drained soil of average fertility, with a pH of 6.0 to 7.0.

WHEN TO PLANT:
African marigolds take a long time to reach blooming size. For best results with these, start seeds indoors 8 to 9 weeks before the average date of your last spring frost and set out plants when all danger of frost is past. Seeds germinate in 5 to 7 days at a soil temperature of 70 to 75° F.

French marigolds bloom quickly and are good candidates for direct-sowing. Sow these seeds outdoors when all danger of frost is past.

In Zones 9 and 10, marigolds can be sown in fall for winter flowers.

SPACING:
Spacing depends on variety, ranging from 6 to 9 inches for dwarf plants to 12 to 22 inches for tall African types.

PLANTING DEPTH:	Sow seeds ¼ to ½ inch deep.
PROPAGATION:	Seeds.
PLANTING TIPS:	Marigolds are easy to grow and versatile in the garden. Plant dwarf cultivars as edgings or in containers, larger varieties in beds and borders, and the tallest varieties in the back of the garden.

Vegetable gardeners like to plant marigolds, especially the African type, among crops because their roots give off a substance that repels nematodes.

TROPAEOLUM

T. majus, Climbing nasturtium
T. minus, Dwarf nasturtium

WHERE TO PLANT:	Full sun, in well-drained soil of average fertility, with a pH of 6.0 to 7.0. Rich soil will produce lots of leaves but few flowers.
WHEN TO PLANT:	Direct-seed about 1 to 2 weeks before the average date of your last frost, when the danger of heavy frost is past. Germination takes 7 to 12 days.
	In warm climates (Zones 9 and 10), plant in fall for winter flowers.
SPACING:	Space climbing plants 2 to 3 feet apart, dwarf varieties 12 inches apart.
PLANTING DEPTH:	Sow seeds ¼ inch deep. Cover seeds completely as darkness is needed for germination.
PROPAGATION:	Direct-seeding; nasturtiums do not transplant well.
PLANTING TIPS:	Train climbing nasturtiums on a trellis or strings for vertical accents or screens, or let them trail from hanging baskets. All climbing nasturtiums will need to be tied to their support, as they lack tendrils for grasping.

Plant dwarf varieties as edgings or ground covers, or grow them in containers.

Leaves and flowers are edible, with a flavor similar to watercress. Buds can be picked and used as a substitute for capers.

Nasturtiums are very prone to aphids.

VERBENA

V. × hybrida, Garden verbena

WHERE TO PLANT:	Full sun, in well-drained soil of average fertility, with a pH of 6.0 to 7.0. Verbena also adapts to sandy and poor soils.
WHEN TO PLANT:	Sow seeds indoors 11 to 12 weeks before the average date of your last spring frost and set out plants when all danger of frost is past.
SPACING:	Space plants approximately 10 to 12 inches apart, depending on the variety.
PLANTING DEPTH:	Sow seeds on the surface of completely moist soil. The fine seeds need darkness to germinate. Cover flats or pots with black plastic and keep moist until germination—about 3 weeks.
PROPAGATION:	Seeds started indoors.
PLANTING TIPS:	Verbena is charming as an edging for beds and borders; it also is suitable for rock gardens and containers. The bigger varieties are good for cutting.

Plants bloom from seed in about 3 months.

ZINNIA

Z. elegans

WHERE TO PLANT:	Full sun, in well-drained soil of average fertility and rich in organic matter, with a pH between 6.0 and 7.0. Zinnias are prone to mildew and need a location with good air circulation.
WHEN TO PLANT:	Sow seeds indoors 4 to 6 weeks before the average date of your last spring frost and set out plants when all danger of frost is past for flowers in midsummer. Seeds germinate in 5 to 7 days at 70 to 75° F. Sow seeds of the tallest varieties in individual peat pots because they do not transplant well. Double-flowered varieties should always be direct-seeded into the garden because these types often revert to single flowering after they are transplanted. For flowers in late summer, direct-seed when frost danger is past and the soil has warmed.
SPACING:	Set plants 6 to 12 inches apart, depending on the variety.
PLANTING DEPTH:	Sow seeds ¼ inch deep.

PROPAGATION: Seeds.

PLANTING TIPS: Zinnias are easy to grow, handsome additions to beds and borders, and make good cut flowers. Plant giant varieties in the back of the garden, medium-size varieties in the middle ground, and dwarf varieties as edgings. They can also be grown in containers.

The flowers come in many warm shades, from pastels to brights.

Zinnias grow best when temperatures are at least 50° F and thrive in hot, dry weather.

Perennials, Ground Covers & Ornamental Grasses

ACHILLEA

A. species, Yarrow

WHERE TO PLANT: Full sun, in well-drained soil of average fertility, with a pH of 5.5 to 7.0. Achillea is drought-resistant, grows well in Zones 3 to 10, but does not flourish in heavy, wet soils.

WHEN TO PLANT: Set out nursery plants in spring. Divide mature clumps of plants in spring in cool and temperate climates or fall in warm climates. Start seeds indoors in February in Zones 8 through 10, in March farther north. Set out transplants when the danger of heavy frost is past.

SPACING: Set plants 1 to 1½ feet apart.

PLANTING DEPTH: Do not cover seeds with soil. Achillea needs light to germinate.

PROPAGATION: Division or seeds. Achillea needs division about every 3 years.

PLANTING TIPS: Grow in beds and borders. The flat-topped flower heads are good for both cutting and drying.

Achillea is very versatile, flourishing in cold and hot climates.

Plants started from seed will bloom the next year.

AJUGA
A. reptans, Bugleweed

WHERE TO PLANT: Full sun to full shade, in practically any well-drained soil of average fertility, with a pH of 5.5 to 7.0. Hardy from Zones 3 to 9 and in the California portion of Zone 10.

WHEN TO PLANT: Set out plants in spring or fall.

SPACING: Set plants 6 to 8 inches apart.

PLANTING DEPTH: Plant divisions or rooted stolons at the same depth they were growing previously.

PROPAGATION: Division or stem cuttings. Divide established plants in spring or fall, or take stem cuttings in late summer.

PLANTING TIPS: An attractive ground cover for either sun or shade, ajuga bears little spikes of tiny purple flowers in late spring to early summer. Some cultivars have red or bronze foliage. Ajuga tolerates dry shade. It will flourish in sun or shade as long as the soil contains plenty of organic matter. Ajuga spreads easily and can become invasive.

AQUILEGIA
A. species and cultivars, Columbine

WHERE TO PLANT: Light shade, in moist but well-drained soil of average fertility, with a pH of 5.5 to 7.0. In northern gardens, columbines will tolerate full sun. Plants are hardy in Zones 4 to 8.

WHEN TO PLANT: Set out nursery plants or direct-seed in spring, when danger of frost is past. Or start seeds earlier indoors and set out plants when frost danger is past. Columbine seeds started indoors should be stratified for 3 weeks before being placed under lights for germination.

SPACING: Set plants 12 to 15 inches apart.

PLANTING DEPTH: Press seeds gently into soil, but do not cover them, because they need light to germinate. Set plants or divisions at the same depth they were growing previously.

AQUILEGIA—*Continued*

PROPAGATION:
Division or seeds purchased commercially. Seeds collected from garden plants may not produce plants like the parents. Species forms often self-sow and can spread through the garden. Divide plants every 3 years.

PLANTING TIPS:
The graceful spurred blossoms of columbines are lovely in beds and borders. The smaller varieties work best in rock gardens.

In Zones 4 and 5, mulch columbines in winter to prevent frost heaving that can push them out of the soil.

ARABIS
A. species, Rock cress

WHERE TO PLANT:
Full sun to partial shade, in light, coarse-textured, well-drained soil with a pH of 5.5 to 7.0. Hardiness varies with species; rock cress is hardy from Zones 4, 5, or 6 to 9.

WHEN TO PLANT:
Fall is generally the best time to set out plants. Divide and replant mature plantings in spring or fall. Start seeds in spring, indoors when you start annuals, or directly outdoors when danger of frost is past. Or take cuttings in spring after plants finish blooming.

SPACING:
Set plants about 9 inches apart.

PLANTING DEPTH:
Do not cover seeds with soil; they need light for germination.

PROPAGATION:
Seeds or division. Plants are easy to divide; dig them up, slice them into sections, and replant.

PLANTING TIPS:
Arabis is low-growing and spreading, nice in rock gardens, as edgings for beds and borders, or in wall gardens. Some varieties have variegated foliage that is pretty all season.

Arabis is evergreen in most climates.

ARMERIA
A. maritima, Thrift, Sea pink

WHERE TO PLANT:
Full sun, in well-drained, sandy soil of average fertility, with a pH of 5.5 to 7.0. Armeria grows well in Zones 4 to 9 and is a good plant for seashore gardens.

WHEN TO PLANT: Set out plants in spring. You can also take stem cuttings in July or August after plants finish blooming, but cuttings are difficult to root. Named varieties can be divided in early spring or early fall. You can collect and plant seeds of species in August (named varieties do not always come true from seed). Soak seeds for 6 to 8 hours before planting. Seeds germinate in 2 to 3 weeks at a soil temperature of 70° F.

SPACING: Set plants about 9 inches apart.

PLANTING DEPTH: Plant seeds ¹⁄₁₆ to ⅛ inch deep.

PROPAGATION: Seeds for species or division for named varieties.

PLANTING TIPS: Armeria forms a low, grassy, dense mound that is lovely in the front of beds and borders, or in rock gardens.

ARTEMISIA

A. species, Wormwood, Southernwood, Mugwort

WHERE TO PLANT: Full sun, in well-drained (ideally sandy) soil of average fertility, with a pH of 5.5 to 7.0. Artemisias cannot tolerate soggy soil and do best in climates where summer weather is not terribly humid. They are good plants for seashore gardens. Hardiness varies with the species; most thrive in Zones 5 to 9, but *A. arborescens* will not survive winters north of Zone 9.

WHEN TO PLANT: Set out plants in spring. Spring is also the time to take stem cuttings or divide crowded plants.

SPACING: From about 10 to 18 inches apart, depending upon plant size.

PLANTING DEPTH: Set plants at the same depth they grew in the nursery container.

PROPAGATION: Division or purchased nursery stock.

PLANTING TIPS: Artemisias are grown for their silvery, lacy foliage, which is a lovely addition to flower beds and borders, and is also useful in arrangements. Artemisias planted in poorly drained soil develop crown rot.

A. lactiflora, A. ludoviciana 'Silver King', and *A. stellerana* are easy to divide; *A. schmidtiana* 'Silver Mound' must be divided with care.

ASTER

A. novae-angliae, Michaelmas daisy, New England aster
A. novi-belgii, Michaelmas daisy, New York aster

WHERE TO PLANT: Full sun, in moist but well-drained, fertile soil rich in organic matter, with a pH of 5.5 to 7.0. Asters prefer moist soil while they are in active growth and drier soil when dormant. They tend to do best in cooler climates, and will not grow well in Florida or along the Gulf Coast. Michaelmas daisies in general are hardy in Zones 4 to 9, but hardiness varies with the cultivar, and buying plants locally may be your best bet.

WHEN TO PLANT: Set out nursery plants or divide established plants in spring or fall.

SPACING: Set plants 1 to 2 feet apart.

PLANTING DEPTH: Plant divisions or nursery plants at the same depth they were growing previously.

PROPAGATION: Division; plants need to be divided every 2 to 3 years. When dividing plants, discard the old central part of the root clump and replant sections from the younger outer parts of the clump. Plants spread through underground rhizomes and often self-sow, but do not come true from seed.

PLANTING TIPS: Asters are beautiful with chrysanthemums in late-summer and autumn beds and borders.

ASTILBE

A. species

WHERE TO PLANT: Partial shade, in moist but well-drained soil rich in organic matter, with a pH of 5.5 to 7.0. Good drainage is especially important in winter when plants are dormant. In very moist soils, astilbe can tolerate full sun. The plants are heavy feeders, so enrich the soil every fall with compost and peat moss. Astilbes are hardy from Zones 4 to 8.

WHEN TO PLANT: Set out nursery plants or start seeds indoors in spring. Seeds germinate in 3 to 4 weeks at a soil temperature of 60 to 70° F.

SPACING: Set plants 10 to 15 inches apart, depending on variety.

PLANTING DEPTH: Set nursery plants or divisions at the same depth they were growing previously.

PROPAGATION: Division. Divide established plants in spring when the new shoots are 1 inch tall.

PLANTING TIPS: The feathery flower plumes of astilbes are heavenly in beds and borders with light shade. Flowers bloom in shades of red, pink, and white.

Plenty of moisture and soil rich in organic matter are important for the best flowers.

Plant astilbes in groups of five or more, and divide them every 3 or 4 years. They take division and transplanting well, and plants can be moved intact anytime during the growing season, even when in bloom, if you leave a good soil ball around the roots.

AUBRIETA
A. deltoidea, False rock cress

WHERE TO PLANT: Partial shade, in light, well-drained soil of average fertility, with a pH of 5.5 to 7.0. Aubrieta is hardy from Zones 5 to 9.

WHEN TO PLANT: Set out plants or divide established plants in spring. Aubrieta can also be started by sowing seed indoors 4 to 6 weeks before the last expected frost. Seeds germinate in 1 to 2 weeks at a soil temperature of 65° F.

SPACING: Set plants 1 foot apart.

PLANTING DEPTH: Do not cover the fine seeds with soil. Set nursery plants or divisions at the same depth they were growing previously.

PROPAGATION: Stem cuttings and seeds. Take stem cuttings in midsummer.

PLANTING TIPS: False rock cress is a low, spreading evergreen plant that is attractive in rock gardens or as an edging for beds and borders.

AURINIA
A. saxatilis, Basket-of-gold

WHERE TO PLANT: Full sun, in very well-drained soil of average or below average fertility, with a pH of 5.5 to 7.0. Basket-of-gold tends to rot in hot, humid climates. Hardy from Zones 4 to 10.

WHEN TO PLANT: Set out nursery plants or divide established plantings in spring. Take stem cuttings in early summer (June). Direct-seed in spring

AURINIA—*Continued*

WHEN TO PLANT:
(continued)

or summer, or start seeds indoors in early spring when you start annuals.

SPACING:
Set plants 1 foot apart.

PLANTING DEPTH:
Plant nursery plants or divisions at the same depth they were growing previously. Do not cover seeds; they need light to germinate.

PROPAGATION:
Division or seeds.

PLANTING TIPS:
Basket-of-gold is easy to grow and is pretty in rock gardens, or for carpeting open areas in beds and borders. You may find the plant listed in catalogs under its old name, *Alyssum saxatile*. Aurinia self-sows prolifically. Cut back plants after flowering to prevent self-seeding. Rich soil causes this plant to become shapeless and lacking in vigor.

BAPTISIA

B. australis, Blue false indigo

WHERE TO PLANT:
Full sun to partial shade, in loose, well-drained soil of average fertility, with a pH of 5.5 to 7.0. False indigo can tolerate dry soil and grows well in Zones 3 to 10.

WHEN TO PLANT:
Direct-seed in spring in cool climates, in fall in warmer climates. If planting in spring, soak the seeds for 48 hours before sowing.

Baptisia can be divided in spring, but division is difficult because of the plant's long taproot.

SPACING:
Most gardeners grow false indigo as a specimen plant, having only one clump in the garden. If you want several clumps, space them 1½ to 2½ feet apart.

PLANTING DEPTH:
Plant seeds ⅛ to ¼ inch deep.

PROPAGATION:
Seeds. Do not divide the plants unless the number of flowers decreases substantially.

PLANTING TIPS:
Plants bloom 2 or 3 years after seeds are sown. Baptisia is handsome in beds and borders or wild gardens. It grows quite large—up to 6 feet high—so give it a lot of space.

The small, pealike flowers are deep violet-blue and are excellent cut flowers.

Plants may self-sow, and the young seedlings may be transplanted in spring.

BOLTONIA

B. asteroides 'Snowbank'

WHERE TO PLANT: Full sun to partial shade, in light, moist but well-drained soil of average fertility, with a pH of 5.5 to 7.0. Boltonia tolerates a range of soil types. Plants are hardy in Zones 3 to 8 and are tolerant of hot, humid weather.

WHEN TO PLANT: Set out plants or divide established clumps in spring or fall.

SPACING: Set plants 1½ to 2 feet apart.

PLANTING DEPTH: Plant nursery plants or divisions at the same depth they were growing previously.

PROPAGATION: Division.

PLANTING TIPS: Boltonia is easy to grow and valuable for its summer to autumn flowers. It is a nice background plant for chrysanthemums or Michaelmas daisies.

The species form of the plant is very large and can be ungainly, but this white-flowered cultivar is more manageable. Plant it at the back of the garden.

Plants spread rapidly in light, fertile soil.

BRUNNERA

B. macrophylla, Siberian bugloss

WHERE TO PLANT: Prefers partial shade, especially in warm climates, but will tolerate full sun. Adapts to a range of soils, but thrives in moist but well-drained soils of average fertility and rich in organic matter, with a pH of 5.5 to 7.0. Plants are hardy from Zones 3 to 10.

WHEN TO PLANT: Set out plants or take root cuttings (1½- to 2-inch-long pieces of thick roots) in spring. Direct-seed in fall. Or divide established plants in early spring or fall.

BRUNNERA—*Continued*

SPACING:

Set plants 12 to 15 inches apart.

PLANTING DEPTH:

Plant seeds ⅛ to ¼ inch deep. Set plants at the same depth they were growing previously.

PROPAGATION:

Division or transplanting of self-sown seedlings. Plants in beds and borders should be divided every 2 or 3 years, when the center of the clump begins to deteriorate.

PLANTING TIPS:

Brunnera is very easy to grow; its tiny blue flowers and big heart-shaped leaves are attractive in beds and borders. The plants can be hard to keep under control in the garden, but are pretty when allowed to naturalize among shrubs.

Plants often self-sow; transplant the volunteers in early spring.

CAMPANULA

C. carpatica, Carpathian harebell
C. glomerata, Clustered bellflower
C. persicifolia, Peach-leaved bellflower

WHERE TO PLANT:

All three species will bloom in either full sun or partial shade. Where summer temperatures routinely go over 90° F, give campanulas some afternoon shade. All of the bellflowers like moist but well-drained soil rich in organic matter. The ideal pH is 7.0 to 7.5. Most campanulas can be grown in Zones 3 to 9.

WHEN TO PLANT:

Sow seeds outdoors in late spring for flowers the following year, or start seeds indoors 6 to 8 weeks before the last expected frost and set out plants when all danger of frost is past.

Take stem cuttings in spring. Divide established plants in spring or early fall.

SPACING:

Set *C. carpatica* 10 to 12 inches apart, the other species 12 to 15 inches apart.

PLANTING DEPTH:

Do not cover the fine seeds of campanula with soil. Light aids germination.

PROPAGATION:

Seeds or division.

PLANTING TIPS:

Bellflowers are easy to grow and are dependable plants for beds and borders. Plant low-growing Carpathian harebell near the front of the garden, clustered and peach-leaved bellflowers in the middle ground.

Campanulas are generally trouble-free except for a susceptibility to snails and slugs.

CAREX

C. morrowii, Japanese sedge

WHERE TO PLANT:	Full sun to partial shade, in well-drained soil of average fertility. Hardy from Zones 5 to 9.
WHEN TO PLANT:	Set out plants in spring or fall.
SPACING:	Set plants 2 feet apart.
PLANTING DEPTH:	Plant at the same depth plants were growing previously.
PROPAGATION:	Nursery plants.
PLANTING TIPS:	Japanese sedge is a handsome, easy-to-grow ornamental grass (although not a true grass) that is good for edging beds and borders, grouped in specimen plantings, or in rock gardens. It grows in neat clumps and is evergreen in warm climates.

CENTAUREA

C. macrocephala, Globe centaurea
C. montana, Mountain bluet

WHERE TO PLANT:	Full sun, in dry, well-drained soil of average fertility, with a pH of 5.5 to 7.0. Both species are hardy from Zones 3 to 8.
WHEN TO PLANT:	Divide established plants in spring. Direct-seed in spring or summer for flowers the following summer. Globe centaureas should be divided every 3 to 4 years; mountain bluets may need dividing every other year to keep them vigorous and producing lots of flowers.
SPACING:	Space plants 1 to 1½ feet apart.
PLANTING DEPTH:	Cover seeds lightly with soil.
PROPAGATION:	Seeds or division.
PLANTING TIPS:	Plant both these species in beds and borders. Mountain bluets are good cut flowers, but they tend to flop over as they grow. They also spread aggressively and can become invasive. Globe centaureas attract butterflies. Centaureas will not survive the winter in areas with poor drainage.

CHRYSANTHEMUM

C. × *morifolium* cultivars, Garden or florists' chrysanthemum

WHERE TO PLANT:	Full sun, in fertile, moist but well-drained soil rich in organic matter, with a pH of 5.5 to 7.0. Chrysanthemums have shallow roots, so they need regular fertilization and plenty of moisture. Plants grow from Zones 4 to 10, but should be given a winter mulch in the North.
WHEN TO PLANT:	Set out nursery plants or divide established plants in spring. You can also start new plants from stem cuttings taken in spring.
SPACING:	Space plants 1 to 2 feet apart, depending on the variety.
PLANTING DEPTH:	Set nursery plants or divisions at the same depth they were growing previously.
PROPAGATION:	Division or cuttings.
PLANTING TIPS:	Chrysanthemums require a lot of work, but they are the mainstay of many autumn beds and borders. Breeding has extended the blooming period and given us an enormous range of plant sizes, flower forms, and colors from which to choose.

To maintain plant vigor and top flower quality, divide chrysanthemums every year.

When buying plants for your garden, purchase garden-center plants intended for outdoor growing instead of gift plants from the florist, which are often forced into bloom outside their normal season and may not survive winter outdoors.

When dividing plants, discard the woody central portion of the rootstock and replant the young outer shoots.

Gardeners in the northern parts of the growing range can dig plants in late fall and move them to a cold frame over winter. Protect them with a good layer of salt hay, shredded leaves, or other loose mulch.

CLEMATIS

C. species and cultivars

WHERE TO PLANT:	Full sun to partial shade, in fertile, moist but well-drained, cool soil rich in organic matter, with a pH of 5.5 to 7.0. The soil must be neither soggy nor dry, and not too light in texture. If your soil is

sandy, work in plenty of compost and leaf mold before planting clematis. Mulching in spring will help keep the soil cool. Most clematis grow well in Zones 4 to 9, although some species are more hardy than others.

WHEN TO PLANT:
Set out nursery plants in spring. Take stem cuttings in summer to start new plants that will bloom the following year.

SPACING:
Space plants 1½ to 2 feet apart.

PLANTING DEPTH:
Set out nursery plants at the same depth they were growing previously.

PROPAGATION:
Nursery plants or stem cuttings. Some varieties can be started from seed. Sow seeds in flats of a good germination medium, and place them in your freezer for 3 weeks. Then place in a very warm location, with soil temperatures of 80 to 85° F. Germination will be slow and erratic. If seeds fail to germinate, repeat the cold/hot cycle.

PLANTING TIPS:
Most clematis are vines that are lovely when trained on a fence or trellis.

Clematis does not need division—plants can be left in place permanently after planting.

Although clematis thrives in full sun, it also requires a constantly cool, moist root zone.

COREOPSIS
C. grandiflora
C. lanceolata
C. verticillata, Threadleaf coreopsis

WHERE TO PLANT:
Full sun, in practically any well-drained soil, with a pH of 5.5 to 7.0. Coreopsis tolerates poor soil, but blooms best in soils of average fertility. Threadleaf coreopsis grows well in Zones 3 to 10; the other two species are hardy to Zone 4.

WHEN TO PLANT:
Set out plants or sow seeds outdoors in spring or early summer. Seeds may also be sown indoors 8 to 10 weeks before the average last frost date. Germination takes approximately 3 weeks at a soil temperature of 55 to 70° F. Divide established plants in spring or fall.

SPACING:
Space plants 1 to 2 feet apart, depending on the variety.

COREOPSIS—*Continued*

PLANTING DEPTH:
Set divisions at the same depth they were growing previously. When sowing seeds, do not cover with soil as light is required for germination.

PROPAGATION:
Seeds or division.

PLANTING TIPS:
Coreopsis is easy to grow, and its sunny yellow flowers, which bloom all summer long, are a bright addition to beds and borders.

Although coreopsis is easy to start from seed, a few cultivars should be propagated by division because they don't always come true from seed.

The flowers are excellent for cutting and last long in the vase.

DELPHINIUM
D. elatum hybrids

WHERE TO PLANT:
Full sun, in moist but well-drained, highly fertile, deeply dug soil, rich in organic matter, with a pH of 5.5 to 7.0. Delphiniums need rich soil and several applications of balanced fertilizer during the growing season. Although they are hardy from Zones 3 to 9, they grow best in climates where summer weather is cool and moist, especially at night. New England and the Pacific Northwest are two good areas for delphiniums. In the southern parts of the growing range, delphiniums are best treated as hardy annuals, with new plants set out each year.

Give delphiniums a spot protected from wind.

WHEN TO PLANT:
Set out nursery plants or divide established plants in early spring. Direct-seed in summer (fall, in warm climates) for plants that will bloom the following year. Or sow seed indoors 8 to 10 weeks before the average last frost date. Seeds germinate best at a soil temperature of 65 to 75° F. Germination takes 1 to 2 weeks.

SPACING:
Space plants 1 to 2 feet apart; do not crowd them or you may encounter disease problems.

PLANTING DEPTH:
Set plants or divisions so that the crowns (where roots and stem meet) are 1 to 2 inches below the soil surface. Sow seeds about ¼ inch deep. Be sure to totally cover seeds as they require darkness to germinate.

PROPAGATION:	Seeds, cuttings, or division. Take stem cuttings in late spring. The plants need division every couple of years, and many gardeners find it best to start with new seedlings every few years.
PLANTING TIPS:	Although they are demanding to grow, delphiniums are magnificent in beds and borders, where they are heavenly with flowers of creamy white, pale yellow, blue, or pink.
	Handle delphiniums carefully when transplanting—the roots break easily.
	The plants are highly susceptible to slugs and fungus diseases.
	When the young shoots are about 6 inches tall, thin to leave about three of the strongest shoots on each plant. Thinning will prevent crowding, which can invite disease and reduce the size of the flowers.
	Delphiniums are greedy feeders and demand a soil heavily amended with organic matter to thrive.

DIANTHUS

D. × allwoodii, D. deltoides, D. gratianopolitanus, D. plumarius,
Garden pinks

WHERE TO PLANT:	Full sun, in light, well-drained, preferably sandy soil of average fertility, with a pH around 7.0. All dianthus varieties prefer a neutral to slightly alkaline soil. All these species (and their cultivars) are hardy from Zones 4 to 8.
WHEN TO PLANT:	Set out plants from the nursery or garden center in spring. Divide and replant established plants in midsummer when they finish blooming. Or divide established plants in spring.
	You can also start plants by sowing seeds outdoors in spring or early summer. Or sow seeds indoors about 4 weeks before the average last frost date. Germination takes 2 to 3 weeks at a soil temperature of 70° F.
SPACING:	Space plants about 8 to 12 inches apart.
PLANTING DEPTH:	Crowns must be even with the soil surface; do not bury the stems of plants, divisions, or rooted cuttings. Sow seeds ⅛ inch deep.
PROPAGATION:	Stem cuttings, division, or layering. Take cuttings from or layer established plants in midsummer when they finish blooming. Cuttings root more easily if taken with a heel.

DIANTHUS—*Continued*

PLANTING TIPS:
Spicy-scented garden pinks are delightful in the front of beds and borders.

The plants need good air circulation, especially around their roots, so do not mulch them.

Add ground limestone if your soil is distinctly acid.

Plants lose their vigor after 2 or 3 years, so be sure to keep starting new plants each year.

DICENTRA
D. spectabilis, Bleeding-heart
D. eximia, Fringed bleeding-heart

WHERE TO PLANT:
Partial shade is best, although plants will tolerate full sun if the soil is moist. Plant in deeply dug, moist but well-drained loamy soil rich in organic matter, with a pH of 5.0 to 6.0. Bleeding-heart grows well in Zones 3 to 7. Farther south the plants are short-lived because they do not like long, hot summers.

WHEN TO PLANT:
Set out nursery plants in spring. Divide established plants in early spring when the first shoots appear. Handle divisions with care— they are delicate. You can also start plants from stem or root cuttings in spring, or by direct-seeding in fall. Bleeding-heart can also be started from seed sown indoors in late winter. Seed should be stratified in a freezer for 6 weeks before sowing. Germination takes 4 to 6 weeks. Seeds germinate best at a soil temperature of 55 to 60° F.

SPACING:
Space plants 1½ to 2½ feet apart.

PLANTING DEPTH:
Cover seeds lightly with soil.

PROPAGATION:
Plants from the nursery or garden center, or division. Fringed bleeding-heart tends to self-sow.

PLANTING TIPS:
Bleeding-heart is charming in beds and borders, and easy to grow if you can provide the right environment. The plants do not need to be divided unless you notice that flower production has declined.

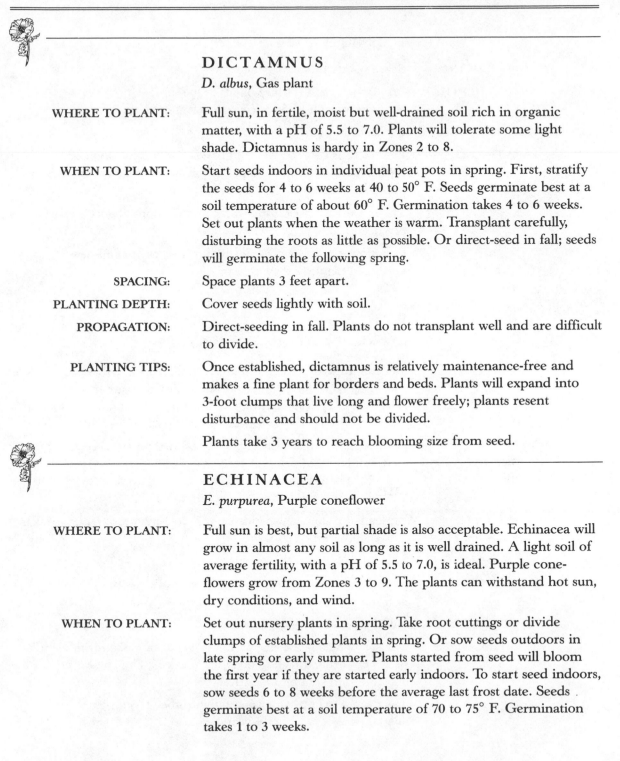

DICTAMNUS

D. albus, Gas plant

WHERE TO PLANT: Full sun, in fertile, moist but well-drained soil rich in organic matter, with a pH of 5.5 to 7.0. Plants will tolerate some light shade. Dictamnus is hardy in Zones 2 to 8.

WHEN TO PLANT: Start seeds indoors in individual peat pots in spring. First, stratify the seeds for 4 to 6 weeks at 40 to 50° F. Seeds germinate best at a soil temperature of about 60° F. Germination takes 4 to 6 weeks. Set out plants when the weather is warm. Transplant carefully, disturbing the roots as little as possible. Or direct-seed in fall; seeds will germinate the following spring.

SPACING: Space plants 3 feet apart.

PLANTING DEPTH: Cover seeds lightly with soil.

PROPAGATION: Direct-seeding in fall. Plants do not transplant well and are difficult to divide.

PLANTING TIPS: Once established, dictamnus is relatively maintenance-free and makes a fine plant for borders and beds. Plants will expand into 3-foot clumps that live long and flower freely; plants resent disturbance and should not be divided.

Plants take 3 years to reach blooming size from seed.

ECHINACEA

E. purpurea, Purple coneflower

WHERE TO PLANT: Full sun is best, but partial shade is also acceptable. Echinacea will grow in almost any soil as long as it is well drained. A light soil of average fertility, with a pH of 5.5 to 7.0, is ideal. Purple coneflowers grow from Zones 3 to 9. The plants can withstand hot sun, dry conditions, and wind.

WHEN TO PLANT: Set out nursery plants in spring. Take root cuttings or divide clumps of established plants in spring. Or sow seeds outdoors in late spring or early summer. Plants started from seed will bloom the first year if they are started early indoors. To start seed indoors, sow seeds 6 to 8 weeks before the average last frost date. Seeds germinate best at a soil temperature of 70 to 75° F. Germination takes 1 to 3 weeks.

ECHINACEA—*Continued*

SPACING: Space plants 1½ to 2 feet apart.

PLANTING DEPTH: Set divisions and nursery plants at the same depth they were growing previously. Sow seeds ¼ to ½ inch deep.

PROPAGATION: Division or seeds.

PLANTING TIPS: Echinacea is easy to grow and handsome in beds and borders. It pairs beautifully with Rudbeckia. Purple coneflowers are also nice in prairie gardens in the Midwest.

The flowers are good for cutting, and the cone-shaped flower heads dry beautifully.

Coneflowers self-sow prolifically, but it is easy to cull new, unwanted plants as they appear.

ECHINOPS

E. species and cultivars, Globe thistle

WHERE TO PLANT: Full sun, in well-drained soil of average fertility, with a pH of 5.5 to 7.0. The plants like regular moisture when they are growing actively, but because the roots go deep into the soil, the plants can tolerate drought. Globe thistles are hardy in Zones 3 to 10.

WHEN TO PLANT: Set out nursery plants or divide established plants in spring. Sow seeds outdoors in spring or early summer. Or start seeds indoors 6 to 8 weeks before the average last frost date. Seeds germinate in 2 to 3 weeks at a soil temperature of 65 to 75° F.

You can also start new plants from 2- to 3-inch root cuttings taken in early autumn.

SPACING: Space plants 1½ to 2 feet apart.

PLANTING DEPTH: Plant divisions or nursery plants at the same depth they were growing previously. Cover seeds lightly with soil.

PROPAGATION: Division, root cuttings, or seeds.

PLANTING TIPS: The steely blue globe-shaped flower heads of globe thistles lend a somewhat exotic touch to beds and borders. The color is especially effective with cool pinks and yellows.

The deep roots make division rather difficult, but plants need dividing only every 3 or 4 years.

EPIMEDIUM
E. species

WHERE TO PLANT: Partial shade to shade, in moist, fertile, deeply dug soil rich in organic matter, with a pH of 5.5 to 7.0. Plants grow well in Zones 5 to 8 and with winter protection will succeed in Zone 4 or even Zone 3. They tolerate dry soil if planted in a shady spot and can withstand sun if the soil is moist.

WHEN TO PLANT: Set out nursery plants in spring. Divide clumps of rhizomes of established plants in early spring before they flower or in fall.

SPACING: Space plants 8 to 10 inches apart.

PLANTING DEPTH: Plant divisions or plants at the same depth they were growing previously, with crowns at soil level.

PROPAGATION: Division.

PLANTING TIPS: Epimediums are excellent in rock gardens.

They don't need dividing unless you want to start new plants.

Some varieties are evergreen and make excellent ground covers, although they do not spread rapidly.

FESTUCA
F. cinerea, F. ovina var. *glauca*, Blue fescue

WHERE TO PLANT: Full sun, in well-drained soil of average fertility. Hardy from Zones 4 to 9.

WHEN TO PLANT: Set out plants in spring or fall. Direct-sow in spring.

SPACING: Space plants 1½ feet apart.

PLANTING DEPTH: Cover seeds lightly with soil.

PROPAGATION: Nursery plants or seeds.

PLANTING TIPS: Blue fescue is prized for its low clumps of slender blue-green leaves. Plant it as an edging, in the front of beds and borders, or in the rock garden. Attractive year-round.

GAILLARDIA

G. × grandiflora, Blanketflower

WHERE TO PLANT: Full sun, in light, loose soil of average fertility, with a pH of 5.5 to 7.0. The plants withstand heat and drought, and grow well in Zones 3 to 9.

WHEN TO PLANT: Divide established plants or take root cuttings in spring for flowers the same year. Or direct-sow seed outdoors in late spring. Some varieties can be started from seed early indoors and will bloom the same year.

SPACING: Space plants 10 to 18 inches apart, depending on the variety.

PLANTING DEPTH: Set divisions at the same depth they were growing previously. Do not cover seeds with soil as light is necessary for germination.

PROPAGATION: Division, root cuttings, or seeds.

PLANTING TIPS: Blanketflowers are durable and colorful additions to beds and borders, and make good cut flowers. Plants tolerate drought and poor soil, but they become sprawling and untidy as fall approaches.

GALIUM

G. odoratum, Sweet woodruff

WHERE TO PLANT: Partial shade to shade, in moist but well-drained soil rich in organic matter, with a pH of 5.5 to 6.5. Plants are hardy from Zones 4 to 9.

WHEN TO PLANT: Set out plants or divide established plantings in spring or fall. Sow seeds outdoors in the fall for new plants in the spring. Sweet woodruff seed is difficult to germinate. You might try sowing seeds in flats in the fall and leaving them outdoors to freeze and thaw over the winter.

SPACING: Space plants 6 to 8 inches apart.

PLANTING DEPTH: Cover seeds lightly with soil. Plant nursery plants or divisions at the same depth they were growing previously.

PROPAGATION: Division.

PLANTING TIPS: A lovely ground cover in shady beds and borders, and planted under shrubs such as rhododendrons. The aromatic leaves, used to flavor May wine, stay green well into autumn, and delicate white flowers appear in late spring to early summer.

You may find sweet woodruff listed in catalogs under its old name, *Asperula odorata*.

GERANIUM

G. species and cultivars, Cranesbill, Hardy geranium

WHERE TO PLANT: Full sun to partial shade, in any well-drained soil of average fertility, with a pH of 5.5 to 7.0. Cranesbills grow best where summers are cool; in regions where summer weather is hot, make sure they get some shade. Hardiness varies with species, but most grow from Zones 4 to 8.

WHEN TO PLANT: Set out nursery plants or divide established plants in spring. Sow seeds outdoors in spring or sow indoors 4 to 6 weeks before the average last frost date. Germination takes 3 to 6 weeks at a soil temperature of 70° F.

SPACING: Space plants about 1 foot apart.

PLANTING DEPTH: Press seeds lightly into soil. Set nursery plants or divisions at the same depth they were growing previously.

PROPAGATION: Division. Geraniums are very easy to divide; you don't even need to dig up the plants. Simply uncover a portion of the root clump and break or tear off sections to replant.

PLANTING TIPS: Hardy geraniums (not to be confused with the popular bedding and pot plants also known as geraniums, but actually belonging to the genus *Pelargonium*) are lovely in beds or planted around the base of trees and shrubs. They spread rapidly, and the more shade-tolerant plants make fine ground covers in woodland gardens.

The plants can be left undisturbed unless you want divisions to start new plants.

If you are starting new plants from seed, sow them right away—the seed does not store well.

GEUM
G. species

WHERE TO PLANT:
: Full sun to partial shade, in fertile, moist but well-drained soil rich in organic matter, with a pH of 5.5 to 7.0. Geums grow well in Zones 5 to 9.

WHEN TO PLANT:
: Set out plants or divide established clumps of plants in spring. Or sow seed outdoors in late spring. Seeds may also be started indoors 7 to 8 weeks before the average last frost date. Seeds germinate in 3 to 4 weeks at a soil temperature of 70 to 80° F.

SPACING:
: Space plants 12 to 15 inches apart.

PLANTING DEPTH:
: Cover seeds lightly with soil. Set plants or divisions at the same depth they were growing previously.

PROPAGATION:
: Division.

PLANTING TIPS:
: Geums have a long blooming period—an asset in summer beds and borders. In hotter climates they do better with partial shade.

Divide them every 3 years to keep the plants vigorous and floriferous.

GYPSOPHILA
G. *paniculata*, Perennial baby's-breath

WHERE TO PLANT:
: Full sun, in deeply dug, well-drained soil containing plenty of organic matter, with a pH of 6.5 to 7.5. Plants grow well in Zones 3 to 8.

WHEN TO PLANT:
: Set out nursery plants or direct-seed in spring. You can also take stem cuttings in late spring (May).

SPACING:
: Space plants 1½ to 2½ feet apart.

PLANTING DEPTH:
: Sow seeds ¼ inch deep. Set plants at the same depth they were growing previously. Many nursery plants are grafted; plant them with the graft union (recognizable as a knobby bump where the stem joins the roots) 1 inch below the soil level.

PROPAGATION:
: Nursery plants or direct-seeding. Seedlings do not transplant well, and established plants are difficult to divide.

PLANTING TIPS: Baby's-breath is lovely in beds and borders, and is a classic flower for cutting and drying.

In Zones 3 and 5, the plants need a winter mulch.

Taller varieties grow up to 3 feet high and usually need support to remain erect. Baby's-breath does best in a more alkaline soil and responds well to lime added to acid soil.

HEDERA
H. helix, English ivy

WHERE TO PLANT: Partial shade, shade, or sun, in any well-drained soil of average fertility and pH 6.0 to 7.0. Ivy growing in full sun needs a good winter mulch to protect it from cold winds in Zones 4 to 6. Most cultivars are hardy from Zones 4 to 9.

WHEN TO PLANT: Set out plants or rooted cuttings in spring or fall. Softwood or hardwood cuttings root easily and can be taken practically anytime during the growing season.

SPACING: Space plants 1½ to 2 feet apart.

PLANTING DEPTH: Set plants or rooted cuttings at the same depth they were growing previously.

PROPAGATION: Softwood or hardwood cuttings.

PLANTING TIPS: English ivy is an excellent ground cover for shady places and banks and slopes. It will also climb walls. Many cultivars are available, with a variety of leaf sizes and variegations.

HELENIUM
H. autumnale, Sneezeweed

WHERE TO PLANT: Full sun, in moist, fertile soil rich in organic matter, with a pH of 5.5 to 7.0. Helenium is tolerant of most average garden soils, but does best in rich, moist soil. Hardy from Zones 3 or 4 to 9.

WHEN TO PLANT: Spring or fall, but most often planted in spring. Divide established plants in early spring.

Sow seeds indoors 8 to 10 weeks before the last expected frost and set out seedlings when all danger of frost is past. Seeds germinate in 7 to 10 days at a soil temperature of 70° F.

HELENIUM—*Continued*

SPACING: Space plants 1½ to 2 feet apart.

PLANTING DEPTH: Cover seeds lightly with soil. Plant divisions at the same depth they were growing previously.

PROPAGATION: Division; plants need dividing every 2 or 3 years.

PLANTING TIPS: The daisylike flowers in shades of yellow, gold, and mahogany bloom in late summer and fall. Plants are tall and tend to become weedy, so put them at the back of beds and borders.

HELIOPSIS
H. helianthoides

WHERE TO PLANT: Prefers full sun but will tolerate partial shade, especially in warmer climates. Plant in well-drained soil rich in organic matter, with a pH of 5.5 to 7.0; plants can tolerate poorer, drier soils as well. Hardy from Zones 4 to 9.

WHEN TO PLANT: Spring or fall. Sow seeds outdoors in spring or early summer. Or start seeds indoors 6 to 8 weeks before the average last frost date. Germination takes 10 to 15 days at a soil temperature of 70° F.

SPACING: Space plants 1½ to 2 feet apart.

PLANTING DEPTH: Cover seeds lightly with soil. Plant divisions at the same depth they were growing previously.

PROPAGATION: Species forms can be grown from seed and may self-sow in the garden. Cultivars are best propagated by division.

PLANTING TIPS: The sunny, daisylike flowers of heliopsis are lovely in beds and borders and good for cutting. The plants are generally easy to grow.

HEMEROCALLIS
H. species and cultivars, Daylilies

WHERE TO PLANT: Daylilies bloom best in full sun, but will also succeed in partial shade. They tolerate almost any soil, but flourish in moist but well-drained soils of average fertility, rich in organic matter, with a pH of 5.5 to 7.0. Daylilies are hardy from Zones 3 to 9; in warm climates they appreciate some shade in the afternoon.

WHEN TO PLANT:	Set out tuberous roots from the nursery in spring. Divide established plants in spring or early fall, every 3 or 4 years. Slice the root clump into sections with a sharp spade or knife, making sure each division has three shoots.
SPACING:	Space plants 1½ to 2 feet apart, depending on the variety.
PLANTING DEPTH:	Plant divisions at the same depth they were growing previously, with crowns at soil level.
PROPAGATION:	Division.
PLANTING TIPS:	Daylilies are easy to grow and lovely in beds and borders, massed in the landscape, or planted along driveways and sidewalks.

Breeding has produced cultivars that bloom in early, mid-, and late summer and has extended the color range well beyond the orange of the tawny daylily that is such a familiar summer sight along roadsides in the eastern part of the United States.

Not all daylilies grow well in all gardens. Local nurseries or garden centers should stock cultivars that will thrive in your area.

HOSTA

H. species, Plantain lily

WHERE TO PLANT:	Partial shade to shade, in fertile, well-drained soil rich in organic matter. The soil should be moist in summer but drier in winter. Ideal pH is 5.5 to 7.0. The plants will also grow in full sun, if the soil is moist and fertile. Hardy from Zones 3 to 9.
WHEN TO PLANT:	Set out nursery plants or divide established clumps of plants in either spring or fall. Sow seeds indoors or directly in the garden in spring. Germination takes 2 to 3 weeks at a soil temperature of 70° F.
SPACING:	Space plants 1½ to 2 feet apart.
PLANTING DEPTH:	Plant divisions or plants at the same depth they were growing previously. Lightly cover seeds with soil.
PROPAGATION:	Division. Hostas seldom need division and can be left undisturbed for years. If you want to start new plants without disturbing an established clump, push up a sharp spade into the soil near the outside of the clump, slice off a few pieces of the root clump, dig them up, and fill the hole with compost. Replant the divisions in

HOSTA—*Continued*

PROPAGATION:
(continued)

prepared soil. This operation is easiest to perform in early spring while the leaves are still small.

PLANTING TIPS:

Bold-leaved hostas, with foliage in a host of variegation patterns and varying shades of green, white, and gold, are invaluable in shady beds and borders. They can also be planted along walks and paths, or as a ground cover. Although most valuable for their foliage, hostas send up spikes of small, occasionally fragrant, lilylike flowers in summer or fall.

Plants do not like moisture when they are dormant. They are favorite targets of slugs and snails.

Hostas are easy and undemanding to grow.

IBERIS
I. sempervirens, Perennial or evergreen candytuft

WHERE TO PLANT:

Full sun to partial shade, in moist but well-drained soil of average fertility, with a pH of 5.5 to 7.0. Iberis thrives in Zones 3 to 10.

WHEN TO PLANT:

Set out new plants or divide established plants in either spring or fall. Or start seeds indoors about 8 weeks before the last expected frost; seeds germinate in 2 to 3 weeks at a soil temperature of 55 to 65° F. Set out seedlings or direct-seed after all danger of frost is past and the soil begins to warm.

SPACING:

Space plants 1½ to 2 feet apart.

PLANTING DEPTH:

Set plants or divisions at the same depth they were growing previously. Sow seeds ¼ inch deep.

PROPAGATION:

Division, seeds, or cuttings (both hardwood and softwood).

PLANTING TIPS:

A low, mound-forming plant with tiny white flowers and evergreen foliage, perennial candytuft is lovely in rock gardens, as edging for beds and borders, and as a companion to spring bulbs.

IMPERATA
I. cylindrica 'Red Baron', Japanese blood grass

WHERE TO PLANT:

Full sun, in well-drained soil of average fertility. Hardy from Zones 6 to 9. Tolerates a range of soils.

WHEN TO PLANT:	Set out plants in spring or fall.
SPACING:	Space plants about 1½ feet apart.
PLANTING DEPTH:	Set plants at the same depth they were growing previously.
PROPAGATION:	Nursery plants.
PLANTING TIPS:	A striking grass whose leaves combine red and green in spring and summer, then turn brilliant scarlet in fall. Imperata grows 18 to 24 inches high and makes a good plant for edging or mass planting in the middle of a border.

IRIS

I. species and cultivars

WHERE TO PLANT:	There are many kinds of irises, and growing conditions vary according to species. Most do best in full sun, although some perform well in light shade. Bearded irises generally prefer moist but well-drained, fertile soil with a pH of 7.0 to 8.0. Siberian and most other irises prefer a humus-enriched soil of average fertility, moist but well-drained, with a pH of 5.5 to 7.0. Hardiness varies with the species. Bearded, crested, and Siberian irises are hardy from Zones 4 to 9; Japanese irises and *I. pseudacorus* (both of which favor marshy or boglike sites) grow from Zone 5 to 9. Pacific Coast irises grow best in the area for which they are named, while Louisiana irises do well in the Southeast, where summers are hot and humid.
WHEN TO PLANT:	Most nurseries ship iris rhizomes for late summer planting. If you live where hot weather lingers and winter arrives late, wait until early fall to plant irises. You can also plant rhizomes in spring. Cut back and divide established plants in summer, after they have finished blooming. Dutch irises and *I. reticulata*, which grow from bulbs, are planted in fall. Japanese iris may be started from seeds. Seeds need a cold period before they will germinate—refrigerate them 3 to 4 weeks before sowing outdoors in spring, or start seeds in a cold frame in autumn.
SPACING:	Space plants 1 to 2 feet apart for rhizomatous types, depending on the species. Space Dutch iris bulbs 3 to 6 inches apart, and *I. reticulata* 4 inches apart.

IRIS—*Continued*

PLANTING DEPTH:
Set rhizomatous irises so the top of the rhizome is even with the soil surface. The top surface of the rhizome should not be covered. In hot climates (Zone 9) set the rhizome slightly below the surface. Plant Dutch iris and *I. reticulata* bulbs 4 inches deep.

PROPAGATION:
Division every 3 to 4 years. Species forms can also be grown from seed.

PLANTING TIPS:
Irises are favorite flowers for beds and borders. Their range of heights, colors, and blooming times makes them a versatile group of plants.

Make sure the fan of leaves attached to the rhizome is pointing in the direction you want the plant to grow; if planting a group or bed of irises, the leaf fans should all point in the same direction.

LAVANDULA

L. angustifolia, English lavender

WHERE TO PLANT:
Full sun, in well-drained soil of average fertility, with a pH of 6.5 to 7.5. Lavender is hardy from Zones 6 to 9, but can often survive Zone 5 winters with a good mulch; mulch in Zone 6 as well. Soil that is too rich will decrease the plant's hardiness. Lavender responds well to lime added to acid soil.

WHEN TO PLANT:
Set out plants in spring, when all danger of frost is past, or in fall. Lavender seeds are difficult to germinate, but seeds can be sown indoors about 10 weeks before you want to plant them out. First stratify the seeds for 4 to 6 weeks at 40 to 50° F. Sow seeds in a sterile medium. Germination takes 2 to 3 weeks at a soil temperature of 70° F.

SPACING:
Space plants 1½ to 2 feet apart.

PLANTING DEPTH:
Set plants or rooted cuttings at the same depth they were growing previously. Sow seeds ⅛ inch deep.

PROPAGATION:
Softwood cuttings. Because lavender seed is difficult to germinate, softwood cuttings, taken with a bit of the heel from the older wood, provide the surest method of propagation. Take the cuttings from young growth during the summer. Root in moist, sandy soil in a shaded cold frame or other protected area.

PLANTING TIPS:　Beloved of herb gardeners for its refreshing scent, lavender is also a charming addition to flower beds and borders. In mild climates it can also be grown as a low hedge. Lavender bears its wands of tiny purple flowers in summer.

The flowers can be dried for use in potpourris and sachets.

LIRIOPE
L. muscari, Lilyturf

WHERE TO PLANT:　Partial shade to shade, in moist, fertile soil rich in organic matter. Plants are hardy from Zones 6 to 9; the roots may survive farther north, but the foliage is usually ruined by winter weather.

WHEN TO PLANT:　Plant divisions in spring or fall. Sow seeds outdoors anytime from late fall through midsummer. Or sow indoors in late winter. Seeds germinate best if soaked in warm water for 24 hours before planting. Germination occurs in about 4 weeks at a soil temperature of 65 to 70° F.

SPACING:　Space plants 1 to 1½ feet apart.

PLANTING DEPTH:　Plant divisions or nursery plants at the same depth they were growing previously. Cover seeds lightly with soil.

PROPAGATION:　Division in the spring.

PLANTING TIPS:　Lilyturf is most often used as a ground cover, an edging for sidewalks and driveways, or planted at the base of trees. The plants spread by stolons (underground stems) and can become invasive in beds and borders.

The spikes of small violet or white flowers look like large grape hyacinths. Some cultivars have striped leaves.

If foliage looks brown or tattered at the end of winter, cut it back before growth resumes in spring.

LYCHNIS
L. chalcedonica, Maltese cross
L. coronaria, Rose campion

WHERE TO PLANT:　Plant Maltese cross in full sun to partial shade, rose campion in full sun. Both like well-drained, fertile soil rich in organic matter. Lychnis will not tolerate "wet feet" in the winter. Ideal pH is 5.5 to

LYCHNIS—*Continued*

WHERE TO PLANT:
(continued)

7.0 for Maltese cross, 6.5 to 8.0 for rose campion. Both species will grow from Zones 3 to 10, although they will not flourish in the excessive heat along the Gulf Coast and south Florida.

WHEN TO PLANT:

Set out divisions in the spring or early summer. Or direct-seed outdoors in spring or early summer. Seeds may also be started indoors 7 to 8 weeks before the average last frost date. Seeds germinate in 3 to 4 weeks at a soil temperature of 70° F.

SPACING:

Space plants 1 to 1½ feet apart.

PLANTING DEPTH:

Seeds need light to germinate. Press them lightly into the soil but do not cover.

PROPAGATION:

Propagate Maltese cross by division. Rose campion does not respond well to division, but can be grown from seed and self-sows readily in many gardens.

PLANTING TIPS:

Maltese cross has heads of scarlet flowers; rose campion has brilliant magenta flowers borne one to a stem. Both plants are lovely in beds and borders.

Rose campion is a biennial or short-lived perennial, but new, self-sown seedlings may bloom their first year.

These plants have been reclassified several times, and you may also find them listed as *Agrostemma*, *Silene*, or *Viscaria* instead of *Lychnis*.

MISCANTHUS
M. sinensis, Eulalia grass, Maiden grass

WHERE TO PLANT:

Full sun, in well-drained soil of average fertility; tolerates a range of pH. Hardy from Zones 5 to 9.

WHEN TO PLANT:

Set out nursery plants in spring or fall, or direct-seed in spring.

SPACING:

Set plants 2 feet apart.

PLANTING DEPTH:

Set plants at the same depth they were growing previously. Lightly cover seeds with soil.

PROPAGATION:

Nursery plants.

PLANTING TIPS:

One of the best of the ornamental grasses, handsome in specimen plantings and the back of beds and borders. Grows 5 to 8 feet tall and is carefree and long-lived.

Miscanthus bears feathery flower plumes in late summer.

MONARDA

M. didyma, Beebalm

WHERE TO PLANT: Full sun to partial shade, in moist but well-drained soil of average fertility, with a pH of 5.5 to 7.0. Where summers are cool, plant in full sun; where summers are hot, plants generally do better in partial shade. Beebalm grows from Zones 4 to 9, but tends to be short-lived in the South.

WHEN TO PLANT: Set out plants in spring or fall. Or sow seeds outdoors from early spring through midsummer. Seed may be started indoors 4 to 6 weeks before the average last frost date. Germination takes 2 to 3 weeks at a soil temperature of 60 to 70° F.

SPACING: Space plants 12 inches apart.

PLANTING DEPTH: Set plants or divisions at the same depth they were growing previously. Cover seeds lightly with soil.

PROPAGATION: Seeds or division. Plants spread rapidly and need to be divided every 2 to 3 years.

PLANTING TIPS: The rounded heads of brilliant scarlet, pink, or red-violet flowers are attractive to bees and are striking toward the back of beds and borders. The leaves can be used in tea or in potpourris, and the plant is also grown in herb gardens.

Beebalm is easy to grow but needs good air circulation to prevent powdery mildew and rust.

MYOSOTIS

M. scorpioides, Forget-me-not

WHERE TO PLANT: Partial shade to shade, in moist soil of average fertility and rich in organic matter, with a pH of 5.5 to 7.0. If the soil is sufficiently moist, the plants can tolerate full sun; forget-me-nots are hardy from Zones 3 to 8.

WHEN TO PLANT: Set out plants in spring or fall.

You can also sow seeds outdoors in late summer. Plants will germinate, overwinter, and bloom the following spring.

Seeds are easy to start indoors. Sow in flats 4 to 6 weeks before the average last frost date. Germination takes 1 to 2 weeks at a soil temperature of 55 to 70° F.

MYOSOTIS—*Continued*

SPACING:	Space plants 1 foot apart.
PLANTING DEPTH:	Cover the seeds with soil; they need darkness to germinate.
PROPAGATION:	Division, seeds, or cuttings. Divide established plants in early spring or take stem cuttings in spring. Cuttings root best in a mixture of soil and builder's sand, or in pure sand. Keep the medium evenly moist until cuttings root.
PLANTING TIPS:	Forget-me-nots bloom in spring and summer and are lovely planted with bulbs and other perennials. They are especially nice planted on the banks of a stream or in shady woodland gardens.
	The flowers are sky blue—one of the few true blues of the garden.
	Forget-me-nots thrive when they are a bit crowded.

NEPETA

N. mussinii, Catmint

WHERE TO PLANT:	Full sun, in light, sandy, well-drained soil of average fertility, with a pH of 5.5 to 7.0. Hardy from Zones 3 to 9. Nepeta will thrive in hot, dry, poor, or sandy soils.
WHEN TO PLANT:	Sow seeds outdoors or set out plants in spring or summer. Or sow seed indoors 4 to 5 weeks before the average last frost date. Seeds germinate in about 1 week at a soil temperature of 60 to 70° F. Divide established plants in early spring or fall.
SPACING:	Set plants 1 foot apart.
PLANTING DEPTH:	Cover seeds lightly with soil. Set plants or divisions at the same depth they were growing previously.
PROPAGATION:	Division or seeds.
PLANTING TIPS:	The blue-violet or white flower spikes of catmint are handsome in beds and borders. A close relative of catnip, catmint is also attractive to cats.
	Plants tend to look a bit weedy and are best suited to informal garden styles.

OENOTHERA

O. species, Evening primrose, Sundrops

WHERE TO PLANT: Full sun, in well-drained soil of average fertility, with a pH of 5.5 to 7.0. The plants tolerate heat, drought, and poor soil, and grow well in Zones 4 or 5 (depending on the species) to 9. Good drainage is important, especially in winter when plants are dormant.

WHEN TO PLANT: Direct-seed in spring or fall. Take stem cuttings in late summer. Divide established plants in early fall. Sow seeds outdoors in late summer, fall, or early spring. Or start seeds indoors 4 to 5 weeks before the average last frost date. Seeds germinate in 2 to 3 weeks at a soil temperature of 70 to 85° F.

SPACING: Space plants 12 to 15 inches apart.

PLANTING DEPTH: Cover seeds lightly with soil. Plant divisions at the same depth they were growing previously.

PROPAGATION: Division or seeds.

PLANTING TIPS: Evening primrose and sundrops are handsome flowers for the front of the border. The plants spread and reseed aggressively, and will need to be divided about every other year. Plants are useful as a quick ground cover and for erosion control.

PACHYSANDRA

P. terminalis, Japanese spurge

WHERE TO PLANT: Partial shade to shade, in moist, loose soil of average fertility and rich in organic matter, with a pH of 6.0 to 7.0. The leaves will turn yellow in full sun. Plants are hardy from Zones 4 to 8.

WHEN TO PLANT: Set out plants in early spring or fall. Take stem cuttings in summer from new growth, and root them in a mixture of half garden soil and half builder's sand. Keep the cuttings shaded and watered until roots form. Divide established plantings in fall.

SPACING: Space plants 8 to 12 inches apart.

PLANTING DEPTH: Set stem cuttings ½ to 1 inch deep in loose, humusy soil. Plant divisions or rooted cuttings at the same depth they were growing previously. Cover seeds lightly with soil.

PACHYSANDRA—*Continued*

PROPAGATION: Stem cuttings or division.

PLANTING TIPS: Pachysandra is one of the most widely planted ground covers in the United States. Its evergreen leaves are variegated with white in some cultivars. The plants spread quickly and make a handsome carpet under trees and in shady beds, and a lovely background for bulbs and perennials.

Plants send up small white flowers in spring but are most valuable for their foliage.

PAEONIA

P. officinalis and hybrids, Common peony
P. tenuifolia, Fernleaf peony

WHERE TO PLANT: Full sun to partial shade, in moist but well-drained soil of average fertility and rich in organic matter, with a pH of 5.5 to 7.0. Most hybrid peonies are hardy from Zones 2 to 8; fernleaf peony is hardy to Zone 4. In the southern parts of the growing range, peonies appreciate some afternoon shade.

WHEN TO PLANT: Set out plants or divide established plants in fall—September in the North or October in the South.

SPACING: Space plants 3 feet apart.

PLANTING DEPTH: Depth is critical for peonies; set the crowns so that the red buds on the fleshy roots are no more than 2 inches below the soil surface or plants will not bloom.

PROPAGATION: Division. To divide, dig up the root clump, wash it clean of soil, and cut apart the roots with a sharp knife, making sure each division has three to five eyes.

PLANTING TIPS: Beloved of flower gardeners, peonies are easy to grow, and their foliage remains attractive all season until it dies back to the ground in fall. The big flowers, many of them fragrant, in shades of pink, red, and white, are wonderful for cutting.

Peonies seldom need division unless you want to start new plants. They transplant well and can be moved anytime, as long as you leave lots of soil around the roots.

Peonies need a cold dormant period in winter and will not grow well south of Zone 8. In Zone 8 and the warmer parts of Zone 7, plant early-blooming varieties, because later varieties may not flower well in intense summer heat. Gardeners in the South may also have to induce dormancy by cutting back the stems in fall and withholding water in winter.

Peonies are sometimes prone to botrytis blight.

A third type of peony, *P. suffruticosa*, the tree peony, is a shrub that retains its woody stems from year to year. Tree peonies are graft products and should be planted with the graft union 6 to 7 inches below the soil surface.

PAPAVER

P. orientale, Oriental poppy

WHERE TO PLANT: Full sun, in well-drained soil of average fertility, with a pH of 5.5 to 7.0. Oriental poppies grow best from Zones 3 to 7; they do not grow well where winters are warm. In Zone 7, plant poppies where they will get some shade in the afternoon.

WHEN TO PLANT: Set out roots or divide established plants in late summer or fall; divide when growth resumes after a summer dormant period. Start seeds indoors 8 to 10 weeks before the average last spring frost date and set out plants when frost danger is past.

Seeds germinate best in cool temperatures of about 55° F. Seeds germinate in 10 to 20 days; plants bloom the first year from seed.

SPACING: Space plants 2 to 3 feet apart.

PLANTING DEPTH: Plant roots 3 to 4 inches deep. Seeds need light to germinate; press them lightly into the soil but do not cover them.

PROPAGATION: Root cuttings or division, although plants seldom need to be divided unless you want to start new plants.

PLANTING TIPS: The ruffled, tissue-paper flowers of Oriental poppies come in many warm shades from pastels to brights, and are lovely additions to beds and borders. Poppies go dormant in summer after blooming and leave a gap in the garden. Try planting expansive plants like baby's-breath or Russian sage near the poppies to help cover the vacant area.

PAPAVER—*Continued*

PLANTING TIPS:
(continued)

Oriental poppies must have well-drained soil, especially in winter, or they may rot.

Transplant with care if you grow poppies from seed; they do not transplant easily. Poppies resent disturbance. If you want to move or divide established plants, do so when they emerge from summer dormancy.

PENNISETUM

P. species, Fountain grass

WHERE TO PLANT: Full sun, in well-drained soil of average fertility; tolerates a range of pH. Hardy from Zones 7 to 9.

WHEN TO PLANT: Set out plants in spring or fall. Direct-sow in spring.

SPACING: Space plants 1 to 1½ feet apart.

PLANTING DEPTH: Set plants at the same depth they were growing previously. Lightly cover seeds with soil.

PROPAGATION: Seeds or nursery plants.

PLANTING TIPS: Gracefully arching clumps of slender leaves, and feathery flowers in summer, make these plants lovely as edgers or specimen plantings, or in the middle of beds and borders.

Although perennial species are not hardy in the North, an annual species, *P. villosum*, can be planted instead.

PENSTEMON

P. barbatus, Beard-tongue

WHERE TO PLANT: Full sun, in well-drained soil of average fertility, with a pH of 5.5 to 7.0. Crowns will rot in soggy soil; if your soil drains slowly, plant in raised beds or on slopes. Plants are hardy to Zones 3 or 4. In warm climates, plant in partial shade to prolong the life of the plants.

WHEN TO PLANT: Sow seeds outdoors or set out plants in spring or late summer. Or sow seeds indoors 4 to 5 weeks before the average last frost date. Seeds germinate best in cool temperatures, around 55° F. They take 2 to 3 weeks to sprout.

SPACING:	Space plants 1 to 1½ feet apart.
PLANTING DEPTH:	Cover seeds lightly with soil. Set plants at the same depth they were growing previously.
PROPAGATION:	Seeds or nursery plants.
PLANTING TIPS:	Penstemons bear their spikes of tubular red, pink, or purple flowers in late spring or summer. Plant them in the middle of beds and borders.

Penstemons are native to the Midwest and Rocky Mountain area, and many of them tend to grow best in this part of the country.

PHALARIS

P. arundinacea, Ribbon grass, Gardener's garters

WHERE TO PLANT:	Full sun to partial shade, in well-drained soil of average fertility; tolerates a range of pH. Hardy from Zones 4 to 9.
WHEN TO PLANT:	Spring or fall.
SPACING:	Space plants 1 to 1½ feet apart.
PLANTING DEPTH:	Set plants at the same depth they were growing previously.
PROPAGATION:	Nursery plants.
PLANTING TIPS:	This handsome grass spreads quickly and can be used as a ground cover. Plants are 2 to 3 feet tall, with slender green and white striped leaves (depending on the variety) that turn light tan in winter.

PHLOX

P. divaricata, Blue phlox
P. paniculata, Garden phlox
P. subulata, Mountain pink

WHERE TO PLANT:	Garden phlox and mountain pinks both grow best in full sun; blue phlox does best in partial shade or shade. Blue phlox and garden phlox like fertile, moist but well-drained soil rich in organic matter, with a pH of 5.5 to 7.5. Mountain pinks prefer soil of average fertility. *P. divaricata* is hardy from Zones 3 to 8, *P. paniculata* from Zones 4 (3 with winter protection) to 9, and *P. subulata* from Zones 4 to 9.

PHLOX—*Continued*

WHEN TO PLANT: Spring or fall. Take cuttings from or divide blue phlox and mountain pinks in fall; divide garden phlox in autumn after the plants finish blooming. You can also start blue and garden phlox from seed sown outdoors in fall for spring germination. Or sow seeds indoors in late winter. Stratify seeds for 3 to 4 weeks at 40 to 50° F. Germination takes 4 to 5 weeks at a soil temperature of 70° F.

SPACING: Space *P. divaricata* about 1 foot apart, *P. paniculata* 15 to 18 inches apart, and *P. subulata* 1 foot apart.

PLANTING DEPTH: Sow garden and blue phlox seed ⅛ to ¼ inch deep. Be sure to cover seeds as darkness is needed for germination.

PROPAGATION: Division or cuttings. Garden and blue phlox can both be grown from seed. Garden phlox is propagated commercially from root cuttings, but division and stem cuttings are the easiest, most reliable methods of propagation for home gardeners. Garden phlox develops clumps of stems with eyes at the base. When dividing, pull the clumps apart, or chop them apart with a sharp spade, making sure that each division has several eyes.

Mountain pinks are also easily propagated by division, or cuttings taken in late fall and rooted in sand in a cold frame. To divide mountain pinks, cut back the plants lightly in fall, and a couple of weeks later dig them up and pull the clumps apart. Replant the divisions immediately.

PLANTING TIPS: *P. divaricata* is a low, creeping perennial that makes an attractive ground cover in a woodland setting. Its lilac-blue or white flowers bloom in spring. It tends to be susceptible to powdery mildew.

Garden phlox is a tall, clump-forming perennial, bearing showy pyramids of flowers on 3- to 5-foot stems. It blooms from midsummer to fall. Flowers come in shades of red, pink, purple, and white. This type of phlox is prone to powdery mildew. Do not crowd plants in the garden.

The carpets of mountain pinks are a familiar sight on banks and slopes, in rock gardens, and in flower beds in early spring. The small flowers come in shades of pink—pastel to bright—lavender, and white. The plants spread quickly.

Divide phlox, especially garden phlox, every 3 to 4 years.

RUDBECKIA
R. fulgida, Coneflower

WHERE TO PLANT: Full sun, in moist but well-drained soil of average fertility, with a pH of 5.5 to 7.0. Hardy from Zones 3 to 9.

WHEN TO PLANT: Sow seeds in a cold frame in early spring and move seedlings to the garden as soon as they are big enough to handle. Seeds take 2 to 3 weeks to germinate.

Set out nursery plants when danger of heavy frost is past. Divide established plants in early spring (March or April), before new growth begins in earnest.

SPACING: Space plants 2 feet apart.

PLANTING DEPTH: Plant divisions at the same depth they were growing previously. Sow seeds ¼ inch deep.

PROPAGATION: Division or seeds. Not all varieties come true from seed; 'Goldsturm', the most popular cultivar, must be propagated by division.

PLANTING TIPS: These summer flowers are garden versions of the black-eyed Susan—golden yellow daisies with deep brown centers. They are attractive in beds and borders and easy to grow.

In light, moist soil in warm climates, the plants spread quickly and will need to be divided every couple of years; otherwise they generally need dividing every 4 years.

SALVIA
S. azurea var. *grandiflora*, Pitcher's sage
S. × superba, Violet sage

WHERE TO PLANT: Full sun, in well-drained soil of average fertility, with a pH of 5.5 to 7.0. Pitcher's sage is hardy from Zone 4 to 9; violet sage, from Zones 5 to 9.

WHEN TO PLANT: Plant cuttings or divisions in early spring or fall, but generally in the spring. Sow seeds outdoors from spring through midsummer. Or sow seeds indoors 6 to 8 weeks before the average last frost date. Germination takes 12 to 15 days at 70° F.

SPACING: Set plants 1½ feet apart.

SALVIA—*Continued*

PLANTING DEPTH: Plant divisions at the same depth they were growing previously. Sow seeds ⅛ to ¼ inch deep.

PROPAGATION: Propagate pitcher's sage from seeds, cuttings, or divisions; propagate violet sage by division.

PLANTING TIPS: The upright flower spikes of these sages are lovely additions to the front or middle of beds and borders. Pitcher's sage has blue or white flowers, and violet sage has blossoms of deeper purple. Violet sage blooms in midsummer; pitcher's sage blooms in late summer.

Give S. *azurea* var. *grandiflora* a winter mulch north of Zone 6.

Another blue-flowered sage, S. *farinacea* (mealycup sage), is covered under Annuals, but is perennial in frost-free climates.

SEDUM

S. 'Autumn Joy'

WHERE TO PLANT: Full sun to partial shade, in well-drained soil of average fertility, with a pH of 5.5 to 7.0. Good drainage is particularly important in winter when plants are dormant; they can tolerate more moisture when in active growth. Hardy from Zones 3 to 9.

WHEN TO PLANT: Spring or fall.

SPACING: Space plants 15 to 18 inches apart.

PLANTING DEPTH: Plant divisions, rooted cuttings, or nursery plants at the same depth they were growing previously. Cover seeds lightly with soil.

PROPAGATION: Division, stem cuttings, leaf cuttings, or seeds. Seeds need 2 to 3 weeks to germinate.

PLANTING TIPS: Many sedums are low growers that are handsome in rock gardens. This 2-foot-tall cultivar is one of the best perennials for beds and borders. The succulent green foliage is attractive in spring, and the immature flower heads resemble broccoli. The long-lasting flowers open in mid- to late summer, beginning as light pink, then gradually deepening to rosy red, then an impossible-to-describe shade of coppery bronze, then deep rust, and eventually, brown. The dry flower heads endure through fall and winter, and provide interest in the garden when little else is available. The dried flowers are also useful in indoor arrangements.

'Autumn Joy' sedum is an easy-to-grow plant that seldom needs division.

TANACETUM

T. vulgare var. *crispum*, Tansy

WHERE TO PLANT:	Full sun to partial shade, in light, well-drained soil of average fertility, with a pH of 5.5 to 7.0. Hardy from Zones 3 to 9.
WHEN TO PLANT:	Sow seeds outdoors in spring or fall. Sow indoors 8 to 10 weeks before the last expected frost; set out plants when danger of frost is past.
SPACING:	Space plants 1 to 1½ feet apart.
PLANTING DEPTH:	Cover seeds lightly with soil. Plant divisions at the same depth they were growing previously.
PROPAGATION:	Seeds or division.
PLANTING TIPS:	Tansy is most often seen in herb gardens, but can also be included in flower beds and borders. The plants grow 2 to 4 feet tall, with ferny foliage and clusters of tiny, yellow, buttonlike flowers.

In rich, moist soil the plants can become invasive and will need to be divided often.

Tansy is valued as an herb for its aromatic leaves; it is not edible.

THERMOPSIS

T. caroliniana, Carolina lupine

WHERE TO PLANT:	Full sun to partial shade, in light, well-drained soil of average fertility, with a pH of 5.5 to 7.0. Plants are drought resistant in sun and light soil, less so in richer, moist, shady locations. Hardy to Zone 3.
WHEN TO PLANT:	Direct-sow in fall; seeds will germinate the following spring. Or sow seeds indoors 4 to 5 weeks before average last frost date. To increase germination rate, scarify and soak seeds overnight in warm water before planting. Seeds germinate in 2 to 3 weeks at 70° F.
SPACING:	Set plants 2 to 3 feet apart.
PLANTING DEPTH:	Cover seeds lightly with soil.
PROPAGATION:	Direct seeding.
PLANTING TIPS:	Carolina lupine's yellow flower spikes are an unusual sight in flower beds and borders. The plants grow 4 to 5 feet tall, need lots of

THERMOPSIS—*Continued*

PLANTING TIPS:
(continued)

space, and bloom for a short time. They are best planted in large gardens.

When starting from seed, use only fresh seed; old seeds germinate poorly.

Plants are difficult to divide and seldom require division, but can be divided in spring if you want more plants.

TRADESCANTIA
T. × andersoniana, T. virginiana, Spiderwort

WHERE TO PLANT: Full sun to partial shade, in moist soil of average fertility, with a pH of 5.5 to 7.0. A moist but well-drained soil is ideal, but plants also will grow in boggy soils. They do not do well in dry soils. Plants are hardy to Zone 5.

WHEN TO PLANT: Sow seeds outdoors from early spring through summer. Or sow indoors 8 to 10 weeks before the average last frost date. Germination takes about 4 weeks at 70° F. You can also allow plants to self-sow in fall, divide established plants in spring, or take stem cuttings in summer.

SPACING: Set plants 12 to 15 inches apart.

PLANTING DEPTH: Cover seeds lightly with soil.

PROPAGATION: Division or self-sown seeds.

PLANTING TIPS: *T. virginiana* is a wildflower native to the woodlands of the northeastern United States; *T. × andersoniana* includes numerous hybrid forms with larger flowers. Flowers are violet, pink, or white and appear in summer.

The grassy foliage tends to become straggly and floppy by midsummer, so locate the plants where other plants will camouflage the leaves, or cut back the foliage when plants finish blooming. Spiderworts are easy to grow.

VALERIANA
V. officinalis, Common valerian

WHERE TO PLANT: Full sun, in very moist but well-drained soil of average fertility and rich in organic matter, with a pH of 5.5 to 7.0. Hardy to Zone 5.

WHEN TO PLANT:	Direct-sow or divide established plants in early spring or fall.
SPACING:	Set plants 3 feet apart.
PLANTING DEPTH:	Plant divisions at the same depth they were growing previously. Cover seeds lightly with soil.
PROPAGATION:	Division of crowns or collection of offsets that grow on runners sent out by the mother plant. Seeds germinate poorly.
PLANTING TIPS:	Valerian is easy to grow and its fragrant pink, lavender, or white flowers are handsome additions to the middle or back of summer beds and borders. Plants tend to be weedy and are best used in informal gardens.

VERONICA
V. species, Speedwell

WHERE TO PLANT:	Full sun to partial shade, in well-drained soil of average fertility that is neither soggy nor dry, with a pH of 5.5 to 7.0. Most veronicas are hardy from Zones 4 to 9.
WHEN TO PLANT:	Set out nursery plants in spring or fall. Take stem cuttings in summer. Divide established plants in late summer or early fall when plants have finished blooming. Or sow seeds outdoors in spring or early summer. You may also start seeds indoors 4 to 5 weeks before the average last frost date. Seeds germinate in 2 to 3 weeks at 70° F.
SPACING:	Space plants 1 foot apart.
PLANTING DEPTH:	Set plants or divisions at the same depth they were growing previously. Cover seeds lightly with soil.
PROPAGATION:	Division or cuttings.
PLANTING TIPS:	The blue flower spikes of veronica are lovely in beds and borders and good for cutting. There are some prostrate and trailing species nice for rock gardens. There are also shrubby types (now classified in the genus *Hebe*) that are popular among British gardeners, but those species are not recommended for most American gardens, for they are not tolerant of heat or cold. The herbaceous plants tolerate heat well.

VINCA
V. minor, Periwinkle, Myrtle

WHERE TO PLANT:
Full sun, partial shade, or shade, in well-drained soil of average fertility, with a pH of 5.5 to 7.0. Plants tolerate a wide range of conditions, but flower best in partial shade. They are hardy from Zones 4 to 9.

WHEN TO PLANT:
Set out bare-rooted nursery plants in fall or early spring, container-grown plants in spring or early summer. Divide in spring or fall. Take stem cuttings or use continuous layering in early summer.

SPACING:
Set plants 6 inches apart.

PLANTING DEPTH:
Set plants or divisions at the same depth they were growing previously.

PROPAGATION:
Division; plants spread by running stems on top of the soil. These runners root readily and are easy to divide.

PLANTING TIPS:
Periwinkle is one of the most popular evergreen ground covers, and deservedly so. It is easy to grow as an edging for beds and borders, a backdrop for spring bulbs, or a ground cover for shady places. The purple flowers (breeding has also produced white-flowered forms) appear in spring.

Periwinkle can also be planted in window boxes or hanging baskets; it will trail over the sides of the container.

VIOLA
V. cornuta, Horned violet
V. odorata, Sweet violet

WHERE TO PLANT:
Partial shade, in fertile, moist but well-drained soil rich in organic matter, with a pH of 5.5 to 7.0. Hardy from Zones 6 to 9.

WHEN TO PLANT:
Set out nursery plants in spring or fall. Sow seeds outdoors in spring after stratifying in a refrigerator for several days. Or start violas indoors 8 to 10 weeks before the average last frost date. Sprinkle the seeds on a flat of damp soil, and stratify the entire flat for several days in a refrigerator. Store the flat of stratified seeds in a dark closet and remove to a light source at the first signs of germination. Seeds will germinate in 1 to 3 weeks. Set out the young plants near the average last frost date.

Divide established clumps in late summer after plants have bloomed or in early fall.

SPACING:	Set plants 5 to 8 inches apart.
PLANTING DEPTH:	Viola seeds are quite fine and should be planted as close to the soil surface as possible. All violas need darkness to germinate, however; seeds must be covered with enough soil to eliminate light.
PROPAGATION:	Seeds, divisions, or offsets. Sweet violet plants spread by means of underground runners; the small offsets that grow at the ends of the runners can be lifted and transplanted.
PLANTING TIPS:	Horned violets resemble pansies and come in shades of violet, apricot, yellow, white, and red. Sweet violets are fragrant and come in shades of violet, purple, and white. Both plants are only about 6 inches high, and make lovely edgings for spring beds and borders. Sweet violets spread and can be used as a ground cover.

YUCCA

Y. filamentosa, Adam's needle
Y. glauca, Soapweed

WHERE TO PLANT:	Full sun, in sandy, well-drained soil of average fertility, with a pH of 5.5 to 7.5. Good drainage is especially important in winter, when plants are dormant. Hardy to Zones 4 or 5.
WHEN TO PLANT:	Set out nursery plants in spring or fall. Remove and transplant offsets produced around the base of established plants and plant them in fertile, well-drained soil.
SPACING:	Space plants 2 to 3 feet apart.
PLANTING DEPTH:	Set plants at the same depth they were growing previously.
PROPAGATION:	Division of offsets and root cuttings. Yuccas can be grown from seed, but the process is slow and tedious. Seeds germinate in 4 to 5 weeks and must be kept at a relatively cool soil temperature—around 55° F.
PLANTING TIPS:	These bold plants with their stiff, sword-shaped leaves look like they would be most at home in the desert, but these species are hardy in much of the country. A bold accent plant for beds and borders, in summer yuccas produce tall spikes of big, bell-shaped white flowers.

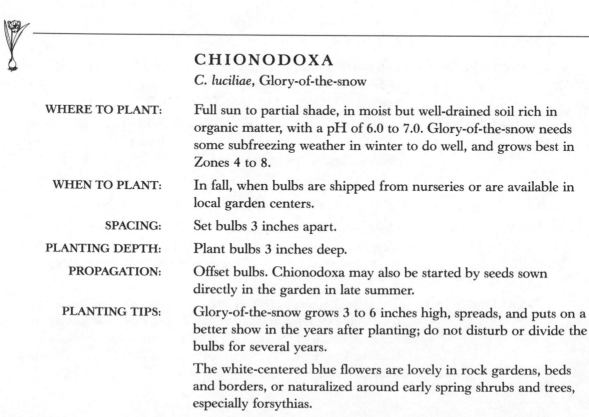

Bulbs, Corms & Tubers

CHIONODOXA
C. luciliae, Glory-of-the-snow

WHERE TO PLANT: Full sun to partial shade, in moist but well-drained soil rich in organic matter, with a pH of 6.0 to 7.0. Glory-of-the-snow needs some subfreezing weather in winter to do well, and grows best in Zones 4 to 8.

WHEN TO PLANT: In fall, when bulbs are shipped from nurseries or are available in local garden centers.

SPACING: Set bulbs 3 inches apart.

PLANTING DEPTH: Plant bulbs 3 inches deep.

PROPAGATION: Offset bulbs. Chionodoxa may also be started by seeds sown directly in the garden in late summer.

PLANTING TIPS: Glory-of-the-snow grows 3 to 6 inches high, spreads, and puts on a better show in the years after planting; do not disturb or divide the bulbs for several years.

The white-centered blue flowers are lovely in rock gardens, beds and borders, or naturalized around early spring shrubs and trees, especially forsythias.

CROCUS
C. species and cultivars

WHERE TO PLANT:
Full sun, in well-drained soil of average fertility, with a pH of 6.0 to 7.0. Crocus need cold winter weather and can be grown in Zones 3 to 8.

WHEN TO PLANT:
Plant spring-blooming crocus in autumn; autumn crocus in summer for bloom just a few months later.

SPACING:
Set corms 3 to 5 inches apart.

PLANTING DEPTH:
Set corms 3 to 4 inches deep.

PROPAGATION:
Corms. Mature corms produce cormels, which can be planted and will grow to blooming size in 1 or 2 years. Dig and separate cormels after foliage dies down in late spring.

Crocus may also be started by seeds sown directly in the garden in late summer.

PLANTING TIPS:
Plant crocus in the front of beds and borders, in rock gardens, along paths and pavements, near deciduous shrubs, or naturalize them in a lawn that can be left unmowed until the crocus foliage yellows. You can also naturalize crocus with ground covers such as ivy and vinca.

DAHLIA
D. cultivars

WHERE TO PLANT:
Full sun, in well-drained, loamy soil rich in organic matter and well supplied with phosphorus and potassium, with a pH of 6.0 to 7.0. Add sand to heavy clay soils to lighten them. Dahlias are winter-hardy only in Zones 9 and 10.

WHEN TO PLANT:
Start seeds indoors 8 to 9 weeks before the average date of your last spring frost. Or set out plants or plant tubers (actually tuberous roots) when all danger of frost is past. Some mail-order nurseries also sell plants started from cuttings; plant them as soon as they arrive. If it is too cold to plant outdoors, put the plants in pots until the weather turns warmer.

SPACING:
Set plants 10 inches to 3 feet apart, depending on the variety. Plant in rows 3 to 4 feet apart, or the same distance apart in all directions in beds.

DAHLIA—*Continued*

PLANTING DEPTH: Sow seeds ¼ inch deep. Set tubers 4 to 6 inches deep, placed horizontally in the hole with the eye (bud) facing upward. Cover the tuber with 2 or 3 inches of soil when planting. Gradually add more soil as the shoot grows until the hole is filled.

PROPAGATION: Division of tuber clumps. Dahlias are tender and their tuberous roots must be dug in fall and stored indoors over winter everywhere except in Zones 9 and 10. To divide clumps of tubers, cut apart a large clump with several stems, making sure each division has an eye.

Many varieties will bloom the first year from seed.

PLANTING TIPS: Dahlias are demanding to grow, but the range of sizes and flower forms is tremendous.

Plant dwarf varieties as edgings in beds and borders or in pots or window boxes. Plant medium-size varieties in the middle of beds and borders. Grow tall cultivars in the back of the garden. All dahlias make lovely cut flowers.

Medium and tall varieties need to be staked; to avoid injuring the tubers, put the stakes in place before planting.

GLADIOLUS

G. species and cultivars

WHERE TO PLANT: Full sun, in deeply dug, fertile, well-drained soil rich in organic matter, with a pH of 6.0 to 7.0. Gladiolus grows well in most soils except heavy clay. It is winter-hardy only in Zones 8 to 10.

WHEN TO PLANT: After all danger of frost is past in spring. For continuous bloom, make succession plantings every 2 weeks until midsummer, up to 90 days before the first expected fall frost.

In Zones 9 and 10, gladiolus is grown for winter flowers; dormant corms can be planted at any time, but the usual planting time is September to March.

SPACING: Varies, from 3 to 6 inches apart, according to the size of the corm and eventual size of the plant. In beds and borders, set corms 6 inches apart in all directions. In cutting gardens, plant in rows 2 to 2½ feet apart. Plants will grow taller and produce larger flowers when spaced farther apart.

PLANTING DEPTH: Varies with the size of the corm. Plant small corms (½ inch or less in diameter) 3 inches deep, medium-size corms (½ to 1 inch in diameter) 4 to 5 inches deep, and large corms (1¼ inches or more in diameter) 6 to 8 inches deep.

Plant in a trench and cover corms with a few inches of soil, adding more soil as the plants grow.

PROPAGATION: Corms. Gladiolus corms produce offsets that can be removed and planted, to grow into blooming-size corms in 1 or 2 years.

Gladiolus can also be grown from seed, but it will take several years to get corms of blooming size.

PLANTING TIPS: Gladiolus is tender and must be dug 6 weeks after plants finish blooming and stored indoors over winter in all zones north of Zone 8. Separate the old corms and discard them; save the new corms and cormels (which formed during the growing season) for planting next spring.

Plant gladiolus in beds and borders, with tall varieties at the back of the garden. Or plant them in rows in a cutting garden; they are classic cut flowers.

HYACINTHUS

H. orientalis, Hyacinth

WHERE TO PLANT: Full sun is best, but hyacinths will tolerate partial shade. Plant in reasonably fertile, well-drained soil rich in organic matter, with a pH of 6.0 to 7.0. Hyacinths can be grown from Zones 4 to 10, although the bulbs deteriorate quickly in Zones 9 and 10 where winters are warm. Gardeners in these zones may find it best to dig up and discard the bulbs after blooming and plant new bulbs each year.

WHEN TO PLANT: Plant bulbs in autumn when they are shipped from mail-order nurseries and available in local garden centers.

SPACING: Set bulbs 4 to 8 inches apart.

PLANTING DEPTH: Place bulbs 4 to 5 inches deep. Plant 8 to 10 inches deep if the soil is sandy, or if you plan to overplant the bulbs with summer annuals.

HYACINTHUS—*Continued*

PROPAGATION:
Bulbs. Bulbs can also be propagated by cutting them into lengthwise sections as described on page 82 under Dividing Bulbs.

Hyacinths can be induced to form bulblets if you scoop out or score the base of a bulb with several diagonal cuts that reach about halfway through the bulb. Score or scoop out bulbs in late summer, and place the bulbs in a warm, dry, light place until October or November, when bulblets have formed along the injured areas. Plant the bulb along with its bulblets about 5 inches deep. The following summer, dig the bulbs and separate the young ones. Replant the young bulbs in fall. They will reach blooming size in 2 to 5 years.

PLANTING TIPS:
Plant hyacinths in beds by themselves, or in drifts or clumps in mixed beds and borders. They can also be grown under deciduous trees.

Hyacinths can also be used as cut flowers and for forcing.

LILIUM
L. species and cultivars, Lilies

WHERE TO PLANT:
Some lilies grow best in full sun, while others prefer partial shade. Many lilies like to have their topgrowth in the sun and their roots in the shade. All require excellent drainage. Plant them in light, moist but very well-drained, loamy soil rich in organic matter. They are adaptable in terms of pH, growing well in either acid or alkaline soil. The hardiness of lilies varies with the species or hybrid group.

WHEN TO PLANT:
Some lilies, such as the Asiatic Hybrids, are planted in spring; others, such as the Madonna lily (*L. candidum*), are planted in fall.

If bulbs for fall planting arrive from the mail-order nursery too close to frost to safely plant them, store the bulbs over winter, in a box of dry sand or vermiculite in a cool, dry, frost-free place. Do not let the bulbs dry out; mist them occasionally if necessary. Plant them out the following spring.

SPACING:
Plant lily bulbs in groups of 3 or more, 8 to 12 inches apart.

PLANTING DEPTH:
As a general rule, plant bulbs 3 times as deep as the height of the bulbs. For example, a 2-inch bulb should have its bottom 6 inches

deep, and its top 4 inches below the soil surface. One exception is the Madonna lily, which should have only 1 inch of soil above the top of its bulb.

PROPAGATION: Bulbs from the nursery, or bulblets. Divide overgrown clumps of lilies when plants are crowded and quality and quantity of bloom declines. In fall, dig up the clumps, gently separate the bulbs, and replant quickly before the bulbs have a chance to dry out.

Lilies can also be propagated from scales or bulblets that form at the base of the stem or in leaf axils. Remove scales from the mother bulb early in summer and store them in a shady place in plastic bags full of moist vermiculite. In late summer, put them in the refrigerator for 6 to 8 weeks while bulblets form.

In fall plant bulblets (whether grown from scales or removed from stems or leaf axils) in pots of rich, well-drained growing medium and keep the medium moist all winter. In early spring, repot the bulblets and move the pots to a cold frame. The following year you can plant the young bulbs in the garden. It takes 1 to 4 years to grow blooming-size bulbs.

Lilies can also be grown from seed, but it takes a minimum of 2 years to grow bulbs large enough to bloom.

PLANTING TIPS: Lilies are classic summer flowers for beds and borders, and make good cut flowers, too. Small varieties are nice in rock gardens.

Most lilies grow best when given a deep mulch of organic material or when overplanted with a ground cover.

Do not plant lilies near vigorous-rooted perennials or shrubs that will compete with them for moisture and nutrients.

NARCISSUS

N. species and cultivars, Daffodils and Narcissus

WHERE TO PLANT: Full sun to partial shade, in well-drained soil rich in organic matter, with a pH of 6.0 to 7.0. Most daffodils and narcissus can be grown in Zones 4 to 8. In Zones 9 and 10, many gardeners dig the bulbs in summer when the foliage yellows, store them in the refrigerator over summer, and replant in fall, or discard the bulbs and plant new ones each year. The bulbs can, however, often remain in the ground in warm climates for a few years before they decline.

NARCISSUS—*Continued*

WHEN TO PLANT:
In autumn, at least a month before the soil turns really cold. In cool and temperate climates (Zones 4 to 6 or 7) plant in late September or October. In warm climates (Zone 8) do not plant until the soil temperature drops below 70° F or the bulbs may rot.

SPACING:
Set bulbs 4 to 8 inches apart, depending on their size.

PLANTING DEPTH:
Set bulbs 4 to 8 inches deep. A general rule of thumb is to plant bulbs 1½ times as deep as the height of the bulb. Bulbs planted too shallowly will form lots of offsets that will not bloom.

Plant bulbs at the shallow depth if you want them to form a lot of offsets.

PROPAGATION:
Bulbs. In a few years bulbs produce offsets that can be divided from the parents in midsummer and planted; they will grow to blooming size in a year or two. Or dig and divide mature bulbs in midsummer by cutting into lengthwise pieces.

PLANTING TIPS:
Plant narcissus in drifts in beds and borders, along paths and pavements, near trees and shrubs, or naturalize them in meadows or open woodlands. Smaller varieties are lovely in rock gardens.

Daffodils and narcissus make good cut flowers.

SCILLA

S. siberica, Siberian squill

WHERE TO PLANT:
Full sun to partial shade in sandy, well-drained soil rich in organic matter, with a pH of 6.0 to 7.0. The bulbs spread quickly in rich, light soil. Siberian squill is hardy to Zone 4. It needs subfreezing winter temperatures and doesn't grow well below Zone 8.

WHEN TO PLANT:
Early autumn.

SPACING:
Space bulbs approximately 3 inches apart.

PLANTING DEPTH:
Set bulbs 3 to 4 inches deep.

PROPAGATION:
Bulbs. Plantings spread quickly, but if you want even more squills, dig up clumps of bulbs in fall, separate the newer offsets, and replant.

PLANTING TIPS:
Mass squills in beds and borders, plant them in rock gardens, or use them as ground covers under trees and shrubs. They are pretty with windflowers (*Anemone blanda*), and grow well under evergreen

trees where few other flowers will thrive. Siberian squills are pretty planted at the edge of woodlands.

For the best effect, plant a lot of these small bulbs.

TULIPA
T. species and cultivars, Tulips

WHERE TO PLANT: Full sun to filtered, partial shade, in light, well-drained, sandy soil rich in organic matter, with a pH of 6.0 to 7.0. Tulips grow best in Zones 3 to 7.

WHEN TO PLANT: Late fall.

SPACING: Space bulbs 4 to 8 inches apart, depending on variety and size of bulb.

PLANTING DEPTH: Set bulbs 6 to 10 inches deep. Deep planting keeps bulbs producing good quality flowers for several years—longer than bulbs planted less deeply—but bulbs will produce fewer offsets.

PROPAGATION: Bulbs. Some gardeners, especially in the South, buy new bulbs each year.

Tulips need division every 2 or 3 years, in midsummer when the leaves wither.

You can also propagate from small offset bulbs that form on bulbs after a year or two on the garden. Remove any first-year blooms from these offsets to strengthen the bulb.

PLANTING TIPS: The range of tulip colors is extensive, and there are a number of different flower forms. Planting types with different blooming times can give you tulips over a 6-week period, from late March to May.

Plant tulips in beds by themselves, in clumps or drifts in beds and borders, or in front of shrubs.

Tulips can be used as cut flowers, too.

Vegetables

ASPARAGUS
Asparagus officinalis

WHERE TO PLANT: Full sun, in well-drained, sandy loam rich in organic matter, with a pH of about 6.5 to 6.8. The soil should be loose and crumbly to a depth of 18 inches. If your soil is heavy clay, work in coarse builder's sand to lighten it. Asparagus is hardy in Zones 3 to 8.

WHEN TO PLANT: Plant crowns from the nursery as soon as soil can be worked in spring, near the average date of your last spring frost.

To start from seeds sow seeds indoors 12 to 14 weeks before planting-out date for seedlings. Soak seeds in very warm water for 48 hours before planting. They germinate best when the soil temperature is 75 to 80° F. Plant seedlings 5 to 6 weeks after the average date of your last spring frost, when plants are about 12 inches tall.

SPACING: Plants started from seed should be set out in a nursery bed in full sun, 3 to 5 inches apart. In the second year, these young plants should be transplanted to the permanent bed at a spacing of 1½ to 2 feet. Plant nursery crowns 1½ to 2 feet apart, in trenches spaced 3 to 4 feet apart.

PLANTING DEPTH: For either crowns or seedlings, plant 6 inches deep in average soils. In very light, sandy soils, plant 8 inches deep. For larger spears (and slightly later harvest), plant 10 inches deep.

PROPAGATION: From one-year-old crowns from the nursery.

PLANTING TIPS: Asparagus needs elaborate bed preparation before planting because it is a perennial crop that will remain in place indefinitely. Once it is planted it will tolerate only a minimum of disturbance. To plant crowns, dig a trench 18 inches deep and 12 to 15 inches wide. Reserve the topsoil, but discard the subsoil. Fork compost, leaf mold, peat moss, or well-rotted manure into the bottom of the trench and work it into the soil (asparagus thrives with lots of organic matter). To provide plenty of phosphorus and potassium (asparagus stalks are flower stems), add some bone meal or rock phosphate and greensand or granite dust and work them in also.

It is a good idea to soak the crowns in lukewarm water for an hour or so before planting.

Make a mound of soil every 2 feet along the trench. Set one crown or seedling on top of each mound. Set crowns so the eyes (growth points) face upward, and spread the roots down and over the sides of the mound. Cover crowns with 2 inches of soil, working it carefully around the roots with your fingers. If planting seedlings, draw 2 inches of soil around the base of the plant. Water to settle plants or crowns into the soil and eliminate air pockets around the roots.

As plants grow, add 1 to 2 more inches of soil to the trench periodically until the trench is level with the surrounding soil surface by around the middle of the growing season.

Asparagus is particularly susceptible to a fungal disease called rust. Plant rust-resistant varieties.

BEANS
Phaseolus species

WHERE TO PLANT: Full sun, in well-drained, humusy soil well supplied with potassium and phosphorus, with a pH of 6.0 to 7.5.

WHEN TO PLANT: One week or more after the last frost, when soil temperature is at least 60° F. Lima beans are more cold-sensitive than other types;

BEANS—*Continued*

WHEN TO PLANT:
(continued)

plant them at least 2 weeks after the last frost, when soil temperature is 65° F or more.

Beans do not transplant well. If you live in a cool climate with a short growing season, plant fast-maturing varieties or start seeds indoors in peat pots 2 to 3 weeks before the last expected frost.

SPACING:

Plant bush snap beans and shell beans (except for limas) 3 to 4 inches apart in rows 18 to 30 inches apart, or 6 inches apart in all directions in intensive beds. Make successive sowings 2 weeks apart to extend the harvest. Plant pole snap beans 4 to 6 inches apart in rows 2 to 3 feet apart, or in hills 3 feet apart. Plant six seeds per hill and later thin to the sturdiest three or four plants.

Plant bush lima beans 3 to 6 inches apart in rows 24 to 30 inches apart, or 8 inches apart in all directions in intensive beds. Plant pole limas 6 to 10 inches apart in rows 30 to 36 inches apart.

PLANTING DEPTH:

Plant 1 inch deep in heavy clay soil or 1½ inches deep in light, sandy soils.

PROPAGATION:

Direct-seed in the garden.

PLANTING TIPS:

Beans are tender annuals. They need warm weather to grow well and will not tolerate even a light frost. Do not plant them too early, because seeds may rot in cold, wet soil.

To improve the plants' ability to fix nitrogen in the soil, treat seeds with a legume inoculant powder (available from mail-order seed companies and at garden centers) before planting. Do not soak or pre-sprout bean seeds before planting; they are prone to rotting.

Pole beans produce their crop more slowly than bush beans, but they bear more heavily and over a longer period of time. Baby lima beans bear earlier than large varieties.

Supports for pole beans should be in place before seeds are planted. Beans planted in rows can be trained on trellises, vertical strings, or plastic grow netting. Beans planted in hills can be supported with teepees or tripods made of three slender poles lashed together at the top.

BEETS
Beta vulgaris

WHERE TO PLANT: Full sun to partial shade, in well-drained, sandy soil rich in organic matter, with a pH around 6.5. The soil must be finely textured, free of stones, and loose to a depth of 10 inches so roots can develop easily. Enrich the planting area with compost and wood ashes or rock phosphate. Avoid using fresh manure around beets. If your soil is acid (with a pH lower than 6.0), work in ground limestone to raise the pH to near neutral.

WHEN TO PLANT: Direct-seed 1 to 2 weeks before the average date of your last spring frost, when soil temperature is 40° F or more. Start seeds indoors in peat pots 8 weeks before the frost-free date. Set out transplants 4 weeks before the expected frost-free date.

You can make successive plantings every 3 weeks until midsummer.

For a fall crop, plant 10 weeks before the first expected frost. In hot climates (Zones 9 and 10), plant in fall for a winter crop.

SPACING: Sow 2 to 6 inches apart in rows 8 to 12 inches apart. Thin (or set transplants) to 3 to 4 inches apart in rows, or 6 inches apart in all directions in beds. Beet seeds are actually clusters of seeds and will *always* require thinning. Thin twice: once when seedlings develop their first true leaves, and again when plants are 6 inches tall. Use the thinnings in salads.

PLANTING DEPTH: Plant ½ to 1 inch deep.

PROPAGATION: Direct-seeding.

PLANTING TIPS: Soak seeds for at least 12 hours before planting. In hot, dry weather, cover seeds with shredded leaf mold or compost to prevent a crust from forming on the soil.

Seeds germinate slowly; sow radish seeds along with beets to mark the row. Radishes will be ready to harvest before beets grow large enough to become crowded.

Beets will not germinate in soil temperatures of 85° F and above. Plan spring beet sowings so that harvest can take place before your average daily temperatures reach 85° F. Beets that mature in hot weather become tough and woody and lack flavor.

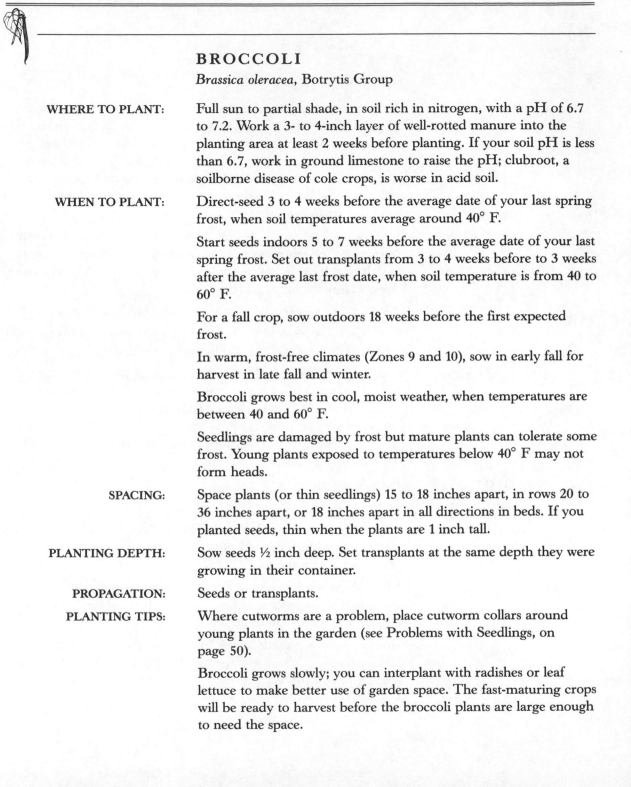

BROCCOLI
Brassica oleracea, Botrytis Group

WHERE TO PLANT: Full sun to partial shade, in soil rich in nitrogen, with a pH of 6.7 to 7.2. Work a 3- to 4-inch layer of well-rotted manure into the planting area at least 2 weeks before planting. If your soil pH is less than 6.7, work in ground limestone to raise the pH; clubroot, a soilborne disease of cole crops, is worse in acid soil.

WHEN TO PLANT: Direct-seed 3 to 4 weeks before the average date of your last spring frost, when soil temperatures average around 40° F.

Start seeds indoors 5 to 7 weeks before the average date of your last spring frost. Set out transplants from 3 to 4 weeks before to 3 weeks after the average last frost date, when soil temperature is from 40 to 60° F.

For a fall crop, sow outdoors 18 weeks before the first expected frost.

In warm, frost-free climates (Zones 9 and 10), sow in early fall for harvest in late fall and winter.

Broccoli grows best in cool, moist weather, when temperatures are between 40 and 60° F.

Seedlings are damaged by frost but mature plants can tolerate some frost. Young plants exposed to temperatures below 40° F may not form heads.

SPACING: Space plants (or thin seedlings) 15 to 18 inches apart, in rows 20 to 36 inches apart, or 18 inches apart in all directions in beds. If you planted seeds, thin when the plants are 1 inch tall.

PLANTING DEPTH: Sow seeds ½ inch deep. Set transplants at the same depth they were growing in their container.

PROPAGATION: Seeds or transplants.

PLANTING TIPS: Where cutworms are a problem, place cutworm collars around young plants in the garden (see Problems with Seedlings, on page 50).

Broccoli grows slowly; you can interplant with radishes or leaf lettuce to make better use of garden space. The fast-maturing crops will be ready to harvest before the broccoli plants are large enough to need the space.

Do not plant broccoli in the same place in which it or another member of the cabbage family grew last year. Rotating cole crops reduces the risk of clubroot, a disease to which all members of the family are susceptible.

Broccoli heads often burst into bloom when daytime temperature reaches 85° F. Plant broccoli early enough to complete the spring harvest before summer heat sets in, or plant in midsummer for harvest in fall.

BRUSSELS SPROUTS
Brassica oleracea, Gemmifera Group

WHERE TO PLANT: Full sun, in well-drained soil rich in organic matter, with a pH of 6.0 to 6.8. Brussels sprouts do better in heavy soil than in light, sandy soil.

WHEN TO PLANT: Brussels sprouts grow best in cool weather, with temperatures averaging 60 to 65° F; the flavor is improved by frost. Direct-sow 5 to 6 weeks before the average last frost date. Or sow indoors 10 to 12 weeks before the average last frost date, and set out transplants 5 to 6 weeks before the last frost date.

For a fall crop, direct-sow 10 to 12 weeks before the first expected killing frost. In areas where the growing season is extremely short (Zones 3 and 4), start seeds indoors in early summer. Brussels sprouts do not grow well in areas with long, hot, dry summers (Zones 8, 9, and 10), except as a fall or winter crop.

SPACING: Sow seeds about 2 inches apart, then thin plants to stand 18 to 24 inches apart in rows 30 to 36 inches apart, or 18 inches apart in all directions in beds. If you planted seeds, thin when plants are about 6 inches tall.

PLANTING DEPTH: Plant seeds ½ inch deep. Set transplants so that the bottom leaves are just above the soil surface.

PROPAGATION: Seeds or transplants.

PLANTING TIPS: Plants need 10 to 12 weeks to mature; you can plant fast-maturing crops like radishes and lettuce between brussels sprouts to make more efficient use of garden space.

Cutworms love brussels sprouts, so protect the seedlings with cutworm collars (see Problems with Seedlings, on page 50).

(continued)

BRUSSELS SPROUTS—*Continued*

PLANTING TIPS:
(continued)

Do not plant brussels sprouts where they or other members of the cabbage family grew last year, to reduce the risk of clubroot, a soilborne disease.

Since a more alkaline pH discourages clubroot, the addition of ground limestone to the soil several weeks before planting may also prevent this disease.

CABBAGE

Brassica oleracea, Capitata Group

WHERE TO PLANT:
Full sun to partial shade, in rich, moist but well-drained, loamy soil high in organic matter, with a pH between 6.0 and 6.8. If clubroot is a problem in your garden, add lime to raise the pH to 7.2. Moisture is essential; cabbage will grow well in either clay or sandy soils as long as they are moist and drain well.

WHEN TO PLANT:
Start seeds of early varieties indoors 7 to 9 weeks before the average last frost date, for transplanting outdoors 2 to 3 weeks before the last frost date. Seedlings should be 4 to 5 inches tall at transplanting time. Direct-sow midseason varieties 1 to 2 weeks after the last frost date, and late-season varieties 4 weeks later.

Seeds germinate fastest when soil temperature is 75° F, but plants grow best when the air temperature is 55 to 65° F, making indoor sowing the ideal way to start a crop.

Cabbage can tolerate temperatures as low as 20° F and grows best in cool weather. In Zones 9 and 10, can be planted in fall for a winter crop, or in early winter for a spring crop.

SPACING:
Sow seeds 1 inch apart, later thinning so plants stand 14 to 18 inches apart for early varieties, 16 to 18 inches apart for midseason varieties, or 18 to 24 inches apart for late varieties. Space rows 28 to 36 inches apart. Intensive spacing for growing beds is 12 to 15 inches apart in all directions, but close spacing will yield smaller heads. Compact varieties are the best choice for intensive spacing.

PLANTING DEPTH:
Sow seeds ½ inch deep. Set transplants with the lowest leaves slightly above the soil surface.

PROPAGATION: Seeds or transplants.

PLANTING TIPS: Conventional practice is to start early varieties indoors and sow midseason varieties directly in the garden.

Three weeks after transplanting (or when direct-seeded plants are 7 to 8 inches tall), side-dress with well-rotted manure or water with manure tea, fish emulsion, or seaweed concentrate.

Do not plant cabbage in the same spot where it or another member of the cabbage family grew last year, to reduce the risk of clubroot.

Cabbage grows best in cool, moist soil. Mulch with an organic material (not plastic) during summer months to keep soil temperatures down. Choose varieties carefully: midseason varieties mature best in warm weather; early and late-season varieties do best in cool weather. And varieties sold as long-keeping are intended for fall harvest and storage in a root cellar.

CARROTS

Daucus carota var. *sativus*

WHERE TO PLANT: Full sun to partial shade in light, loose, sandy loam that retains some moisture but drains well. The soil should be deeply dug—loose to a depth of 10 or 12 inches—and free of stones and lumps. Carrots prefer a pH around 6.0 to 6.5 but will tolerate a pH range of 5.5 to 6.8.

WHEN TO PLANT: Carrots grow best when temperatures average 60 to 65° F, but tolerate everything from light frost to summer heat. They are usually planted in spring and summer in northern and temperate gardens (Zones 3 to 8) and in fall, winter, and early spring in southern gardens (Zones 9 and 10.)

Direct-seed about 6 weeks before average last frost date, or when soil temperature is about 55° F. Sow seeds up to 12 weeks before the first fall frost for an autumn crop. Seeds germinate in soil temperatures from 55 to 75° F.

Make successive sowings 2 to 3 weeks apart for an extended harvest.

CARROTS—*Continued*

SPACING:
Thin plants when 2 inches tall, to stand 3 to 4 inches apart in rows 12 inches apart, or 3 inches apart in all directions in beds. To avoid disturbing roots, snip off unwanted seedlings at soil level rather than pulling them up.

PLANTING DEPTH:
Cover seeds with ¼ to ½ inch of fine soil, or, to prevent crusting, cover with sand or vermiculite instead.

PROPAGATION:
Direct-seeding; carrots do not transplant well.

PLANTING TIPS:
If your soil is heavy, plant round or half-long varieties instead of long-rooted types. These are also the best varieties for container growing.

Use only well-rotted manure for carrots; fresh manure contains too much nitrogen, which causes forked, hairy roots.

Soak seeds overnight before planting, to hasten germination.

Carrot seeds are very tiny. One way to space seedlings properly is to sprout seeds between two damp paper towels. Plant the seeds as soon as tiny roots appear (handle *very* carefully). For other tips on handling extremely fine seeds, see page 32.

If you'd like to grow a single row of carrots, you can dig a single V-shaped trench 10 inches deep and 3 inches wide. Fill it with a mixture of equal parts compost and sand. This provides a perfect growing medium for a row of straight, full carrots without all the work of turning over an entire bed.

Carrots make a good succession crop and are often planted to follow peas.

CAULIFLOWER
Brassica oleracea, Botrytis Group

WHERE TO PLANT:
Full sun, in rich, humusy, moist but well-drained soil with a pH of 6.0 to 7.0. Where clubroot is a problem, add lime to raise the pH to 7.0 or higher. The soil needs adequate amounts of trace elements, particularly boron; cauliflower is very sensitive to boron deficiency. Soils rich in organic matter are rarely boron-deficient; however, boron may be unavailable to plants in soils that are strongly alkaline. To ensure the availability of this trace element,

maintain soil pH close to the recommended range. Work in lots of compost or well-rotted manure before planting, along with rock phosphate and granite dust—both good sources of boron. Cauliflower is a very heavy feeder, requiring a steady supply of nitrogen to allow it to grow as rapidly as possible to maturity.

WHEN TO PLANT: Cauliflower does not grow well in extremely cold or hot weather. It does best when temperatures average 60 to 65° F. Plant cauliflower to mature in spring, before summer heat sets in, or in fall, after the hot weather subsides. Exposure to unseasonably warm temperatures may cause failure of a spring crop.

Start spring crops from seed indoors 6 to 8 weeks before the average last frost date, for transplants to set out from 2 to 4 weeks before the last frost date.

For fall crops sow seeds in flats or pots 12 weeks before the first expected fall frost and set out transplants 4 weeks later. Seeds germinate best at a soil temperature of 70 to 75° F. Seeds for a fall crop may also be sown directly in the garden 12 weeks before the average date of your first fall frost.

In warm climates (Zones 9 and 10), plant in fall for a winter or early spring crop.

Transplants should be large enough to have three true leaves when they go into the garden. They should also have a small bud in the center of the plant; this is where the head will form.

SPACING: Space plants or thin seedlings to stand 24 inches apart in rows 36 inches apart, or 18 inches apart in all directions in beds. Thin seedlings when plants are 1 inch tall.

PLANTING DEPTH: Sow seeds ½ inch deep.

PROPAGATION: Seeds or transplants.

PLANTING TIPS: Start spring crops from transplants, either from the garden center or from seed sown indoors. Direct-seed fall and winter crops or use transplants.

Spring crops are harder to grow because of timing the start of hot weather. If you are growing cauliflower for the first time, try a fall crop instead.

Plant fast-maturing crops like lettuce and radishes between young cauliflower plants to make better use of space.

(continued)

CAULIFLOWER—*Continued*

PLANTING TIPS:
(continued)

Do not plant cauliflower where it or other cabbage family members grew last year, to reduce the risk of clubroot.

Self-blanching varieties will produce white heads without the traditional practice of tying the leaves together.

CELERY
Apium graveolens var. *dulce*

WHERE TO PLANT: Full sun to partial shade, in very rich soil that contains lots of organic matter and holds moisture but is well drained, and has a pH between 5.8 and 6.7. The soil should be deeply dug, loose to a depth of 18 inches. Work in as much organic material as you can. Like cauliflower, celery needs the trace element boron. If your soil is deficient in boron, a quick fix for a 30-foot row of celery is to dissolve 1 teaspoon of household borax in 1 gallon of water and pour it evenly over the soil. Good drainage is critical.

WHEN TO PLANT: Celery grows best when temperatures average 60 to 65° F. Plants can stand heat after they become established, but temperatures of 40 to 55° F cause damage that may not show up until the plants mature. Young plants exposed to sudden cool weather—temperatures below 50° F—may bolt to seed.

Start seeds indoors 6 to 8 weeks before setting out transplants. Celery needs a soil temperature of 60 to 70° F for best germination. Germination is slow in any case, taking 3 to 4 weeks. Transplants can go into the garden about 3 weeks after your last frost date, when temperatures no longer drop below 50° F. Transplant before seedlings are 3 to 5 inches high; bigger plants develop a taproot that makes transplanting more difficult.

Direct-seed only in mild climates, when temperatures will not drop below 50° F. In Zone 10, celery can be grown as a winter crop.

SPACING: Set plants 6 inches apart in rows 24 inches apart, or 9 inches apart in all directions in beds.

PLANTING DEPTH: Sow seeds ¼ inch deep in fine soil. Set transplants so the crown is level with the soil surface.

PROPAGATION: Transplants started indoors or purchased from a nursery or garden center.

PLANTING TIPS:
Celery needs a long growing season with stable temperatures to do well and is a demanding crop to grow. Because the plant is 94 percent water, it demands a constant supply of moisture through the growing season.

If growing celery from seed, soak the seeds for several hours before planting them. Keep the soil evenly moist until the seeds germinate.

CORN
Zea mays

WHERE TO PLANT:
Full sun, in loose, well-drained soil well supplied with nitrogen and humus, and with a pH between 6.0 and 6.8. The soil should be loose to a depth of 6 inches. Corn needs 70 to 100 days of frost-free weather to mature a crop. Corn is a heavy feeder requiring lots of nitrogen. For this reason, rotate corn plantings into areas where you have grown legumes or where you have turned in a leguminous cover crop.

WHEN TO PLANT:
Direct-seed early varieties a week or so after your last frost date; sow midseason and late varieties about 10 days later. Corn will not germinate in soil that is 50° F or colder in temperature. Seed planted in cold soil will rot. A black plastic mulch will help warm cool soil. Corn germinates best in a soil temperature of 60 to 70° F.

Corn does not transplant well, but in areas with a very short growing season, seeds can be started indoors in peat pots 2 to 3 weeks before the frost-free date and carefully moved to the garden 2 to 3 weeks after the average last frost date.

SPACING:
Plant standard varieties 3 inches apart in rows 30 inches apart. Dwarf varieties can be planted in rows 24 inches apart. When plants are 2 to 4 inches tall, thin standard varieties to 12 inches apart in the row, and dwarf varieties to 8 inches. In beds, space plants 18 inches apart in all directions. Or plant in hills 6 feet apart in all directions, with six seeds per hill, later thinning to the four strongest plants in each hill.

PLANTING DEPTH:
Plant seeds 1 to 2 inches deep. Planting depth should increase as the soil temperature increases. Use the 2-inch depth for midsum-

CORN—*Continued*

PLANTING DEPTH:
(continued)

mer sowings in very warm soil. Supersweet varieties germinate best when planted less than 1 inch deep. In heavy soils plant slightly shallower; in light, sandy soils plant slightly deeper.

PROPAGATION:

Direct-seeding.

PLANTING TIPS:

If you have heavy clay soil, plant late-maturing varieties; in light, sandy soil plant early varieties.

For better wind pollination of small plantings, plant corn in squares with at least four rows of plants containing 4 plants per row. For any planting that is smaller than 16 plants, pollinate by hand to ensure an adequate crop.

To extend the harvest make two or three successive plantings of early varieties 3 weeks apart, or plant an early, a midseason, and a late variety.

CUCUMBERS •
Cucumis sativus

WHERE TO PLANT:

Full sun, in well-drained soil rich in organic matter, with a pH between 6.0 and 7.0.

WHEN TO PLANT:

Direct-seed at least 2 weeks after the average date of your last spring frost when soil temperature is 65° F or higher. Cucumber seed will rot in soil that is 60° F or colder. Cucumbers are very sensitive to cold; once germinated they grow well when temperatures are 65 to 85° F.

SPACING:

Plant in hills 4 feet apart with the hills in rows 6 feet apart for standard varieties, somewhat closer for bush and dwarf types. Plant six seeds per hill, later thinning to the three strongest plants. In beds, plant standard varieties 18 inches apart in all directions, bush and compact varieties somewhat closer.

PLANTING DEPTH:

Plant ½ to 1 inch deep in most soils; plant 2 inches deep in very light, sandy soils.

PROPAGATION:

Direct-seeding. Cucumbers don't transplant well. If you must start seeds indoors, plant in individual peat pots for best results when transplanting.

PLANTING TIPS:

Cucumbers can be planted in rows of early corn, where they will take over the space after the corn is harvested. To save garden space, vining cucumbers can be trained to climb a fence or trellis. Plant seeds 4 inches apart along the trellis, later thinning plants to 8 inches apart.

EGGPLANT
Solanum melongena var. *esculentum*

WHERE TO PLANT:

Full sun, in rich, loose, loamy, well-drained soil, with a pH between 5.5 and 6.8. Do not plant in heavy, very wet soil.

WHEN TO PLANT:

Sow seeds indoors 4 to 6 weeks before the average date of your last spring frost. Seeds germinate best when soil temperature is around 70° F. When seedlings develop their first set of true leaves, transplant to individual containers. Set out transplants 4 to 6 weeks after the last frost date. Another way to determine transplant time is to wait until the average nighttime temperature remains above 55° F. Eggplant grows best in warm weather, when temperatures are between 70° and 85° F. It cannot tolerate cold and will not bear a crop in temperatures below 60° F.

SPACING:

Set transplants 2 feet apart in rows 2 to 3 feet apart, or 2 feet apart in all directions in beds.

Small-fruited and dwarf varieties make good container plants.

PLANTING DEPTH:

Sow seed ¼ inch deep. Set transplants at the same depth they were growing in their container.

PROPAGATION:

Transplants started indoors or purchased from a nursery or garden center.

PLANTING TIPS:

Long-season varieties grow best in areas where summers are hot and fall weather is mild. Elsewhere, plant early varieties.

When hardening off eggplant prior to transplanting, do *not* expose the seedlings to cold or to water withdrawal as you would for other types of transplants. Eggplant seedlings exposed to cold may fail to flower and set fruit.

KALE
Brassica oleracea, Acephala Group

WHERE TO PLANT: Full sun to partial shade, in loamy, well-drained, moist but not soggy soil of average fertility and not too rich in nitrogen, with a pH of 6.5 to 6.8. Very light, sandy soil and very heavy clay soil adversely affect the flavor.

WHEN TO PLANT: Kale grows best in cool weather and its flavor is improved by exposure to frost, so it makes a good fall crop.

Start seeds indoors 5 to 7 weeks before the average last frost date. Transplant out from 2 weeks before to the week of the last frost date. Or direct-sow 2 to 4 weeks before the last frost date or as soon as soil can be worked in spring. Seeds will germinate in cool soil, but sprout best when soil temperature is around 70° F. For a fall crop, direct-sow 10 weeks before the first expected fall frost. In Zones 8 to 10 you can sow in fall for a winter or early spring crop.

Soil temperature must be 40° F or higher for good germination. Plants grow best when the soil temperature averages 60 to 65° F.

SPACING: Space plants 12 to 15 inches apart in rows 18 to 24 inches apart, or 15 to 18 inches apart in all directions in beds.

PLANTING DEPTH: Sow seeds ¼ to ½ inch deep.

PROPAGATION: Seeds or transplants.

PLANTING TIPS: Make several successive plantings 2 to 3 weeks apart to prolong the harvest in spring or fall. Spring-sown kale will continue to grow during the hot summer months, but the leaves will be bitter and tough. To harvest the sweetest crop, keep spring-sown kale growing through the fall and begin harvest only after the leaves have been touched by frost. In some northern zones, kale can be banked with snow and harvested throughout the winter.

KOHLRABI
Brassica oleracea, Gongylodes Group

WHERE TO PLANT: Full sun to partial shade, in loose, light, moist soil rich in organic matter, with a pH between 6.0 and 7.0. The soil should be loose to a depth of 8 inches, and free of stones and lumps. Kohlrabi needs plenty of potassium to produce a good crop; enrich the soil with wood ashes, greensand, or granite dust.

WHEN TO PLANT: Kohlrabi grows best in cool weather, when temperatures are 60 to 65° F. Direct-seed 2 to 4 weeks before the average date of your last spring frost. In areas with a very short growing season, start seeds indoors 6 to 10 weeks before the last frost date and set out transplants from 2 weeks before to 2 weeks after the last frost date. Kohlrabi germinates best when soil temperature is 70 to 75° F. Germination generally takes 12 to 15 days.

For a fall crop, direct-seed approximately 10 weeks before the first expected fall frost.

SPACING: Set transplants 9 inches apart in rows 18 inches apart, or 9 inches apart in all directions in beds.

PLANTING DEPTH: Sow seeds ¼ inch deep.

PROPAGATION: Direct-seeding or transplants.

PLANTING TIPS: Although kohlrabi is usually planted in spring, a fall crop will often yield a better-tasting, sweeter crop because the bulbs mature in cool weather.

Kohlrabi tastes best when it has been grown rapidly in cool weather. Standard varieties become woody and bitter when the bulbs grow over 2 inches in diameter. Some hybrids, however, will remain tender and sweet up to 4 inches in diameter.

LETTUCE

Lactuca sativa

WHERE TO PLANT: Full sun for heading varieties, full sun to partial shade for leaf lettuce, in rich, moist, well-drained soil high in organic matter and containing plenty of nitrogen, with a pH between 6.0 and 6.8.

WHEN TO PLANT: Lettuce grows best in cool weather and bolts to seed in summer heat, although some varieties (such as 'Oak Leaf') are more heat-resistant than others. Soil temperature must be 35° F or more for seeds to germinate.

Start seeds indoors 4 weeks before planting out, which can be done from 4 weeks before to 4 weeks after the average last frost date. Seeds germinate best when soil temperature is about 65 to 70° F. Plants can tolerate some freezing temperatures, but grow best when temperatures are 60 to 65° F.

LETTUCE—*Continued*

WHEN TO PLANT:
(continued)

Direct-sow from 4 weeks before to 4 weeks after the last frost date. Although seeds sown indoors will usually germinate in 7 to 10 days, lettuce sown outdoors in cold soil may take up to 2 weeks to germinate.

Make succession plantings every 3 weeks, using heat-resistant varieties in summer. Provide shade for seeds and young plants in summer.

For a fall crop, direct-sow 8 weeks before the first expected frost and make 2 or 3 succession plantings 3 weeks apart.

In areas with mild winters (Zones 9 and 10), plant successively in fall, winter, and early spring.

SPACING:

Set leaf lettuce plants 9 inches apart in rows 14 inches apart, or 9 inches apart in all directions in beds. Set head lettuce plants 12 inches apart in rows 14 inches apart, or 12 inches apart in all directions.

PLANTING DEPTH:

Lettuce needs light to germinate. Do not cover seeds with soil. Until they germinate, protect newly sown seeds from heavy rain and wind with a light covering of hay, shredded peat moss, straw, or an agricultural fabric such as Reemay.

PROPAGATION:

Seeds or transplants.

PLANTING TIPS:

Plant small amounts of lettuce every few weeks for a continuous harvest all season long.

Leaf lettuce is easier to grow than head lettuce.

Many gardeners like to work plenty of manure into the soil the autumn before planting a spring crop of lettuce.

Leaf varieties and dwarf heading varieties make good container crops.

OKRA

Abelmoschus esculentus

WHERE TO PLANT:

Full sun, in well-drained soil rich in organic matter, with a pH between 6.5 and 7.5. The soil should be loose to a depth of 8 inches.

WHEN TO PLANT: Direct-seed 1 or 2 weeks after the average date of your last spring frost, when the soil temperature is at least 70° F. Or start seeds indoors 3 to 4 weeks before the frost-free date and set plants out in the garden 3 to 4 weeks after the frost-free date. Start seedlings in individual containers or peat pots because they transplant best when their roots are not disturbed.

SPACING: Set 10 inches apart in rows 2 to 4 feet apart for dwarf varieties, or 14 inches apart in rows about 4 feet apart for standard varieties. In intensive beds, space plants 18 inches apart in all directions.

PLANTING DEPTH: Sow seeds 1 inch deep in light soils, ½ inch deep in heavy soils.

PROPAGATION: Direct-seeding in most areas; in climates with a very short growing season, start seeds indoors.

PLANTING TIPS: Soak seeds overnight before planting to speed germination.

Okra requires plenty of nitrogen. Planted as a succession crop to early spring peas, it makes good use of the nitrogen fixed in the soil by nodules on the pea roots.

Okra is quite tender and easily damaged by frost. It needs at least 10 weeks of hot, sunny weather to produce a good crop.

ONIONS

Allium cepa

WHERE TO PLANT: Full sun for large-bulbed varieties, full sun to partial shade for bunching onions, in loose, well-drained, loamy soil of average fertility but rich in organic matter, with a pH of 6.0 to 7.5.

WHEN TO PLANT: Direct-seed as soon as the soil can be worked in spring, 3 to 5 weeks before the average date of your last spring frost. In warm climates (Zones 8 to 10), sow in fall for an early spring crop. Or start seeds indoors 4 to 6 weeks before transplanting out to the garden. The optimum soil temperature for starting seeds indoors is 60 to 70° F.

Set out seedlings of bunching onions 3 to 4 weeks before to 3 weeks after the last frost date. Set out bulbing onions 5 weeks before to 3 weeks after the last frost date.

Plant onion sets (small bulbs about ½ inch in diameter) as soon as the soil can be worked in spring.

ONIONS—*Continued*

WHEN TO PLANT:
(continued)

Onions grow best in temperatures that are between 55 and 75° F.

SPACING:

For onions to be harvested as mature bulbs, space 3 to 4 inches apart, in rows 12 to 18 inches apart. Onions to be harvested for scallions can be planted 2 inches apart in rows. In beds, space plants or sets 4 inches apart in all directions. Seeds can be sown as close as ¼ inch apart and the plants thinned later on.

PLANTING DEPTH:

Plant ¼ to ½ inch deep. In most soils, plant sets so that just the stem end is exposed; in heavy soils, plant sets so that one-third of the stem end of the bulb is exposed.

PROPAGATION:

Sets or transplants. In climates with a frost-free growing season of at least 90 days, direct-seeding is also possible.

PLANTING TIPS:

It is important to choose the right onion varieties for your climate. Large, sweet Bermuda and Spanish onions grow best in warm climates. Smaller-bulbed, more pungent varieties grow best in cool climates. Onions are also sensitive to daylength. Short-day varieties will form bulbs when they get 12 hours of light a day and grow best as winter crops in warm climates. Long-day varieties need 13 to 16 hours a day to form bulbs and are grown in spring and summer.

If you start seeds indoors, keep the seedling tops trimmed to ½ to 1 inch long until a week before you transplant them out to the garden. You can use the trimmings like chives.

If you purchase onion sets, select bulbs that are ½ to ¾ inch in diameter. Smaller sets take longer to mature, and larger ones may bolt to seed before the crop matures.

Onions do not need lots of space and can be interplanted among fast-maturing crops. They can also be grown in containers and window boxes.

Some gardeners plant radishes along with direct-seeded onions to mark the rows. The radishes are harvested before the onions need the growing space.

PEAS

Pisum sativum

WHERE TO PLANT:

Full sun to partial shade, in loose, well-drained, very fertile soil, with a pH between 6.0 and 7.0. Peas need ample phosphorus and potassium to produce a good crop; enriching soil with wood ashes, bone meal, granite dust, rock phosphate, or greensand increases phosphorus and potassium levels. In cool climates enrich the soil the autumn before planting. Peas must have lots of air around their roots to nourish the nitrogen-fixing bacteria that live on the plants' roots. To ensure this constant air supply, avoid planting in soil that becomes waterlogged, and avoid compressing the soil in any way after peas are planted.

WHEN TO PLANT: Peas grow best in cool weather, when the temperature averages 60 to 65° F. Hot weather hinders flowering and pod development. Direct-seed as soon as the soil can be worked in spring, 2 to 4 weeks before the average last frost date, when the soil temperature is 40° F or more.

In warm climates (Zones 8 to 10) direct-seed in autumn or early winter for a winter crop.

To extend the harvest, plant two or three varieties that mature at different times.

SPACING: Space 1 to 2 inches apart in rows 24 inches apart for low-growing varieties or 30 to 36 inches apart for tall varieties. Or plant tall varieties in double rows 3 inches apart, or 8 inches apart with a vertical support between them. In beds, space 6 inches apart in all directions.

PLANTING DEPTH: Plant 2 inches deep in sandy soils, 1 inch deep in heavier soils.

PROPAGATION: Direct-seeding.

PLANTING TIPS: Soak seeds for 24 hours before planting and roll them in a legume inoculant powder.

Pea plants are not harmed by light frost, but flowers will be damaged.

Be sure to install a trellis or other support that is at least as tall as your variety is supposed to grow. A trellis that is too short results in a tangled mass of plants and difficulty in finding pods to harvest. The support should be in place before you plant the peas.

Edible-podded peas (snow peas and sugar snaps) are planted the same way as conventional garden peas (peas to be shelled).

PEPPERS
Capsicum annuum var. *annuum*

WHERE TO PLANT:	Full sun, in sandy, well-drained soil that is rich in organic matter. Peppers have a particular need for magnesium; if a soil test shows your soil to be deficient, add epsom salts or dolomitic limestone. The best pH range for peppers is 6.0 to 7.0.
WHEN TO PLANT:	Peppers are tropical plants that need a constantly moist atmosphere, daytime temperatures between 70 and 80° F, and nighttime temperatures between 60 and 70° F. They will not bloom or set fruit and will even drop flowers and immature fruit if exposed to hot, dry, or cold conditions. Start seeds indoors 2 to 4 weeks before the average last frost date and set out plants 4 to 6 weeks after the last frost date, or when nighttime temperatures remain above 60° F and the soil temperature is 60° F or higher. The optimum temperature for germinating seeds is 75 to 80° F.
SPACING:	Set plants 18 to 24 inches apart in rows 36 inches apart, or 15 inches apart in all directions in beds.
PLANTING DEPTH:	Plant seeds ¼ to ½ inch deep.
PROPAGATION:	Seeds started indoors or transplants.
PLANTING TIPS:	If you buy transplants from a nursery, don't buy plants already in bloom or bearing small fruits. Newly planted peppers need several weeks to establish roots; diverting a young plant's energy to producing fruit will result in a permanently stunted plant by midseason.

POTATOES
Solanum tuberosum

WHERE TO PLANT:	Full sun, in loose, well-drained soil that is rich in organic matter. The ideal pH is 5.2 to 5.7, but potatoes will produce a good crop in a pH of 6.0 to 6.5, which is more suitable for other crops. Potato scab, a soilborne fungal disease, can only survive in soil with a pH of 6.0 or greater. Keeping soil on the distinctly acid side cuts down on the incidence of scab. Rotating potatoes to a different planting spot each year also helps control scab.

WHEN TO PLANT:	Potatoes are traditionally planted around the same time as peas. Plant cut-up seed potatoes directly in the garden 1 to 3 weeks before the average last frost date. (A seed potato is a small tuber or piece of a larger tuber that has at least one "eye," or growing point. Buy certified seed potatoes; most supermarket potatoes are treated with chemicals that inhibit sprouting.) In warm climates, plant in autumn or late winter, and be sure to plant varieties bred especially for warm regions. The best temperature for tuber development is 60 to 65° F with a 10-degree drop at night.
SPACING:	Space 12 inches apart in rows 20 inches apart for small varieties, and 15 inches apart in rows 30 inches apart for large varieties. In beds, space plants 12 inches apart in all directions.
PLANTING DEPTH:	Plant 6 inches deep in light soils; 4 inches deep in heavy soils. After the vine emerges, cover it with a light compost/soil mix. Do this at least twice, once when the vines are about 6 inches long and again when they are about 18 inches long.
PROPAGATION:	Certified seed potatoes or seed "eyes." Cut whole seed potatoes into several pieces with each piece having one or two eyes.
PLANTING TIPS:	Let pieces of seed potatoes dry overnight before planting to reduce the chance of rot.
	When planting, set the potato pieces with the cut side facing down. Keep the soil moist but not soggy until shoots poke through the surface.
	An alternate way to plant potatoes is to set them in a shallow trench, then hill up an 18-inch layer of loose mulch (salt hay, for example) on top of them. Planting in mulch makes the harvest easier and cleaner than planting in soil.
	To extend the harvest, plant early, midseason, and late-maturing varieties if enough space is available.

RADISHES
Raphanus sativus

WHERE TO PLANT:	Full sun, in light, loose, moist but well-drained soil containing plenty of organic matter. Avoid soils rich in nitrogen (which will encourage leaf growth instead of roots) and heavy soils (which will produce small, poorly formed roots). Radishes tolerate a pH anywhere between 5.5 and 6.8.

RADISHES—*Continued*

WHEN TO PLANT:
Radishes grow best in cool temperatures between 60 and 65° F; hot weather causes a very sharp, overly pungent flavor. Midseason varieties can stand more heat and are the best type for warm climates.

Direct-sow early varieties when the soil temperature is 40° F or more. Sow early varieties 2 to 4 weeks before the average date of your last spring frost, or in warm climates (Zones 8 to 10) in late autumn for a winter crop. You can make succession plantings every 10 days to 2 weeks until the weather becomes quite warm. A second crop can be sown in fall, about 4 weeks before the first expected frost.

Sow midseason varieties in mid- to late spring, with succession plantings every 2 weeks until midsummer.

Sow late varieties (usually called winter radishes) 10 weeks before the first expected fall frost in northern gardens; in warm climates (Zones 8 to 10), sow 6 weeks before the last frost date to produce a crop in early spring, or in autumn to yield a winter crop.

SPACING:
Space early varieties 2 to 3 inches apart, in single or wide rows 10 to 12 inches apart, or 3 inches apart in all directions in beds.

Space midseason varieties 3 to 5 inches apart in rows 10 to 15 inches apart, or 5 inches apart in all directions in beds.

Space late varieties 6 inches apart in rows 18 to 20 inches apart, or 6 to 8 inches apart in all directions in beds. Early varieties are generally smallest in size, late varieties are largest, hence the difference in spacing.

Seeds can be sown closely together and the seedlings thinned to their final spacing distance when they are 1 to 2 inches tall.

PLANTING DEPTH:
Sow early varieties ½ inch deep; midseason and late varieties ¾ inch deep.

PROPAGATION:
Direct-seeding.

PLANTING TIPS:
Radishes are easy and fast to grow. The early varieties in particular are useful for succession planting and can be interplanted with slower growing crops such as beets to mark rows in the garden. The radishes will be ready to harvest before the other crops need the growing space.

Early radishes tend to bolt to seed as the hours of daylight increase, so be sure to plant them early.

RHUBARB
Rheum rhaponticum

WHERE TO PLANT:	Full sun, in well-drained, sandy soil, with a pH anywhere from 5.0 to 6.8.

Rhubarb is a long-lived perennial that may spread a considerable amount in the garden. It requires a bed with excellent drainage and rich in organic matter. To prepare a rhubarb bed, first dig a trench 18 inches wide and 2 to 3 feet deep. Reserve the topsoil (the first 12 inches of soil) if it is of good quality and discard the subsoil. Fill the lower 1 to 2 feet of the trench with a mixture of compost and well-rotted manure to which you have added a shovelful of bone meal or rock phosphate and a shovelful of greensand or granite dust for each plant. Fill the top foot of the trench with the reserved topsoil.

Rhubarb needs a cold dormant period in winter and grows best in the northern half of the United States (Zones 3 to 7).

WHEN TO PLANT:	In early spring, as soon as the soil can be worked and while crowns are still dormant, or in autumn, before the soil freezes.
SPACING:	Set plants 3 feet apart, in rows 4 feet apart.
PLANTING DEPTH:	Plant at a depth of 2 to 3 inches.
PROPAGATION:	Crowns purchased from a nursery or divided from crowded mature plantings. Make sure each division has at least two eyes (dormant buds).
PLANTING TIPS:	If the average summer temperature in your garden is much above 75° F, rhubarb will probably not grow well for you.

Because rhubarb spreads and takes up its garden space year-round, it is not a good crop for a small garden.

SPINACH
Spinacia oleracea

WHERE TO PLANT:	Full sun to partial shade, in well-drained, sandy loam rich in organic matter, with a pH between 6.0 and 7.0.
WHEN TO PLANT:	Spinach grows best in cool temperatures (60 to 65° F), when days are short; either increasing daylight hours or exposure to heat will

SPINACH—*Continued*

WHEN TO PLANT:
(continued)

cause the plants to bolt to seed. Direct-seed 3 to 5 weeks before the average last frost date, as soon as the soil temperature is 35° F or higher. Spinach will germinate in soil temperatures ranging from 35 to 70° F. To harvest a spring crop before light and heat cause the spinach to bolt, direct-seed spinach as early in the season as possible, as soon as soil can be worked. Sow a fall crop approximately 9 weeks before you expect the first fall frost.

Gardeners in Zones 9 and 10, where winter temperatures do not drop below 20° F, can plant in late fall for a winter crop.

You can make two or three successive plantings 2 to 3 weeks apart to extend the harvest.

SPACING:

Sow 6 inches apart in rows 14 inches apart, or 6 inches apart in all directions in beds. If you sow seeds more closely, you can thin when plants are 4 to 5 inches tall and use the thinnings in salads.

PLANTING DEPTH:

Plant seeds ¼ to ½ inch deep.

PROPAGATION:

Direct-seeding.

PLANTING TIPS:

In order to sow a spring crop as early as possible, prepare the seed bed the previous fall by turning in well-rotted manure and compost.

Germination can be improved by soaking the seeds in water for 24 hours before planting.

Be sure to choose the right variety for the time of year you are planting. Use cold-resistant varieties for early spring and late fall plantings, and bolt-resistant varieties for later spring planting. If you live where spring weather turns hot quickly, or if you want to harvest in summer, plant a heat-tolerant spinach substitute such as New Zealand spinach or Malabar spinach.

SQUASHES AND PUMPKINS

Cucurbita maxima, Banana, Hubbard, Turk's turban squashes
C. mixta, Pumpkins, Cushaw squash, Pie pumpkins
C. moschata, Winter crookneck squashes, Butternut squashes
C. pepo var. *melopepo*, Pattypan or Scallop, Cocozelle and other
Summer crookneck squashes, Zucchini
C. pepo var. *pepo*, Acorn squash

WHERE TO PLANT: Full sun, in rich, fertile soil that is moist but well drained, with a pH of 6.0 to 7.0. Pumpkins can tolerate some shade when plants are young.

WHEN TO PLANT: All squash plants are very tender and grow best in warm temperatures averaging 65 to 75° F. Direct-sow 2 or more weeks after the average date of the last frost, when soil temperature is at least 60° F. In cooler climates, a black plastic mulch laid down 2 weeks before planting will warm the soil.

Gardeners wishing to grow winter squash where the growing season is short can start seeds indoors 4 to 6 weeks before transplanting out. Sow in individual pots to minimize disturbance of roots—squash does not transplant well. The best soil temperature for indoor germination is 70 to 75° F. Set out seedlings of summer squash 4 to 5 weeks after the last frost date, winter squash and pumpkins 3 to 4 weeks after the last frost date.

SPACING: Plant vining squash varieties in hills, six seeds per hill, with the hills 6 to 8 feet apart. Plant vining pumpkins six seeds per hill in hills 10 to 12 feet apart.

Plant bush squashes in hills 4 to 5 feet apart, bush pumpkins in hills 4 to 6 feet apart.

When plants are 2 to 3 inches tall, thin to leave the two strongest seedlings in each hill.

You can also plant in rows. Space vining squashes and pumpkins 3 to 4 feet apart in rows 8 to 12 feet apart. Plant bush squashes and pumpkins 2 to 3 feet apart in rows 4 to 6 feet apart.

In beds, plant bush summer squash 2 feet apart in all directions; bush varieties of winter squash and pumpkins, 3 feet apart.

PLANTING DEPTH: Sow seeds of all varieties 1 inch deep.

SQUASHES AND PUMPKINS—*Continued*

PROPAGATION: Direct-seeding.

PLANTING TIPS: Pumpkins, which unlike other squashes can tolerate some shade when young, are sometimes grown with corn to save on garden space. When the corn is harvested, knock down the stalks so the pumpkins receive full sun.

All squashes and pumpkins are heavy feeders, so a soil rich in organic matter and nutrients is essential for maximum yields.

If you want to grow the huge pumpkins that are featured in giant pumpkin contests, start with special seeds, such as 'Big Max' or 'Big Moon'. Six weeks before transplant time, sow the seeds indoors, using one 8- or 10-inch pot per plant. Carefully transplant the plants at least 20 feet apart in soil that has been deeply enriched with compost and well-rotted manure.

SWEET POTATOES
Ipomoea batatas

WHERE TO PLANT: Full sun, in sandy, well-drained loam that is loose to a depth of 1 foot or more, with a pH between 5.5 and 6.5. The soil must contain lots of potassium but not be overly rich in nitrogen. Sweet potatoes do not grow well in cloudy, rainy climates, in wet soil, or in regions with a short, cool growing season. They are very prone to disease, although an acid soil will help to minimize disease problems.

WHEN TO PLANT: Set out plants 3 to 4 weeks after the average last frost date, when nighttime temperatures no longer dip below 60° F and the soil temperature is 65° F or more.

SPACING: Plant 15 inches apart in ridged rows 36 inches apart, or in hills 12 inches apart in all directions in intensive beds.

PLANTING DEPTH: Set plants 4 to 5 inches deep. Some gardeners report good results with burying the plants horizontally 2 to 3 inches deep with plant nodes underground (a node in this case means the swollen section of stem at each leaf).

PROPAGATION: Plants from the nursery or garden center.

PLANTING TIPS: To ensure good drainage and adequate nutrients, make a furrow 12 inches wide (or holes, if planting in beds) 2 inches deep, and fill with compost. Mound up a ridge of soil 10 inches high on top of the furrow and plant along the ridge. Make sure to flatten the top of the ridge to prevent excessive water runoff and encourage water to penetrate to the root zone.

You can start your own plants by cutting potatoes in half lengthwise and setting them in a moist rooting medium, 6 to 8 weeks before the last frost date. Keep the tubers in a warm place, where temperatures are 70 to 80° F. Rooted sprouts will form at the eyes on the tuber. When the sprouts have grown 4 to 8 inches tall, carefully pinch the slips (young plants) away from the potatoes and plant them in the garden. This propagation method will work only on untreated sweet potatoes. Supermarket sweet potatoes usually have been treated to retard sprouting.

Depending upon the variety, sweet potatoes may require from 100 to 150 days of hot weather to produce a good crop. If you live in Zones 3 to 6, choose a variety that matures quickly.

SWISS CHARD
Beta vulgaris var. *cicla*

WHERE TO PLANT:
Full sun to partial shade, in well-drained soil rich in organic matter, with a pH of 6.0 to 6.8.

WHEN TO PLANT:
Direct-seed 1 to 2 weeks before the average last frost date, as soon as the soil temperature is at least 40° F. Since Swiss chard will germinate in soil temperatures ranging from 40 to 85° F, it can be planted from very early spring to midsummer. In mild climates (Zones 9 and 10), direct-seed in early fall for a winter or early spring crop.

SPACING:
Like beet seed, each Swiss chard seed is actually a cluster of up to eight seeds from which a clump of seedlings will develop. To get the best final spacing, you will have to thin the seedlings.

Sow seeds 3 inches apart in rows 18 inches apart, thinning to 9 inches apart when the plants are about 6 inches tall. In beds, space plants 9 inches apart in all directions. The thinnings can be cooked or used in salads.

PLANTING DEPTH:
Sow seeds ½ to 1 inch deep.

PROPAGATION:
Direct-seeding.

SWISS CHARD—*Continued*

PLANTING TIPS:
Swiss chard is a very adaptable crop, tolerant of both frost and hot weather, and a good hot weather substitute for spinach. If you harvest regularly and keep the soil moist, it will keep producing all summer and into fall.

TOMATOES
Lycopersicon lycopersicum

WHERE TO PLANT:
Full sun, in light, well-drained sandy or loam soil rich in organic matter, with a pH between 6.0 and 7.0. If your soil is heavy and drains poorly, plant in raised beds. In very warm climates, plants will need some shade during the height of summer or they may drop blossoms.

WHEN TO PLANT:
Start seeds indoors 5 to 7 weeks before the average last frost date. Optimum soil temperature for seed germination is 70 to 75° F. During this time indoors, transplant seedlings at least once into flats. Set the plants 2 inches apart and slightly deeper than they grew before. Keep indoor seedlings a little on the cool side—60 to 70° F—to prevent rampant early growth that is difficult to harden off. Transplant seedlings to the garden after all danger of frost has passed and nighttime temperatures no longer dip below 55° F.

In regions with a warm growing season that is at least 10 weeks long, you can direct-seed 1 or 2 weeks after the last frost date, or whenever the soil temperature is 60° F or higher.

SPACING:
When direct-seeding, sow 2 inches apart in rows 3 feet apart for determinate varieties or indeterminate varieties that are staked, or in rows 4 feet apart for unstaked indeterminate plants. When plants are 2 inches tall, thin them to stand 3 inches apart; when 12 inches tall, thin to the spacings recommended for transplants.

Set transplants of determinate tomatoes and staked indeterminate varieties 1½ to 2 feet apart. In beds, space the plants 2 feet apart in all directions. Indeterminate plants that will not be staked need to be 4 feet apart.

PLANTING DEPTH:
Sow seeds ¼ to ½ inch deep. Set transplants 2 inches deeper than they were growing in their containers. Tall, leggy seedlings can be set horizontally in 2- to 3-inch-deep trenches, with only the top

cluster of leaves uncovered. Pinch off all the lower leaves before planting. The buried stem will produce new roots that will help anchor the plant, and the top of the plant will grow straight after several days.

PROPAGATION: Transplants, started indoors or purchased from a nursery or garden center.

PLANTING TIPS: Determinate tomatoes (which include dwarf varieties suitable for container growing) are compact, bushy varieties that produce all of their fruit over a short period, then stop growing. These varieties are best for short growing seasons, and are also convenient for gardeners who want to can or otherwise process the harvest.

Indeterminate tomatoes grow and bear fruit continuously until frost stops them, and are usually staked or caged to keep their rampant growth in bounds.

Set stakes or cages in place at the same time that you plant out transplants. For direct-seeded plants, set stakes or cages in place when you thin seedlings to their final spacing.

TURNIPS
Brassica rapa, Rapifera Group

WHERE TO PLANT: Full sun to partial shade, in loose soil rich in organic matter and potassium, with a pH of 5.5 to 6.8.

WHEN TO PLANT: Turnips grow best in cool weather, when temperatures average 60 to 65° F. Hot weather causes depletion of sugar in the root resulting in woody, sharp-tasting turnips. To get the best-tasting turnips, plan your seed planting for early spring so that turnips are ready to harvest before hot weather sets in. Young turnip plants can withstand temperatures as low as 40° F, but more mature plants may bolt and flower upon prolonged exposure to temperatures below 40° F. Direct-sow 2 to 4 weeks before the average last frost date, when soil temperature is 40° F or higher. Turnips will germinate in soil temperatures ranging from 40 to 85° F, but optimum temperature is 60° F.

For a fall crop, direct-seed approximately 9 weeks before the first expected fall frost.

In warm climates (Zones 8 to 10), sow turnips in early fall through spring for continuous winter crops.

TURNIPS—*Continued*

SPACING:

Seeds can be planted closely together (about three seeds per inch of row) and thinned later. Thin to 1 inch apart when the plants have their first true leaves. When leaves of adjacent plants begin to touch one another, thin again to the final spacing distance and use the thinnings in salads. Final spacing for thinned plants is 4 to 6 inches apart in rows 12 to 15 inches apart, or 6 inches apart in all directions in beds.

PLANTING DEPTH:

Plant seed ¼ to ½ inch deep.

PROPAGATION:

Direct-seeding.

PLANTING TIPS:

Turnips may be grown either for delicious greens or for large, sweet roots. In growing turnips for greens, select a variety designated as a greens turnip and sow the seeds on the same schedule as for turnips grown for roots. Harvest while the weather remains cool—summer heat turns turnip greens bitter.

Herbs

BASIL

Ocimum basilicum

WHERE TO PLANT:
: Full sun, in moist but well-drained soil rich in organic matter. The ideal pH is around 6.0, but basil tolerates a pH range of 5.5 to 7.5.

WHEN TO PLANT:
: Direct-seed or set out transplants in spring, after all danger of frost is past and the soil has warmed to 50° F or more. Seeds may rot in cold, wet soil. Or start seeds indoors, approximately 4 to 6 weeks before the last expected frost. Basil germinates best at a soil temperature of 75° F. Germination takes 7 to 10 days.

SPACING:
: Thin plants to stand 10 to 12 inches apart in rows 18 to 24 inches apart, or 12 inches apart in all directions in beds.

PLANTING DEPTH:
: Sow seeds ⅛ to ¼ inch deep.

PROPAGATION:
: Direct-seeding or transplants.

PLANTING TIPS:
: Keep the soil or germination medium moist (but not soggy) until seeds germinate. Mulch when seedlings are several inches high (or after transplanting to the garden) to conserve moisture and keep down weeds. All basil varieties also grow well in containers when given plenty of moisture. Basil is a tender annual that thrives best in hot, humid weather.

BORAGE
Borago officinalis

WHERE TO PLANT:
Full sun, in light, loose, well-drained and moderately rich soil, with a pH between 6.0 and 7.0. Borage tolerates dry soil of average fertility, but grows better when given plenty of organic matter and regular moisture.

WHEN TO PLANT:
Direct-seed when all danger of frost has passed in spring. Borage germinates best at a soil temperature of 60 to 70° F. Germination takes 7 to 10 days.

SPACING:
Thin seedlings to stand 12 to 18 inches apart.

PLANTING DEPTH:
Sow seeds ½ inch deep.

PROPAGATION:
Direct-seeding; plants have a taproot that makes them difficult to transplant.

PLANTING TIPS:
Borage is a blue-flowering hardy annual that self-sows freely. Enjoy borage flowers over the winter by potting up small volunteer plants in the fall.

CHAMOMILE
Chamaemelum nobile, Roman or English chamomile
Matricaria recutita, German chamomile

WHERE TO PLANT:
Roman chamomile is a low, creeping, half-hardy perennial that grows best in full sun to partial shade. It prefers light, sandy, well-drained soil of average fertility and a pH between 6.5 and 8.0. German chamomile is an upright hardy annual that thrives in full sun, in sandy, moist but well-drained soil with a pH between 6.0 and 7.5.

WHEN TO PLANT:
Direct-seed Roman chamomile in early spring, or plant cuttings or offsets divided from the parent plant. Direct-seed German chamomile either early in the spring as soon as the soil can be worked, or in the fall. Both types may be started from seed sown indoors 6 to 8 weeks before the last expected frost. Set out transplants around the last expected frost. German chamomile

germinates best at a soil temperature of 55° F. Roman chamomile germinates best at 75° F.

SPACING: Space Roman chamomile 18 inches apart; German chamomile 6 inches apart.

PLANTING DEPTH: Scatter the tiny seeds of German chamomile on top of the soil and press them in lightly. Plant rooted cuttings or divisions of Roman chamomile just deep enough to cover the roots.

PROPAGATION: Division is the best way to start Roman chamomile; direct-seeding in spring is best for German chamomile.

PLANTING TIPS: Double-flowered cultivars of Roman chamomile need richer, moister soil than the single-flowered wild type. German chamomile self-sows prolifically and can become invasive.

CHERVIL
Anthriscus cerefolium

WHERE TO PLANT: Partial shade, in moist, fine-textured soil rich in organic matter and with a pH between 6.5 and 7.5.

WHEN TO PLANT: Chervil is a hardy annual that grows best in spring and fall; hot, dry summer weather tends to make it bolt to seed. Direct-seed in early spring and again in late summer to have mature plants in fall. Successive sowings 2 or 3 weeks apart will extend the harvest of leaves.

SPACING: When seedlings are 2 to 3 inches tall, thin them to stand 9 to 12 inches apart.

PLANTING DEPTH: Seeds need light to germinate; sow in a small furrow 1 inch deep but do not cover them with soil. Mist the seeds with water to settle them into the soil.

PROPAGATION: Direct-seeding; chervil does not transplant well.

PLANTING TIPS: Chervil prefers cool temperatures and partial shade. In sunny gardens, plant it in the shade of taller plants to help get it through hot summer weather. It is also a good plant for containers. Chervil self-sows readily.

CHIVES

Allium schoenoprasum

WHERE TO PLANT: Full sun, in well-drained soil of average fertility, with a pH of 6.0 to 7.0. Chives grow best in sun but can tolerate a bit of shade.

WHEN TO PLANT: Sow seeds indoors about 4 to 5 weeks before the last expected frost. Keep the medium constantly moist and provide temperatures of 60 to 70° F until germination, which takes 10 to 14 days. Transplant out when danger of frost has passed. Set seedlings out in clusters, not as individual thin spears. Or direct-seed chives after danger of heavy frost is past. Set out potted clumps from the nursery or divisions from mature clumps of chives in spring or anytime during the growing season.

SPACING: Space clumps 8 to 10 inches apart.

PLANTING DEPTH: Sow seeds ½ inch deep. Set potted clumps or divisions at the same depth they were growing previously.

PROPAGATION: Nursery plants or divisions will grow quickly to harvest size.

PLANTING TIPS: Chives are hardy perennials, so plant them where they can remain for several years. Chives make a good container plant, and can be brought indoors to a sunny windowsill in late fall for use all winter.

CORIANDER

Coriandrum sativum

WHERE TO PLANT: Full sun, in light, moist but well-drained, moderately rich soil with a pH of 6.0 to 7.0. To get the best flavor, avoid soils very high in nitrogen.

WHEN TO PLANT: Coriander is a hardy annual that should be direct-seeded when all danger of frost is past. Coriander is one of the easiest herbs to grow by direct-seeding.

SPACING: Thin seedlings or set plants 5 to 8 inches apart.

PLANTING DEPTH: Sow seeds ½ inch deep. Cover seeds completely to provide the darkness needed for germination. Set nursery plants at the same depth they were growing in their containers.

PROPAGATION: Direct-seeding.

PLANTING TIPS: Since coriander goes to seed quite rapidly as summer progresses, succession planting helps prolong harvest of the leaves. Coriander self-sows in many gardens.

DILL
Anethum graveolens

WHERE TO PLANT:	Full sun, in moist but well-drained, moderately rich soil with a pH between 5.5 and 6.5.
WHEN TO PLANT:	Direct-seed after all danger of frost is past. Seeds can also be sown in fall for a crop the following summer.
SPACING:	Thin seedlings to stand 8 to 10 inches apart if you are growing plants only for their leaves, 10 to 12 inches apart if you want to harvest seed heads.
PLANTING DEPTH:	Sow seeds ½ inch deep.
PROPAGATION:	Direct-seeding. Dill develops a long taproot that makes transplanting difficult.
PLANTING TIPS:	Dill is a hardy annual that often self-sows from seed heads left on the plants. Your dill patch may produce numerous tiny seedlings that need thinning the following spring.

FENNEL
Foeniculum vulgare

WHERE TO PLANT:	Full sun, in light, well-drained, moderately rich soil with a pH of 6.5 to 7.0.
WHEN TO PLANT:	Direct-seed after all danger of frost is past. To extend the harvest, make succession plantings 2 weeks apart until midsummer.
SPACING:	Thin seedlings to stand 6 to 8 inches apart.
PLANTING DEPTH:	Sow ½ inch deep. Cover seeds completely as darkness is required for germination.
PROPAGATION:	Direct-seeding; fennel resents transplanting. Plants may self-sow.
PLANTING TIPS:	Fennel is a half-hardy perennial that is usually grown as an annual. To grow fennel for its anise-flavored bulbous stems, select the variety 'Azoricum'. Sow seeds of 'Azoricum' in midsummer instead of spring. Blanch the fleshy stem bases by hilling soil around them as they mature. If you want to save fennel seeds, do not plant it near coriander, which may keep it from producing seed heads.

LEMON BALM
Melissa officinalis

WHERE TO PLANT:	Full sun to partial shade, in moist but well-drained soil rich in organic matter, with a pH between 6.5 and 7.5. In hot climates where the summer sun is intense, make sure the plants are partially shaded.
WHEN TO PLANT:	Direct-seed in spring, when all danger of frost is past, or in early fall. Or start seeds indoors 6 to 8 weeks before the last expected frost. Seeds germinate within 2 weeks if kept at a soil temperature of about 70° F. Set out plants 1 week after the danger of heavy frost is past. You can also divide or layer mature plants in spring, or plant stem cuttings in spring or summer.
SPACING:	Thin seedlings or set plants to stand 12 inches part.
PLANTING DEPTH:	Seeds need light to germinate; press them lightly into the soil but do not cover with soil. To root cuttings, remove the lower leaves and insert them into soil from one-third to one-half their length.
PROPAGATION:	Direct-seeding, division, or cuttings.
PLANTING TIPS:	Lemon balm is a hardy perennial that needs moist soil but is prone to powdery mildew; do not crowd plants. Plants may self-sow.

LOVAGE
Levisticum officinale

WHERE TO PLANT:	Full sun or partial shade, in moist, fertile, well-drained, deeply dug soil rich in organic matter and with a pH of 6.0 to 7.0.
WHEN TO PLANT:	Direct-seed in late summer to early fall, or start seeds indoors in spring, 8 to 10 weeks before the last expected frost. Set out plants started indoors or purchased from a nursery when all danger of heavy frost is past. Or divide and transplant mature plants in spring.
SPACING:	Plants grow large; if you are growing more than one, space them 1 to 2 feet apart.
PLANTING DEPTH:	Sow seed less than ¼ inch deep.
PROPAGATION:	Direct-seeding, transplants from the nursery, or root division of an established plant.

PLANTING TIPS:	Lovage is a tall hardy perennial that is best planted in the back of the garden. Plants started from seed do not reach usable size until their second growing season. Impatient gardeners will find it more satisfying to plant nursery transplants.

MARJORAM
Origanum majorana

WHERE TO PLANT:	Marjoram is a half-hardy perennial that is grown as an annual north of Zone 10. It prefers full sun, in light, well-drained soil rich in organic matter, and a pH between 7.0 and 8.0.
WHEN TO PLANT:	Sow seeds indoors 4 to 6 weeks before the last expected frost. Set out plants started indoors or purchased from a nursery when all danger of frost is past. In climates with a long growing season, marjoram can be direct-seeded in spring. Seeds can also be started in fall, but plants will have to be moved indoors over winter everywhere but frost-free climates. Stem cuttings can be planted in summer.
SPACING:	Set plants 6 to 8 inches apart in the garden.
PLANTING DEPTH:	Seeds germinate best with light; scatter them on the soil surface and press in gently. Germination takes 2 to 3 weeks at a soil temperature of 70° F.
PROPAGATION:	Marjoram is best propagated by purchasing plants from the nursery. Marjoram seed takes a long time to germinate, and young seedlings are exceptionally fragile. Divisions of mature plants can also be potted up in the fall, maintained in a greenhouse or cold frame, and replanted in the garden the following spring.
PLANTING TIPS:	Keep young seedlings well weeded. After plants are established in the garden, they prefer a dry soil.

MINT
Mentha species

WHERE TO PLANT:	Full sun to partial shade, in moist but well-drained soil rich in organic matter, with a pH of 6.5 to 8.0. Mint is a hardy perennial that spreads aggressively by underground runners. Plant where the roots can be kept from spreading.

MINT—*Continued*

WHEN TO PLANT:
Set out nursery plants anytime in spring. Plant stem or root cuttings from mature plants in summer. Plants can be divided in fall. Mint can also be started from seed sown directly in the garden in early spring or late fall.

SPACING:
Set plants 1 to 2 feet apart.

PLANTING DEPTH:
Plant rooted cuttings or nursery plants at the same depth they were growing previously. Plant root cuttings a couple of inches deep.

PROPAGATION:
Nursery plants or stem cuttings. Cuttings root quickly in water or rooting medium.

PLANTING TIPS:
All mints except Corsican mint spread rapidly and will overwhelm the garden if steps are not taken to contain their roots. To keep mints in bounds, plant in containers or in bottomless containers sunk into the garden. Bottomless containers should extend 10 inches deep into the soil to confine the mint roots.

OREGANO
Origanum vulgare, O. heracleoticum

WHERE TO PLANT:
Full sun, in light, well-drained soil, with a pH of 6.8 to 8.0.

WHEN TO PLANT:
Plant cuttings, root divisions, or nursery plants in spring, when all danger of frost is past.

SPACING:
Set plants 6 to 8 inches apart.

PLANTING DEPTH:
Set plants or divisions at the same depth they were growing previously. Oregano is shallow-rooted.

PROPAGATION:
Most oreganos are half-hardy perennials that are best propagated by stem cuttings, divisions, or nursery plants. Seeds are slow and difficult to germinate.

PLANTING TIPS:
O. vulgare, the species that grows wild on hillsides in the Mediterranean area, is often sold in seed form but generally produces flavorless plants. For the best flavor, plant *O. heracleoticum*, which is also listed as *O. vulgare* subsp. *hirtum*.

PARSLEY
Petroselinum crispum

WHERE TO PLANT: Full sun to partial shade, in moist but well-drained soil rich in organic matter, with a pH of 6.0 to 7.0.

WHEN TO PLANT: Direct-seed in spring as soon as the soil can be worked, 3 to 4 weeks before the last expected frost. Set out nursery plants when the danger of heavy frost is past. Parsley can also be sown indoors 8 weeks before the last expected frost. Seeds germinate best at a soil temperature of 70 to 75° F. Germination takes 2 to 3 weeks.

SPACING: Set plants 6 to 8 inches apart.

PLANTING DEPTH: Sow seeds ¼ inch deep.

PROPAGATION: Direct-seeding or plants from the nursery.

PLANTING TIPS: Parsley is a biennial that is usually grown as an annual because it goes to seed in the second year. Parsley seeds germinate very slowly, taking as long as 3 weeks. Cover seeds completely, as darkness is needed for germination. To hasten sprouting, soak the seeds in warm water for 24 to 48 hours before planting, changing the water once or twice. Or pour hot water over the seeds after planting. Plants often self-sow if you let them go to seed. Set out a few new plants each year to make sure you have plenty of leaves for kitchen use.

ROSEMARY
Rosmarinus officinalis

WHERE TO PLANT: Full sun, in sandy, well-drained soil of moderate fertility, with a pH of 6.5 to 7.5. Rosemary flourishes best in dry, limey soil. If your soil is acid, add lime or wood ashes.

WHEN TO PLANT: Plant rooted stem cuttings or nursery plants in spring, when all danger of frost is past and the soil has warmed.

SPACING: Set plants 1 to 2 feet apart.

PLANTING DEPTH: Plant rooted cuttings or plants at the same depth they were growing previously. Sow seeds ⅛ to ¼ inch deep.

PROPAGATION: Cuttings or nursery plants. Rosemary seeds are slow and difficult to germinate, and the slow-growing plants may take 3 or 4 years to

ROSEMARY—*Continued*

PROPAGATION: *(continued)*	reach harvestable size. Rosemary may also be propagated by layering.
PLANTING TIPS:	Rosemary is a half-hardy perennial shrub that can be wintered over in climates where winter temperatures remain above 10° F (Zones 8 to 10). Plants may survive farther north if well mulched, but a better approach is to grow rosemary in pots that can be brought indoors over winter. Potted rosemary can be clipped as a topiary subject.

SAGE

Salvia officinalis

WHERE TO PLANT:	Full sun, in well-drained soil with plenty of organic matter and a pH between 6.5 and 7.0. Sage flourishes in an alkaline soil.
WHEN TO PLANT:	Late spring, when all danger of frost has passed and the soil has warmed. Tip cuttings can be taken in fall and rooted indoors in pots, then moved to the garden the following spring.
SPACING:	Young plants can be spaced 6 to 8 inches apart; mature plants need 1½ to 2 feet between them.
PLANTING DEPTH:	Sow seeds ½ inch deep.
PROPAGATION:	Sage is a hardy perennial that can be grown from seed, although it takes 2 years to get sizable plants. Most cultivars are better started by rooting cuttings or by layering. Unless you want to grow a lot of plants, the easiest, most reliable source is to buy plants from a nursery or garden center.
PLANTING TIPS:	Some cultivars, notably variegated and purple-leaved varieties, are tender perennials hardy only through Zone 6. Gardeners farther north can winter over these tender varieties by taking cuttings to root in the fall. Over the winter keep the little plants on a sunny windowsill and replant outdoors in the spring.

SAVORY

Satureja hortensis, Summer savory
S. montana, Winter savory

WHERE TO PLANT:	Full sun. Summer savory likes a moist but well-drained soil of average fertility, with a pH of 6.5 to 7.0. Winter savory prefers a lighter, slightly drier soil with a similar pH.

WHEN TO PLANT:	Direct-seed summer savory when all danger of frost is past, or start seeds indoors about 4 weeks before the last expected frost and set out plants around the date of the last frost. Winter savory germinates more slowly; start seeds indoors 6 to 8 weeks before the last expected frost and set out plants around the date of the last frost. Both kinds of savory can also be started from stem cuttings taken in late summer or fall and rooted in pots indoors over winter.
SPACING:	Space summer savory plants 8 to 10 inches apart; winter savory 10 to 12 inches apart.
PLANTING DEPTH:	Sow seeds no more than ⅛ inch deep; summer savory in particular germinates best when seeds receive some light.
PROPAGATION:	For summer savory, seeds or plants from the nursery or garden center. For winter savory, cuttings or nursery plants.
PLANTING TIPS:	Summer savory is a hardy annual that self-sows easily. It can also be grown indoors over winter in a light garden or on a sunny windowsill. Winter savory is a perennial hardy to Zone 6, but its life span is short, and you will need new plants every 2 to 3 years.

TARRAGON
Artemisia dracunculus var. *sativa*

WHERE TO PLANT:	Full sun, in rich, loamy, well-drained soil with plenty of organic matter and a pH between 6.2 and 7.0.
WHEN TO PLANT:	In spring, when all danger of frost is past. Divide mature plants in early spring when new shoots appear; take cuttings a bit later in spring.
SPACING:	Space plants 1 to 2 feet apart.
PLANTING DEPTH:	Set rooted cuttings and nursery plants at the same depth they were growing previously. Sow seeds of Russian tarragon ⅛ inch deep.
PROPAGATION:	French tarragon, which has the best flavor, is a hardy perennial that does not produce seeds. It must be started from cuttings, division, or plants from a nursery or garden center. A less desirable form, Russian tarragon, can be grown from seed, but does not have as good a flavor.
PLANTING TIPS:	Good drainage is essential for tarragon. It is hardy to Zone 4 and in fact grows best in climates where winter temperatures go below freezing, but it will need a winter mulch.

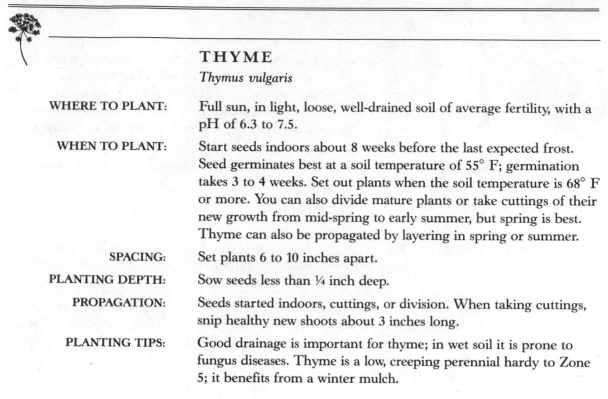

THYME
Thymus vulgaris

WHERE TO PLANT:	Full sun, in light, loose, well-drained soil of average fertility, with a pH of 6.3 to 7.5.
WHEN TO PLANT:	Start seeds indoors about 8 weeks before the last expected frost. Seed germinates best at a soil temperature of 55° F; germination takes 3 to 4 weeks. Set out plants when the soil temperature is 68° F or more. You can also divide mature plants or take cuttings of their new growth from mid-spring to early summer, but spring is best. Thyme can also be propagated by layering in spring or summer.
SPACING:	Set plants 6 to 10 inches apart.
PLANTING DEPTH:	Sow seeds less than ¼ inch deep.
PROPAGATION:	Seeds started indoors, cuttings, or division. When taking cuttings, snip healthy new shoots about 3 inches long.
PLANTING TIPS:	Good drainage is important for thyme; in wet soil it is prone to fungus diseases. Thyme is a low, creeping perennial hardy to Zone 5; it benefits from a winter mulch.

Fruits & Nuts

APPLES
Malus pumila

WHERE TO PLANT: Full sun, in well-drained soil reasonably rich in organic matter, of any type from sandy to clay, with a pH of 6.0 to 7.0. Avoid planting at the bottom of a slope where cold air may settle; also avoid areas where drainage is poor. Apple roots need at least 4 feet of loose soil. Avoid planting where there is hardpan or other obstruction at this depth.

WHEN TO PLANT: Plant trees when they are dormant—early spring in Zones 3 to 7 and in fall in Zones 8 to 10.

SPACING: Plant standard trees 20 feet apart in rows 30 feet apart; semi-dwarf trees 12 feet apart in rows 20 feet apart; dwarf trees 8 feet apart in rows 16 feet apart. Genetic dwarfs (the smallest kind of fruit trees, which are dwarf as a result of breeding rather than grafting) can be planted in large tubs 2 to 2½ feet in diameter or 6 feet apart in the garden.

APPLES—*Continued*

PLANTING DEPTH: Planting hole must be large and deep enough to allow the roots to be spread out. Plant standard and semi-dwarf trees at the depth they grew previously. Plant dwarf trees deeper than they grew at the nursery (look for the soil line on the trunk).

PROPAGATION: Nursery trees or grafting. Use a splice or cleft graft.

PLANTING TIPS: Prune at planting time to develop a central leader shape.

Do not put soluble fertilizers (organic or synthetic) into the planting hole or roots may be burned.

Lay down 2 to 4 inches of loose organic mulch around the tree but not touching the trunk.

Water newly planted trees deeply once a week during dry weather. Trees grafted onto EM IX dwarfing rootstocks must be staked when planted; trees grafted onto EM XXVI or EM VII dwarfing rootstocks may also need to be staked.

Most varieties of apples are *not* self-fruitful. They require cross-pollination from another variety to set fruit. Red Delicious, Winesap, Red Gravenstein, Rhode Island Greening, and triploid crosses (such as Mutsu) need to be planted with a pollinator variety. Stayman and related varieties (including Turley and Arkansas Black Twig) need two pollinator varieties because Stayman cannot pollinate its pollinator variety and that tree will not set fruit unless a third variety is planted. Golden Delicious is a good pollinator for most apple varieties; Winter Banana is also recommended. To set fruit, apples require a cold dormancy period, called the *chill requirement*. Ask your local Extension Agent for the names of varieties with chill requirements that match your climate.

APRICOTS
Prunus armeniaca

WHERE TO PLANT: Full sun, in well-drained soil rich in organic matter, with a pH between 6.0 and 7.0. Apricots generally grow best in sandy soils. Soil too rich in nitrogen causes premature fruit drop and pit burn. Apricots grafted onto myrobalan plum rootstocks can tolerate heavier clay soils. The roots may grow to a depth of 16 feet, so avoid planting where there is hardpan or serious compaction at or above this depth.

If spring in your area tends to bring alternating periods of warm and freezing weather, plant apricots on a north-facing hillside or other location that warms up slowly to delay blooming and lessen the chances that the flowers may be frozen in a late cold snap. Apricots grow best in Zones 5 to 8.

WHEN TO PLANT: Very early spring in Zones 5 to 7; autumn in Zone 8.

SPACING: Standard-size trees should be 30 feet apart.

PLANTING DEPTH: Dig planting holes deep enough to comfortably accommodate all the roots when spread out and to allow the tree to grow at the same depth it grew at the nursery.

PROPAGATION: Trees from a nursery.

PLANTING TIPS: Prune at planting time to encourage an open center or modified central leader form, depending on whether the variety is spreading or upright. Mulch newly planted trees to conserve moisture and to keep down weeds.

Apricots are self-fruitful. You'll get plenty of fruit from only one tree. Be sure to select a variety with a chill requirement that matches your climate.

AVOCADOS
Persea americana

WHERE TO PLANT: Full sun, in moist but well-drained soil rich in organic matter, with a pH anywhere between 4.0 and 10.0. Mexican avocados can tolerate winter temperatures to about 20° F; Guatemalan types withstand temperatures to about 26° F; and West Indian varieties can take temperatures to 28° F.

Avocados can also be grown in containers in a greenhouse where the temperature in summer is 75 to 85° F, and in winter, 55 to 65° F. Use a good all-purpose potting medium.

WHEN TO PLANT: In spring when all danger of frost is past.

SPACING: 20 to 30 feet apart.

AVOCADOS—*Continued*

PLANTING DEPTH:
For either bare-rooted or container-grown trees, make the planting hole about 6 to 8 inches wide and only as deep as the height of the root ball, so the top of the root ball is even with the soil surface. Cover seeds with no more than 1 inch of soil.

PROPAGATION:
Nursery trees, or shield budding onto seedling rootstocks. For container trees, propagate from seed, grafting, or budding. Avocados are easily grown from seed but the fruit is generally of poor quality.

PLANTING TIPS:
Water thoroughly after planting, and during dry weather thereafter. To plant seeds, first remove the hard brown coat. Soak the seed, then dry it, and cut a thin section of the coat from the top and bottom of the seed. Plant with the wide end of the seed down.

Avocados have both male and female flowers. Plant at least two trees in order to get fruit.

BLACKBERRIES

Rubus flagellaris, Dewberry
R. ulmifolius, Thornless blackberry
R. ursinus 'Boysen', boysenberry
R. ursinus 'Logan', loganberry
R. ursinus 'Young', youngberry

WHERE TO PLANT:
Full sun, in well-drained soil of average fertility, with a pH between 6.0 and 7.0. Avoid very acid soils and heavy, poorly drained soils. Dewberries will tolerate drier, rockier soil than other blackberries.

WHEN TO PLANT:
Set out one-year-old plants from the nursery in spring. Most plants ordered through mail-order nurseries will be bare-rooted stock. Handle those according to the instructions on page 98.

Dewberries and loganberries readily layer themselves—the canes will root when their tips touch the ground. Sever the new plants and set them out in the garden as described on page 69.

SPACING:
Space plants 3 feet apart, in rows 5 to 6 feet apart. Give plants plenty of space to help prevent problems with virus and rust diseases.

PLANTING DEPTH:	Plant container-grown nursery plants at the same depth they were growing previously. Set bare root plants with the old nursery soil line 1 inch into the ground.
PROPAGATION:	Nursery plants, tip layering, or root cuttings. To propagate blackberries by root cuttings, dig up the roots of large plants in the fall after dormancy has begun. Cut the roots into pieces 2 to 4 inches long. Store over the winter in moist sand in a cool place not subject to freezing. Plant the cuttings in the spring.
PLANTING TIPS:	Boysenberries, loganberries, and youngberries are planted in mild areas along the Pacific Coast. Dewberries grow best in the South. For other blackberries, choose a variety suited to your region— different cultivars are suited to various parts of the country.
	Blackberries are very susceptible to verticillium wilt; to help prevent it, do not plant blackberries where other wilt-prone plants (such as eggplant, peppers, potatoes, and tomatoes) grew within the last 4 years.
	To minimize the threat of disease, always plant stock that is certified virus-free.

BLUEBERRIES

Vaccinium corymbosum, Highbush blueberry
V. ashei, Rabbit-eye blueberry

WHERE TO PLANT:	Full sun to partial shade, in well-drained, acid soil rich in organic matter. Blueberries tolerate both sandy and clay soils as long as they are acid and well drained. Highbush blueberries need a pH between 4.0 and 5.0, and rabbit-eyes can tolerate a pH up to 5.5 or slightly higher.
	Highbush blueberries can be grown all along the East Coast, and as far west as Michigan, Missouri, and Arkansas. Rabbit-eye berries are better in the Southeast since they tolerate more heat and need less winter chilling.
WHEN TO PLANT:	Plant two-year-old plants in the spring.
SPACING:	Space highbush blueberries 6 feet apart in all directions; space rabbit-eye plants 7 to 8 feet apart.

BLUEBERRIES—*Continued*

PLANTING DEPTH: Set plants at the same depth they were growing at the nursery.

PROPAGATION: Plants from the nursery or mound layering, as described on page 69.

Blueberries can also be propagated from cuttings, although this is difficult to accomplish at home. To propagate from stem cuttings, take 4-inch stem cuttings from the bottom of one-year-old shoots in early spring while plants are still dormant. The cuttings should have no fruit buds on them (fruit buds are fatter than leaf buds). Root the cuttings in a moist rooting medium, preferably in a humidity chamber as described on page 42. Plant them out when roots have formed.

PLANTING TIPS: Blueberries are not self-fruitful. Cross-pollination is essential for good fruit production. Plant at least two cross-fruitful cultivars.

Prune at planting time, cutting back the bushes by one-fourth and removing any low stems near the base of the plant.

CHERRIES

Prunus avium, Sweet cherry
P. cerasus, Sour cherry

WHERE TO PLANT: Full sun, in deep, well-drained, loamy soil with a pH between 6.0 and 8.0. Soils with hardpan closer than 4 feet from the surface will cause shallow rooting that will threaten the trees' well-being in dry years. Soils rich in organic matter benefit cherries; in sandy soils, lots of organic matter is essential to improve the moisture-holding capacity.

Cherries bloom early, so avoid planting in low-lying spots that may act as cold pockets. A north-facing slope that warms slowly in spring is a good place for cherries, because flowering may be delayed, reducing the risk of damage from a late frost. Sweet cherries grow best in Zones 5 to 8, sour cherries in Zones 4 to 7.

WHEN TO PLANT: In cool climates, plant in early spring; in the northernmost parts of the growing range, prepare the soil the autumn before planting. In warm climates, plant in fall.

SPACING:	Space sweet cherries about 15 feet apart in rows 35 feet apart; plant sour cherries about 7 to 8 feet apart in rows 20 feet apart. Genetic dwarf sour cherries can be grown in tubs 2 to 2½ feet in diameter or planted 6 feet apart in the garden.
PLANTING DEPTH:	Set young trees at the same depth they were growing at the nursery.
PROPAGATION:	One- or two-year-old trees from the nursery, or budding.
PLANTING TIPS:	Sour cherries are self-fruitful, but sweet cherries are not, except for the variety 'Stella'. Also sour cherries will not pollinize sweet cherries. Pollination of sweet cherries is extremely complicated, because some varieties have compatible pollen and others are incompatible. Consult a reliable nursery or your local USDA County Extension Agent for information on which varieties are best for cross-pollination in your area.

Prune 4- to 6-foot trees back to 3 feet at planting time to encourage the growth of new branches suitable for scaffolds. Prune 3-foot trees back by about 1 foot.

CITRUS FRUITS

Citrus sinensis, Sweet orange
C. paradisi, Grapefruit
C. limonia, Lemon
C. aurantifolia, Lime

WHERE TO PLANT:	Full sun, in light, well-drained, fertile, loamy soil rich in organic matter and with a pH between 5.0 and 7.0. A south-facing slope offers protection from cold winds. Citrus fruits need a warm climate—Zones 8 to 10 in the United States. Limes are the least hardy of all citrus and in the United States are grown primarily in the Florida Keys. Orange and grapefruit trees can tolerate temperatures in the low 20s, and their fruit withstands temperatures in the upper 20s. Lemons are slightly less hardy.
WHEN TO PLANT:	Citrus can be planted practically anytime, but the best time is late winter or very early spring, when the trees are growing slowly.
SPACING:	Plant trees 20 to 35 feet apart in all directions, depending on the species.

CITRUS FRUITS—*Continued*

PLANTING DEPTH: Plant trees at the same depth they were growing in the nursery.

PROPAGATION: One-year-old balled-and-burlapped trees from a nursery or garden center. Citrus trees can also be propagated by budding buds from mature trees onto seedling rootstocks (shield budding is used), or from tip cuttings, leaf bud cuttings, or whip grafting two twigs to form a scion and rootstock. Tip cuttings are taken in early summer, from the current season's growth. The cuttings should be 3 to 6 inches long. Place cuttings in a moist rooting medium under mist and plant them out when they have formed roots.

PLANTING TIPS: Choose nursery trees carefully. Look for certified trees with a large root system with lots of lateral and feeder roots, straight trunks, and leaves of a good deep green color. The graft union should be from 4 to 12 inches above the soil level, and the trunk an inch above the graft union should be ¾ to 1¼ inches in diameter. Also be sure to select a variety that is matched to your climate. Consult your USDA County Extension Agent for advice on appropriate varieties.

Newly planted trees need lots of water until they become established. In hot, dry areas you will have to water the young trees every 2 to 5 days. In wetter climates they will only need to be watered every 2 or 3 weeks.

Citrus trees can bear fruit without pollination of the flowers, so you need plant only one tree. The fruit which develops from unpollinated flowers will be seedless.

CURRANTS
Ribes sativum

WHERE TO PLANT: Full sun to partial shade, in just about any type of soil of average fertility, from sandy loam to clay, with a pH between 6.0 and 8.0. The soil should be moist but well drained.

WHEN TO PLANT: Set out nursery plants in either spring or fall.

SPACING: Set plants 5 to 6 feet apart.

PLANTING DEPTH: In light soils, plant 1 inch deeper than the plant was growing at the nursery; in heavier soils, plant at the same depth.

PROPAGATION: One-year-old plants from the nursery, hardwood cuttings from established plants, or mound-layering. To mound-layer currants, after they have started to grow in spring, cut back all the branches on a bush to 3 inches. Cover the stumps with soil; when shoots appear and have formed good roots, sever the new plants from the old bush and plant them.

PLANTING TIPS: Red currants are the best type to plant in the United States. White or yellow currants are also acceptable, although they are not generally as productive as red currants. Black currants are a host for the disease white pine blister rust, and their planting is outlawed or strictly regulated in most of the United States.

Currants are also subject to powdery mildew, which is more likely to strike when the plants are grown in partial shade. Currants have shallow roots and benefit from a covering of mulch.

FIGS
Ficus carica

WHERE TO PLANT: Full sun, in fertile sandy loam or clay loam rich in organic matter, moist but well drained, with a pH between 5.0 and 6.5. Figs are cold-sensitive and do not grow readily north of Zone 8; however, gardeners in Zones 6 and 7 can grow figs by planting in a protected location with good southern exposure. To further ensure winter survival, bank the trees with soil and cover the tops with burlap or evergreen boughs before cold sets in.

WHEN TO PLANT: Plant in winter when the plants enter their dormant period and slow their growth.

SPACING: If you are planting an orchard of figs, space them 8 to 25 feet apart, depending on the variety.

PLANTING DEPTH: Make the planting hole 3 to 4 feet deep by 3 to 4 feet wide, and enrich and lighten the soil with compost, peat moss, and sand. Set the tree 2 to 3 inches deeper than it grew in the nursery.

PROPAGATION: Nursery plants. Or take hardwood cuttings in winter or early spring from one- to three-year-old branches that are approximately

FIGS—*Continued*

PROPAGATION:
(continued)

¾ inch in diameter. The top of the cutting should be right above a node, and the bottom cut made right below a node. Cuttings can be 3 to 12 inches long. Insert the cuttings into the rooting medium so that only the top 1½ inches of each cutting are exposed. Keep the soil moist until the cuttings root, which may take several months. Then plant them in the garden or in pots.

Figs can also be propagated by budding, grafting, simple layering, or from seeds.

PLANTING TIPS:

Top-dress newly planted trees with organic sources of nitrogen, phosphorus, and potassium. Apply a 3- to 4-inch mulch of a loose organic material to conserve moisture.

All varieties of figs known as *common types* are parthenocarpic; that is, they will set fruit without a pollinator variety. *Smyrna type* and *San Pedro type* figs must be planted along with a type of wild, inedible fig called a *caprifig* to pollinate them.

FILBERTS

Corylus avellana, European filbert

WHERE TO PLANT:

Full sun in fertile, well-drained soil 8 to 10 feet deep. Filberts flourish best where the soil allows roots to penetrate to a depth of 8 to 10 feet. Trees planted in mediocre, shallow soil will decline in production as the tree matures. Filberts grow well in Zones 5 to 9, but they flourish best in the northwestern part of the United States.

WHEN TO PLANT:

Set out bare-rooted nursery trees in early spring while they are still dormant.

SPACING:

Set trees approximately 18 feet apart.

PLANTING DEPTH:

Set trees at the same depth they were growing at the nursery.

PROPAGATION:

Nursery trees.

PLANTING TIPS:

Plant two varieties to insure pollination. Select only cultivars of European filbert. American filberts (*Corylus americana*) are shrubby plants that produce small, thick-shelled nuts unsuitable for eating.

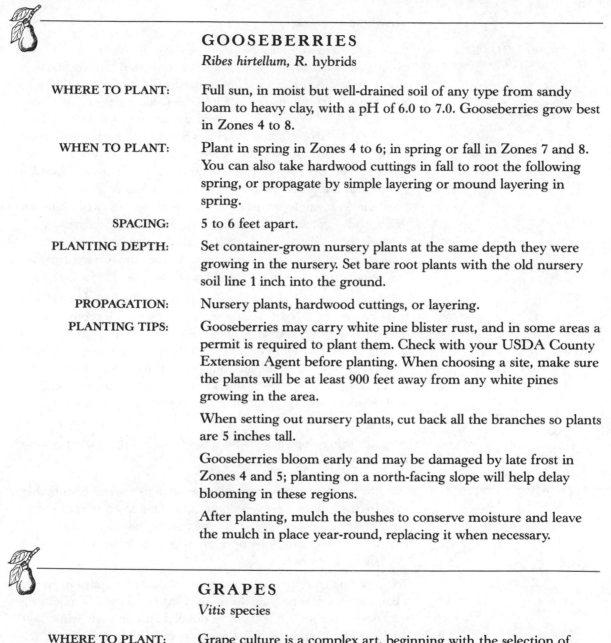

GOOSEBERRIES
Ribes hirtellum, R. hybrids

WHERE TO PLANT:	Full sun, in moist but well-drained soil of any type from sandy loam to heavy clay, with a pH of 6.0 to 7.0. Gooseberries grow best in Zones 4 to 8.
WHEN TO PLANT:	Plant in spring in Zones 4 to 6; in spring or fall in Zones 7 and 8. You can also take hardwood cuttings in fall to root the following spring, or propagate by simple layering or mound layering in spring.
SPACING:	5 to 6 feet apart.
PLANTING DEPTH:	Set container-grown nursery plants at the same depth they were growing in the nursery. Set bare root plants with the old nursery soil line 1 inch into the ground.
PROPAGATION:	Nursery plants, hardwood cuttings, or layering.
PLANTING TIPS:	Gooseberries may carry white pine blister rust, and in some areas a permit is required to plant them. Check with your USDA County Extension Agent before planting. When choosing a site, make sure the plants will be at least 900 feet away from any white pines growing in the area.

When setting out nursery plants, cut back all the branches so plants are 5 inches tall.

Gooseberries bloom early and may be damaged by late frost in Zones 4 and 5; planting on a north-facing slope will help delay blooming in these regions.

After planting, mulch the bushes to conserve moisture and leave the mulch in place year-round, replacing it when necessary.

GRAPES
Vitis species

WHERE TO PLANT:	Grape culture is a complex art, beginning with the selection of varieties. Depending on where you live, and whether you want to grow grapes for eating out of hand or for wine making, there are different types from which to choose.

GRAPES—*Continued*

WHERE TO PLANT:
(continued)

Eastern or *American table* grapes have seeds, are delicious for eating, and will grow well all over the continental United States. *American seedless* grapes are not as hardy as the table grapes, but many varieties grow in Zones 5 to 8. *Muscadine* grapes thrive in Zones 7 to 9, where winter temperatures do not drop below 5° F. *French hybrid wine* grapes are crosses between French wine varieties and native American species. They are hardier and more disease-resistant than the French varieties, and are grown from Zones 5 to 8. *Viniferas* are primarily wine grapes and are difficult to grow. Most viniferas are found in the California wine country, although they are also grown in Maryland, New York, and Pennsylvania. 'Thompson Seedless'—the familiar green grape found in super-markets—also belongs to this group. All varieties are self-fruitful and require no cross-pollination to set fruit.

All grapes need full sun and very well-drained soil, with a pH between 6.0 and 7.0. In rich, loamy soils grapes will produce lush, beautiful vines with large crops of fruit that may tend to be tart or lacking in flavor. In lighter, sandier soils the vines will be smaller and the harvest less abundant, but the fruit will be sweeter and will mature sooner. The type of soil affects the sugar content and flavor of the fruit. The most important soil requirement is excellent drainage.

A south-facing slope is ideal for grapes—they appreciate protection from northwesterly winds.

WHEN TO PLANT:

Plant in late winter or early spring, as soon as the soil is workable. Prepare the soil the previous autumn, digging in compost, rock phosphate, and greensand or granite dust. In warm climates plant in fall. Grapevines must be dormant when you plant them or their buds may be injured.

To propagate from mature vines take hardwood cuttings in late fall when the plants have gone dormant. Cuttings should be about the thickness of a pencil. Tie them in bundles and, in early winter, set them upside down in trenches and cover with 3 inches of soil. In spring, plant the cuttings right side up in soil that is loose but gently tamped around the cuttings.

Grapes can also be propagated by bud cuttings consisting of one bud and part of the stem. Collect budsticks in November. Cut the sticks into single-bud pieces, cutting about ½ inch above and ½ inch below each bud. Split the stem lengthwise through the center. Press the cuttings gently into a moist rooting medium and cover with builder's sand until the buds are just showing. To prevent disease, spread a 1-inch-deep layer of sphagnum moss on top of the sand. Cover the container with a piece of glass and set it in a basement or cool greenhouse for 6 to 8 weeks to form callus. Then move the container to a warmer place to allow roots to form.

To propagate by simple layering during the growing season, choose a healthy, vigorous cane and bend it to the ground, covering it with 3 inches of soil and leaving three buds exposed at the tip. When roots have formed in a few months, sever the new plant and replant it.

Tender grape varieties such as viniferas are often grafted onto hardy rootstocks. The best time to graft is in late winter while plants are still dormant. A cleft graft usually works best.

SPACING: Set nursery plants approximately 8 feet apart in rows 6 feet apart. Muscadines, which grow vigorously, should be spaced 12 to 20 feet apart in rows 9 to 10 feet apart. Plant cuttings 6 inches apart to form roots.

PLANTING DEPTH: Set plants so that the lowest bud on the main stem is even with the soil surface. Plant cuttings deep enough so that only the top bud is exposed.

PROPAGATION: Grapes will not grow true from seeds. They must be propagated by cuttings, layering, or grafting. One-year-old plants from a local nursery are most likely to do well in your area. The vines should be approximately 14 inches long. You can also order bare-rooted plants by mail. Or take hardwood cuttings from established vines.

PLANTING TIPS: Trim roots of nursery plants back to 6 inches before planting, and cut off any broken or damaged roots. Spread out the lowest group of roots in the bottom of the planting hole, and make sure that the lowest bud on the trunk is at soil level.

Press soil around and over the lowest roots, then spread out the upper roots and cover them with soil. Water well to settle the soil around the roots, then fill the rest of the hole with soil and water again.

Cut off all but the two or three strongest stems, and prune those back so that each has two to four buds.

HARDY KIWI
Actinidia arguta

WHERE TO PLANT: Full sun, in light, well-drained loam or sandy loam, with a pH of 6.0 to 7.0. The hardy kiwi is a vine that produces fruit that is smaller than the fuzzy tropical variety sold in supermarkets, but it can be grown from Zones 3 to 9. Avoid areas prone to late frost as new growth is easily damaged by unseasonable cold.

WHEN TO PLANT: Set out bare-rooted plants in early spring while they are still dormant.

SPACING: Set vines 10 feet apart and train them on an arbor or trellis.

PLANTING DEPTH: Set plants at the same depth they were growing in the nursery.

PROPAGATION: Plants from a nursery. Kiwis can also be propagated by grafting, budding, and by hardwood or softwood cuttings.

PLANTING TIPS: Kiwis are dioecious, that is, a vine will produce either all-male or all-female flowers. To produce fruit, both male and female vines are needed. Vines do not begin to flower or set fruit until they are four to seven years old.

MELONS
Cucumis melo, Cantaloupe, Muskmelon, Honeydew
Citrullus lanatus, Watermelon

WHERE TO PLANT: Full sun, in light, loose, sandy, or loamy soil that is fertile and rich in organic matter. Cantaloupes, muskmelons, and honeydews prefer a pH between 6.0 and 8.0; watermelons prefer a pH of 5.5 to 6.5. Melons need good air circulation to minimize the risk of disease.

WHEN TO PLANT: Direct-seed in late spring, when the soil temperature is at least 50° F and the weather is warm. Melons need a long, warm growing season. Although melons do not transplant well, gardeners in the North can get a jump on the season by starting seeds indoors in peat pots 2 to 4 weeks before the soil is warm enough to plant outdoors. Transplant carefully, planting pots and all to minimize disturbance.

SPACING:
: Start plants 2 to 4 feet apart in rows 6 feet apart, or in hills 3 to 5 feet apart. Plant five or six seeds to a hill, later thinning to the two or three strongest seedlings. Compact and bush varieties can be planted closer together.

PLANTING DEPTH:
: Sow seeds ½ inch deep.

PROPAGATION:
: Direct-seeding.

PLANTING TIPS:
: Melons are heavy feeders and require plenty of organic matter. They also require a warm soil. Gardeners in the coldest zones will have greater success by keeping a melon patch mulched with black plastic to warm the soil. Lack of boron will cause melons to produce flavorless fruits. Supply boron by working granite dust into the soil.

PEACHES AND NECTARINES
Prunus persica

WHERE TO PLANT:
: Full sun, in moist but well-drained loamy soil that is loose to a depth of at least 12 inches and has a pH between 6.0 and 8.0.

In cold climates where the weather warms slowly in spring, planting peaches and nectarines on a south-facing slope will encourage them to bloom early and enjoy a longer growing season. In climates where spring brings alternating periods of warm and cold weather, peach blossoms can be damaged by a late cold snap. A north-facing slope would delay blooming but might expose the trees to too much cold in winter. In such locations an eastern or western exposure is probably best. Plant only in areas with very good drainage. Soggy soil causes accumulation of cyanide around tree roots and almost certain decline of the tree. Peaches and nectarines will grow in Zones 5 to 8, but nectarines do not do well in hot, humid summer weather.

WHEN TO PLANT:
: In most gardens, peaches and nectarines are best planted in very early spring when trees are still dormant. In the southern reaches of the growing range, plant in fall.

SPACING:
: Plant standard-size trees 20 to 25 feet apart in all directions, dwarf trees 10 to 12 feet apart. Genetic dwarf trees can be grown in large tubs 2 to 2½ feet in diameter or planted 6 feet apart in the garden.

PEACHES & NECTARINES—*Continued*

PLANTING DEPTH: Set trees at the same depth they were growing at the nursery. Peach trees have shallow root systems and should be positioned so that upper roots are only 1 to 2 inches below the soil surface.

PROPAGATION: One-year-old trees from a nursery or garden center. The trees should be about 4 or 5 feet tall, with branches ½ inch in diameter. Peaches are commercially propagated by budding onto special nematode-resistant peach rootstock. If you would like to bud your own trees, consult your local Extension Agent for the names of rootstocks that do well in your area.

PLANTING TIPS: At planting time prune back the leader of each tree to 2 or 2½ feet to encourage branching, and trim off any dead or broken branches. Peach trees are self-fruitful. You will get plenty of fruit from only one tree. Train the trees to an open-center form. Peaches are graft products; be sure to select a variety *and* rootstock suitable for your hardiness zone.

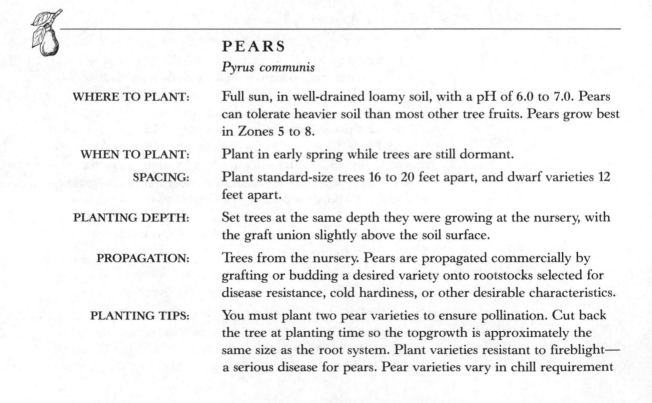

PEARS
Pyrus communis

WHERE TO PLANT: Full sun, in well-drained loamy soil, with a pH of 6.0 to 7.0. Pears can tolerate heavier soil than most other tree fruits. Pears grow best in Zones 5 to 8.

WHEN TO PLANT: Plant in early spring while trees are still dormant.

SPACING: Plant standard-size trees 16 to 20 feet apart, and dwarf varieties 12 feet apart.

PLANTING DEPTH: Set trees at the same depth they were growing at the nursery, with the graft union slightly above the soil surface.

PROPAGATION: Trees from the nursery. Pears are propagated commercially by grafting or budding a desired variety onto rootstocks selected for disease resistance, cold hardiness, or other desirable characteristics.

PLANTING TIPS: You must plant two pear varieties to ensure pollination. Cut back the tree at planting time so the topgrowth is approximately the same size as the root system. Plant varieties resistant to fireblight— a serious disease for pears. Pear varieties vary in chill requirement (number of hours below 45° F needed to set fruit) and in the type of rootstock used to support the tree. Consult your local Extension Agent for the names of varieties and rootstocks that do best in your area.

PECANS
Carya illinoinensis

WHERE TO PLANT:	Full sun, in deep, sandy, well-drained soil. Pecans have a long taproot and require at least 18 inches of topsoil. Pecans thrive primarily in the southeastern portion of the United States, from Zones 7 to 9.
WHEN TO PLANT:	Plant bare-rooted trees in early spring while they are still dormant.
SPACING:	Pecan trees are large; plant them 40 feet apart.
PLANTING DEPTH:	Set trees at the same depth they were growing in the nursery.
PROPAGATION:	Pecan cultivars are budded or grafted onto selected pecan rootstocks. For best results buy named cultivars from a nursery.
PLANTING TIPS:	Pecans cannot tolerate a poorly drained site because wet soil prevents development of the huge taproot necessary to support a mature tree. Pecans will set nuts both with and without cross-pollination. Trees that are cross-pollinated tend to produce superior nuts.

PERSIMMONS
Diospyros virginiana and *D. kaki*

WHERE TO PLANT:	Full sun, in well-drained soil of average fertility, with a pH between 6.0 and 7.0. American persimmons (*D. virginiana*) grow well in Zones 4 to 8. Japanese persimmons (*D.kaki*) grow best in Zones 8 to 10.
WHEN TO PLANT:	Set out bare-rooted nursery trees in early spring while they are still dormant.
SPACING:	Set trees 15 to 20 feet apart.
PLANTING DEPTH:	Plant trees at the same depth they were growing in the nursery.

PERSIMMONS—*Continued*

PROPAGATION:

Nursery trees of named varieties ensure the best fruit. American persimmons can be grown from seed. Plant seeds in fall when the fruit ripens or store them in a plastic bag in the refrigerator over winter and plant out the following spring. If you plant seeds from a wild tree whose fruit is not of good quality, you can graft a better variety onto the seedling after it is a year or two old. Graft when the tree has begun to leaf out in spring. Use a splice graft.

Japanese persimmons are propagated by grafting *D. kaki* varieties onto *D. virginiana* rootstocks.

PLANTING TIPS:

Persimmons are easy to grow and require little maintenance.

If you plant seeds, plant them where you want the trees to grow. Persimmons have a long taproot that makes seedlings difficult to transplant. Some varieties of persimmon are parthenocarpic, setting fruit without seeds and pollination. Other varieties require cross-pollination to set fruit.

PLUMS
Prunus species, American plums
P. domestica, European plum
P. salicina, Japanese plum

WHERE TO PLANT:

Full sun, in any deeply dug, well-drained soil, with a pH between 6.0 and 7.0. Plums can tolerate heavier soils than many other tree fruits. Native American species do best in soils similar to those where they grow wild; the beach plum (*P. maritima*), for example, grows well in sandy soils. American plums are hardiest, growing well in Zones 4 to 7. European plums grow well in Zones 5 to 8, and Japanese plums in Zones 5 to 9.

WHEN TO PLANT:

Set out bare-rooted nursery trees in early spring while they are still dormant.

SPACING:

Plant native American plums 10 to 14 feet apart, named American cultivars and European plums 18 to 24 feet apart, and Japanese plums 14 to 16 feet apart. Dwarf varieties can be spaced 10 to 12 feet apart.

PLANTING DEPTH:	Set trees at the same depth they were growing in the nursery.
PROPAGATION:	Nursery trees grafted onto selected rootstocks. Plums do not come true from seed. They are propagated by budding onto selected rootstocks. If you would like to bud your own trees, consult your local Extension Agent for varieties and rootstocks appropriate to your area.
PLANTING TIPS:	Plant two varieties of Japanese plums to ensure pollination. Most American plums and some European varieties are self-fruitful. Read nursery catalogs carefully to determine the pollination needs of the varieties you want to plant. Prune European plums to develop a modified central leader form; prune Japanese plums to an open-center shape. Most native American species grow as large bushes rather than trees. Keep newly planted trees well weeded and make sure they get plenty of moisture.

RASPBERRIES
Rubus idaeus, Red raspberry, Yellow raspberry
R. occidentalis, Eastern black raspberry
R. leucodermis, Western black raspberry

WHERE TO PLANT:	Full sun to partial shade in well-drained soil of average fertility. The ideal pH is around 6.0, but raspberries tolerate a pH range of 5.5 to 7.0. Depending on the variety, raspberries grow well in Zones 4 to 8.
WHEN TO PLANT:	Set out bare-rooted nursery plants in spring. Red and yellow raspberries produce lots of suckers, which you can dig up and plant during the growing season when they have developed roots. The canes of black raspberries bend to the ground in fall, and their tips root; the new plants that form can be dug up and transplanted the following spring.
SPACING:	Space plants 2 to 3 feet apart in rows 6 to 7 feet apart.
PLANTING DEPTH:	Set bare-rooted nursery plants so the crowns are just below the soil surface. Transplant suckers to the same depth they were growing previously.
PROPAGATION:	Nursery plants or suckers. Raspberries are also easily propagated by tip layering, division, root cuttings, and hardwood cuttings.

RASPBERRIES—*Continued*

PLANTING TIPS:

Raspberries are usually trained on trellises or wires, although you can also plant them in small clumps or in hedgerows.

Raspberries are prone to viral and fungal diseases, so start with nursery stock that is certified virus-free.

Nursery plants come in the form of crowns with a piece of cane growing on them. After planting, when new shoots pop through the soil surface, cut off the old cane and burn it to prevent spread of viral or fungal diseases. Raspberries generally bear fruit on one-year-old canes. Remove and burn old canes immediately after harvest.

STRAWBERRIES
Fragaria species

WHERE TO PLANT:

Full sun, in light, moist but well-drained soil of average fertility but containing lots of organic matter, with a pH around 6.0. Strawberries tolerate a range of soils except for heavy soils with poor drainage. They grow well in Zones 4 to 8. Strawberries prefer a raised bed or raised row system because they do poorly where soil is compacted.

WHEN TO PLANT:

In spring, in cool and temperate climates (Zones 4 to 6 or 7), to bear a crop the following spring. In warm climates (Zone 8 and protected parts of Zone 7), plant in fall for fruit the following spring.

SPACING:

Set plants 18 to 24 inches apart in rows 4 to 5 feet apart. Allow runners to fill in around the rows so that each row is about 30 inches wide and 18 to 30 inches remain between rows. Spaced this way, twenty-five plants will fill about 38 feet of row.

Or use a matted-row system, setting plants 18 inches apart in all directions and allowing runners to fill in between them. In the matted row system, twenty-five plants will fill an area about 10 by 14 feet.

Alpine strawberries do not produce runners and can be planted closer together.

PLANTING DEPTH:	Set plants so that the crown is right at the soil surface, neither above nor below it.
PROPAGATION:	Nursery plants. Strawberries can also be propagated by simple layering. Established strawberry beds are easily rejuvenated by rooting young plants that emerge on runners sent out by mother plants. These baby plants root quite easily if they are pinned down to contact loose soil.
PLANTING TIPS:	There are many strawberry varieties adapted to different parts of the country—read nursery catalogs carefully to select one that will work in your garden. June-bearing varieties bear a heavy crop in early summer when days are long. Everbearing strawberries produce a somewhat smaller crop in early summer and bear a second crop later in the season. Some newer varieties described as day-neutral produce a heavier crop than everbearers, and continue to bloom and bear fruit throughout the rest of summer. Alpine strawberries have small but intensely flavorful berries; the compact plants make nice edgings for gardens and flower beds, and can be grown in containers, too.

When planting strawberries, soak the plants in a bucket of water so the roots don't dry out. Make a small cone of soil in the bottom of each planting hole and gently spread the roots over it. If the roots are long and thick, trim them back to 5 inches before planting. Examine the roots before planting; healthy roots are cream-colored to brown, while wiry black roots are indicative of an old, less than top-quality plant.

Most gardeners remove one-year-old plants in the fall. New plants propagated along runners during the past season will be the prime fruit bearers next season.

WALNUTS

Juglans regia, English walnut or Persian walnut
J. nigra, Black walnut

WHERE TO PLANT:	Full sun. English walnuts produce the best crops in deep, fertile, moist but well-drained soils of medium-heavy texture. Good drainage is essential. English walnuts grow in Zones 5 to 9, but they do not grow well along the Gulf Coast. Black walnuts are

WALNUTS—*Continued*

WHERE TO PLANT:
(continued)

tolerant of a range of soils, but their roots produce a substance (juglone) that is toxic to many other plants and interferes with their growth. Do not plant black walnuts within 100 feet of your garden. Black walnuts are native trees found primarily in the northeastern part of the U.S., and are hardy to Zone 4. They do not thrive south of Zone 8.

WHEN TO PLANT:

In cool and temperate climates (Zones 4 to 7), plant bare-rooted trees in early spring while they are still dormant. In warm climates (Zones 8 and 9), plant in fall.

SPACING:

Trees need to be at least 50 feet apart; some experts recommend 60- to 70-foot spacing.

PLANTING DEPTH:

Set plants at the same depth they were growing in the nursery.

PROPAGATION:

English walnuts do not come true from seed. They are propagated by budding and grafting. Buy nursery trees if you want to grow English walnuts. Wild black walnuts tend to pop up wherever the nuts fall—the volunteer trees can become something of a nuisance. Named cultivars of black walnuts produce nuts with thinner shells and more kernel. These cultivars are propagated by budding and grafting. Buy nursery trees if you want a black walnut cultivar.

PLANTING TIPS:

English walnuts are difficult to grow, and it is important to choose the right variety for your location. You will need to plant two trees to insure good pollination.

Black walnuts need little care once they are established; the trees are tenacious and hardy.

Trees & Shrubs

ABELIA

A. × *grandiflora*, Glossy abelia

WHERE TO PLANT: Full sun to partial shade, in moist but well-drained soil of average fertility, with a pH of 5.5 to 6.5. Hardy from Zones 5 to 9, but grows best from Zone 6 south.

WHEN TO PLANT: Set out balled-and-burlapped or container-grown plants in spring or fall.

HEIGHT AND SPREAD: Shrubs grow 3 to 6 feet tall and 3 to 6 feet across.

PROPAGATION: Softwood cuttings. Take softwood cuttings from summer through fall. You may also start abelia from seeds. Sow seeds as soon as they ripen or store them in an airtight container in a cool place for up to 1 year.

PLANTING TIPS: A shrub with glossy evergreen leaves and pink, bell-shaped flowers in late summer, this species can be used as a specimen plant in masses, as a hedge, or included in borders. A good plant for banks and attractive with other broad-leaved evergreens.

ABIES

A. species, Fir

WHERE TO PLANT:	Firs grow best in cool, moist climates (coastal areas, for example); they do not do well in hot, dry climates. Plant in moist, acidic, but well-drained soil, with a pH of 5.5 to 6.5. Full sun is best, but firs tolerate partial shade. Hardiness varies with species; most are hardy between Zones 3 and 7.
WHEN TO PLANT:	Plant balled-and-burlapped or container-grown plants in spring.
HEIGHT AND SPREAD:	From 30 to 100 feet tall and 15 to 30 feet wide, depending on species.
PROPAGATION:	Seeds or nursery plants. Seeds of different species vary in their dormancy requirements. Seeds should be stratified in a moist medium at about 40° F for 2 to 5 weeks before sowing. Stratification can begin as soon as the seeds ripen, or they can be stored up to a year in an airtight container in a cool, dry place.
	Firs can also be grafted, using another fir species as the understock. Terminal shoots make the best scions, and a side graft is generally used. Most cultivars are grafted.
PLANTING TIPS:	Firs are stately, upright evergreen trees. They are pyramidal or cone-shaped and work best as specimen trees in large landscapes.
	A north-facing slope is an ideal place to plant firs.
	Seedlings need protection from strong sunlight.

ACER

A. griseum, Paperbark maple
A. palmatum, Japanese maple
A. platanoides, Norway maple
A. saccharum, Sugar maple

WHERE TO PLANT:	Full sun to partial shade. Maples grow best in fertile, moist but well-drained soil, but tolerate a range of soils. Paperbark maple (*A. griseum*) can grow in clay soils, and Norway maple (*A. platanoides*) can tolerate sandy or clay soils and hot, dry conditions.

Most maples tolerate a wide pH range; however, Japanese maples (*A. palmatum*) prefer a pH in the acid range.

Japanese maples are best planted under other, taller trees, because their delicate leaves can burn in strong sunlight. Norway maples must be planted far away (200 feet or more) from garden beds and borders because their shallow roots spread far and compete for moisture with those of less tenacious plants.

Hardiness varies with species: paperbark maple is hardy from Zones 4 to 8, but is happiest in northern gardens; Japanese maple thrives in Zones 5 or 6 to 8 or 9 depending on the cultivar; Norway maple is hardy from Zones 3 to 7; and sugar maple from Zones 3 to 8.

WHEN TO PLANT: Set out bare-rooted plants in early spring, balled-and-burlapped or container-grown plants a bit later in spring.

HEIGHT AND SPREAD: Paperback maples grow 20 to 30 feet tall by 10 to 30 feet wide; Japanese maples grow 15 to 25 feet tall and as wide as they are high; Norway maples reach 40 to 50 feet high by 25 to 50 feet wide, and sugar maples grow to 100 feet in the wild, but reach 60 to 70 feet in most gardens, with a spread of 40 to 45 feet.

PROPAGATION: For paperbark maple, take cuttings from seedlings in May or June; it is difficult to grow paperbark maple from seed. For the other species, take softwood cuttings from mature trees or start from seeds. Take softwood cuttings from Japanese maples in July, or collect seeds when they are green or red but before they dry, and plant right away for germination next spring. Take softwood cuttings from Norway maple in June, or collect ripe seeds and stratify them for 3 to 4 months in a moist medium at 41° F. Take softwood cuttings from sugar maple in early June, or collect ripe seeds and stratify them for 2 to 3 months in a moist medium at 41° F.

Softwood cuttings from maples root best if you injure the base of the cutting before planting. With a sharp knife, peel off a strip of bark about 1 inch wide, ending about ¼ inch above the base of the cutting, to expose the cambium layer. Apply rooting hormone to the stripped area, then plant the cutting in a suitable rooting medium.

Cuttings are difficult to bring through a cold winter; take them as early in the season as possible so they will be rooted and well

ACER—*Continued*

PROPAGATION:
(continued)

established by winter. Place the rooted cuttings where the temperature is just about freezing—a refrigerator will work fine if you have the space (wrap the containers in plastic so the cuttings don't dry out). Plant the cuttings outdoors in spring.

PLANTING TIPS:

Paperbark, Norway, and sugar maples are handsome specimen trees to plant on a large lawn. Norway maples tolerate polluted air and are good city plants. Sugar maples have beautiful, flaming autumn foliage. Japanese maples can be planted as specimen trees in shrub borders or in groups.

ALBIZIA

A. julibrissin, Silk tree

WHERE TO PLANT:

The silk tree grows in almost any soil and is particularly tolerant of dry, rocky soils. It can also withstand salty and very alkaline soils and holds up well in strong wind. Hardy from Zones 6 to 9. This tree is attacked by mimosa wilt disease in the South, so look for resistant varieties.

WHEN TO PLANT:

Set out plants in spring or fall.

HEIGHT AND SPREAD:

From 15 to 30 feet high and 20 to 35 feet wide.

PROPAGATION:

Root cuttings. Take root cuttings in spring; they will yield shoots that can be removed and easily rooted.

PLANTING TIPS:

The silk tree has lacy foliage and pink flowers that look like puffballs in summer. It makes a nice specimen tree for lawns and to cast shade on patios, and can also be planted in borders.

ALNUS

A. glutinosa, Black, Common, or European alder

WHERE TO PLANT:

Full sun to partial shade, in moist or even wet soil (the tree will also tolerate dry soil), with an acid or mildly alkaline pH. Alders are hardy from Zones 3 through 8.

WHEN TO PLANT:

Set out plants in spring or fall.

HEIGHT AND SPREAD:

From 40 to 60 feet high by 20 to 40 feet wide.

PROPAGATION:

Start with nursery plants. Black alder is difficult to propagate at home. Cultivars of alders are commonly grafted onto species rootstocks.

Commercial nurseries also propagate alders from seed. The germination rate of alder seeds is not very high, even for commercial nurseries. To start alders from seed, sow freshly collected ripe seeds in fall or stratify dry seeds for 3 months at 41° F before planting.

PLANTING TIPS:

Alders grow well in soil that is too wet for most other trees and shrubs. Because they transpire water at a high rate, keep newly planted trees deeply watered until they are established.

BERBERIS

B. thunbergii, Japanese barberry

WHERE TO PLANT:

Full sun to partial shade, in light, well-drained soil of average fertility. Prefers sandy or loam soils, but grows well in heavier soils, too. Hardy from Zones 4 to 8.

WHEN TO PLANT:

Set out bare-rooted plants in spring or fall.

HEIGHT AND SPREAD:

From 3 to 6 feet high by 4 to 7 feet wide.

PROPAGATION:

Softwood cuttings or seeds. Softwood cuttings can be taken in summer and root easily. Stratify seeds for 15 to 40 days in moist sand at 32 to 41° F. Sow seeds outdoors in fall. Germination occurs the following spring.

PLANTING TIPS:

Barberry is a dense, thorny, deciduous shrub. When it is grown in full sun, its foliage turns bright red in fall. Small red berries persist into winter. Plant barberries as a hedge, as a specimen plant, or in borders. Barberries are resistant to pests and diseases, adaptable to a range of conditions, and good plants for urban areas.

BETULA

B. lenta, Sweet birch
B. papyrifera, Paper birch

WHERE TO PLANT:

Full sun. Paper birch grows best in light, sandy, moist, well-drained soil of average fertility, but will also tolerate richer soil. It will not tolerate air pollution. Paper birch is hardy from Zones 2 to 6.

BETULA—*Continued*

WHERE TO PLANT:
(continued)

Sweet birch prefers deep, rich, moist but well-drained soil, but also tolerates drier, rocky soil. Sweet birch is hardy from Zones 3 to 7 or 8. A slightly acid pH is best for both.

WHEN TO PLANT:

Set out balled-and-burlapped or container-grown plants in spring or fall. Or sow freshly collected seeds of paper birch in fall for germination next spring. Germination rates for all varieties of birch seed are low—typically 20 to 30 percent germination.

HEIGHT AND SPREAD:

Paper birch grows 50 to 70 feet high by 30 to 45 feet wide. Sweet birch reaches 40 to 55 feet high by 35 to 45 feet wide.

PROPAGATION:

Buy nursery trees. Seeds may be germinated with some difficulty and uncertain results. To germinate paper birch, stratify the dried seeds for 2 to 3 months at 41° F before sowing in flats kept at 60 to 70° F. Stratify sweet birch seeds 40 to 70 days at 41° F, then germinate them in flats kept at 90° F during the day and 59° F at night.

PLANTING TIPS:

Paper birch is a lovely specimen tree, with white papery bark and bright yellow foliage in autumn. It is, however, susceptible to canker and birch leaf miner.

Sweet birch is pyramid-shaped when young, and takes on a spreading, rounded form when it matures.

BUXUS

B. sempervirens, Common boxwood

WHERE TO PLANT:

Light, well-drained soil of average fertility. The soil should not be too rich. Hardy from Zones 5 to 8 or 9 depending on the cultivar. This species grows best in moist climates without extremes of hot or cold. Plants flourish best where roots are kept cool and moist.

WHEN TO PLANT:

Set out balled-and-burlapped or container-grown plants in spring or fall.

HEIGHT AND SPREAD:

From 3 to 4 feet high up to 15 to 25 feet high and just as wide. Size depends on the cultivar. Boxwood grows slowly. A ten-year-old plant may be 3 feet high.

PLANTING DEPTH:	Boxwood is shallow-rooted, and its roots will suffocate if it is planted too deeply. However, the roots must not be exposed by soil erosion.
PROPAGATION:	Tip cuttings (they root best when cut at a node). Take cuttings in summer.
PLANTING TIPS:	A dense, slow-growing shrub with tiny, evergreen leaves, boxwood is often planted as a hedge. It responds well to clipping (shear back container-grown plants by one-quarter to one-third at planting time to avoid taxing the roots), and is an essential part of parterres and other elements of formal gardens. Boxwood can also be grown as a specimen (individually or in clumps) or planted in borders. When left unpruned, boxwood develops a round, billowy form. The leaves are aromatic, especially on hot, still days. There are dwarf cultivars.
	Mulch boxwood to keep the roots cool in summer. Shade newly transplanted shrubs from direct sun.

CALYCANTHUS

C. florida, Sweetshrub, Carolina allspice

WHERE TO PLANT:	Partial shade is best, but the plant does well in sun, too. It will grow in any reasonable garden soil, but prefers deep, moist, fertile loam. Sweetshrub tolerates a range of pH, and will grow in either acid or alkaline soil. Hardy from Zones 4 to 9.
WHEN TO PLANT:	Set out nursery plants in spring or fall.
HEIGHT AND SPREAD:	From 6 to 8 feet by 6 to 10 feet.
PROPAGATION:	Seeds or hardwood cuttings. Take hardwood cuttings in July. Collect seeds when they change from green to brown in color (usually in August), break the seed coat, and plant outdoors immediately. Sweetshrub can also be propagated from suckers, by layering, or by division.
PLANTING TIPS:	Sweetshrub is wonderful planted near patios, where its sweet scent can be enjoyed. You can also plant it as a specimen in the lawn or in a shrub border.

CAMELLIA

C. japonica, Common camellia

WHERE TO PLANT:	Partial shade, in fairly light, moist but well-drained soil rich in organic matter, with an acid pH. Camellias are generally hardy only between Zones 7 and 9, but have been know to survive in Zone 6 in protected locations.
	Light is important. Both full sun and deep shade cause loss of flowering.
WHEN TO PLANT:	Set out container-grown plants in spring or fall.
HEIGHT AND SPREAD:	Smaller cultivars grow 4 to 6 feet high; larger cultivars grow 10 to 15 feet high by 6 to 10 feet wide.
PROPAGATION:	Cuttings taken right below the fifth node, or seeds. From May to September, take softwood cuttings of the current season's growth. Sow seed as soon as it ripens in late summer or early autumn, or store and sow the following spring. Soak and scarify dried seeds before planting.
	Camellias can also be air-layered or grafted. Use a cleft graft for large plants, and whip and tongue or splice graft for smaller plants.
PLANTING TIPS:	Broad-leaved evergreen shrubs with glossy deep green leaves, camellias are prized by southern gardeners for their large flowers in white and shades of red and pink. Grow them as specimen plants, espaliered against a wall or on a fence, or in groups.
	Mulch to keep the roots cool in summer.

CARPINUS

C. betulus, European hornbeam
C. caroliniana, American hornbeam

WHERE TO PLANT:	European hornbeam prefers full sun, but will also accept partial shade; American hornbeam grows best in partial shade and will tolerate heavy shade. European hornbeam tolerates many soils, from light to heavy, acid or alkaline, as long as they are well drained. American hornbeam prefers deep, fertile, moist but well-drained soil (although it will tolerate drier soil) with a slightly acid

pH. European hornbeam is hardy from Zones 4 to 7, and American hornbeam from Zones 2 to 9.

WHEN TO PLANT: Set out balled-and-burlapped or container-grown plants in spring.

HEIGHT AND SPREAD: European hornbeam grows 40 to 60 feet high by 30 to 40 feet wide. American hornbeam grows 20 to 30 feet high and as wide.

PROPAGATION: For European hornbeam, cuttings 6 to 8 inches long, or seeds. Take cuttings of European hornbeam when all the tree's leaves have reached full size (usually in July). After the cuttings have rooted, they need a cold dormant period; put them where the temperature can be maintained at 32° F all winter, and plant them out the following March or April. Collect seeds of European hornbeam when the wings turn yellow but before they dry out. Stratify them for 4 weeks at 68° F, then for about 3 months at 41° F before planting.

For American hornbeam, seeds. Collect seeds in early September; stratify them for 2 months at temperatures from 68 to 85° F, then for 2 more months at 41° F.

PLANTING TIPS: Hornbeams can be planted singly on a lawn or near buildings, in groups, or as a screen.

CASTANEA

C. mollissima, Chinese chestnut

WHERE TO PLANT: Full sun, in well-drained, loamy soil, with a pH of 5.5 to 6.5. Chinese chestnut will tolerate a hot, dry climate but not poorly drained soil. Hardy from Zones 4 to 8.

WHEN TO PLANT: Plant container-grown or balled-and-burlapped trees in spring or fall. Plant seeds in fall, as soon as they mature; the seeds do not keep well and must not be allowed to dry out.

HEIGHT AND SPREAD: From 40 to 60 feet tall and as wide.

PROPAGATION: Seeds, or take cuttings from young trees. Stratify seeds in cool, moist conditions for 60 to 90 days before planting.

PLANTING TIPS: Plant this tree as a substitute for American chestnut. The nuts are fine fare, and the tree is resistant to the chestnut blight that attacks American chestnut trees.

CATALPA
C. speciosa, Northern catalpa

WHERE TO PLANT:	Full sun to partial shade; prefers deep, fertile, moist soil, but will tolerate dry soils. Grows well in acid or alkaline soil. Hardy from Zones 4 to 8.
WHEN TO PLANT:	Set out balled-and-burlapped plants in spring or fall.
HEIGHT AND SPREAD:	From 40 to 60 feet high by 20 to 40 feet wide.
PROPAGATION:	Seeds or root cuttings. Collect and sow seeds as soon as they ripen. Take root cuttings in December.
PLANTING TIPS:	Catalpa looks best when planted on a large expanse of lawn; it is not a tree for small spaces. It grows quickly but tends to be rather short-lived.

CEDRUS
C. atlantica, Atlas cedar
C. deodara, Deodar
C. libani, Cedar of Lebanon

WHERE TO PLANT:	Give Atlas cedar full sun or partial shade, cedar of Lebanon and deodar full sun. Atlas cedar prefers deep, moist but well-drained, loamy soil, but will tolerate sandy soil or even clay if it is well drained. Deodar and cedar of Lebanon prefer well-drained loamy soil a little on the dry side. Cedars prefer an acid pH but will also tolerate alkaline soil. Atlas cedar and deodar are hardy from Zones 6 to 9; cedar of Lebanon from Zones 5 to 7.
WHEN TO PLANT:	Set out container-grown plants in spring or fall. Both cedar of Lebanon and Atlas cedar are difficult to transplant—purchase only container-grown plants to minimize transplant shock.
HEIGHT AND SPREAD:	*C. atlantica* and *C. libani* grow to about 40 to 60 feet by 30 to 40 feet; *C. deodara* is somewhat larger.
PROPAGATION:	Seeds. Collect and sow seeds when they ripen in fall. They require no pretreatment, but you can stratify them for 2 weeks at about 40° F to promote consistent germination.

PLANTING TIPS:	The regal cedars work best as specimen plants standing alone in an expanse of lawn.
	Cedar of Lebanon grows best in a dry climate and does not thrive in polluted air.

CERCIS

C. canadensis, Eastern redbud

WHERE TO PLANT:	Full sun to partial shade, prefers deep, moist but well-drained sandy soil, but will tolerate most soils except for soggy and waterlogged conditions. Tolerates a range of pH from acid to alkaline. Hardy from Zones 4 to 9.
WHEN TO PLANT:	Set out bare-rooted plants in early spring or fall, balled-and-burlapped plants in spring or fall.
HEIGHT AND SPREAD:	From 20 to 30 feet high by 25 to 35 feet wide.
PROPAGATION:	Cuttings. Take softwood cuttings in June or July. Place them in moist sand, where temperatures are around 72° F, and they will root in about a month.
	Cuttings work best when started indoors under lights or in a greenhouse. Redbud can also be propagated by layering.
PLANTING TIPS:	Redbud is a lovely tree for home landscapes, with beautiful pink flowers in spring. Especially attractive in woodland and naturalistic gardens, redbud is also nice as a specimen, in groups, or planted in a shrub border. It is a beautiful companion to flowering dogwoods.

CHAENOMELES

C. speciosa, Flowering quince

WHERE TO PLANT:	Blooms best in full sun but also grows well in partial shade. Adapts to a range of soils, even dry ones, and tolerates a range of pH, although the leaves may turn yellow in extremely alkaline soils. Hardy in Zones 4 to 8.
WHEN TO PLANT:	Set out balled-and-burlapped plants in spring or fall.
HEIGHT AND SPREAD:	From 6 to 10 feet tall and as wide.

CHAENOMELES—*Continued*

PROPAGATION:
Cuttings or mound layering. Mound-layer in spring. Take softwood cuttings in August. Dip cuttings in rooting hormone, and root them in a mist chamber or mist them several times daily. You may also perform simple layering in summer. Or take root cuttings or hardwood cuttings in late autumn. Propagation with seeds is unreliable.

PLANTING TIPS:
This shrub is most valuable for its red or pink flowers, which appear in spring. Plant it in borders, as a hedge, or as a specimen.

CORNUS

C. florida, Flowering dogwood
C. kousa, Chinese dogwood

WHERE TO PLANT:
Flowering dogwood is best planted in partial shade, but it also tolerates full sun. *C. kousa* prefers full sun. Both species like moist but well-drained soil rich in organic matter, with a pH in the acid range. *C. kousa* tolerates drought better than *C. florida*. Flowering dogwood is hardy from Zones 5 to 9; *C. kousa* in Zones 5 to 8.

WHEN TO PLANT:
Set out balled-and-burlapped or container-grown plants in spring or fall.

HEIGHT AND SPREAD:
Flowering dogwood reaches 20 to 40 feet and is usually wider than its height; *C. kousa* grows 20 to 30 feet tall and as wide.

PROPAGATION:
Cuttings. Take softwood cuttings as soon as the trees finish blooming; root in damp sand under mist. They should root in about 3 weeks. Take hardwood cuttings in fall. For best results with cuttings, allow newly rooted cuttings to remain undisturbed through one dormancy period. Repot after spring growth begins. Chinese dogwood is a little harder to root than flowering dogwood.

Cuttings taken from pink dogwoods need a dormant period when they have rooted. Root them as early as possible so they will be well established by winter. Wrap the flat of cuttings in plastic and place it in the refrigerator to winter over. Plant the cuttings outdoors in spring, when new growth begins.

PLANTING TIPS:
Dogwoods are most beautiful as specimen trees. Plant them within view of the house.

If you plant flowering dogwood, make sure the nursery stock comes from your part of the country; trees from the South may not survive winters in the North.

Flowering dogwoods are currently at risk from a fungus disease that threatens to decimate them just as Dutch elm disease destroyed so many of America's elm trees. Until disease-resistant hybrids are developed, plant *C. kousa*, which is resistant to the fungus.

CORYLOPSIS

C. glabrescens, Winter hazel

WHERE TO PLANT:	Full sun to partial shade, in moist but well-drained soil rich in organic matter, with a pH in the acid range. Does not like heavy soil. Plant in a sheltered location and away from frost pockets. Hardy from Zones 5 to 8.
WHEN TO PLANT:	Set out balled-and-burlapped plants in spring or fall.
HEIGHT AND SPREAD:	From 8 to 15 feet tall and as wide.
PROPAGATION:	Softwood cuttings. Take softwood cuttings with a heel in summer and root them indoors or in a greenhouse. Allow newly rooted cuttings to go through one dormancy cycle; transplant when new growth begins.
PLANTING TIPS:	Winter hazel is pretty as a specimen plant or in a shrub border. A background of evergreens beautifully sets off its yellow flowers.

The plant blooms in late winter (January to March, depending upon the climate), and its flowers may be damaged in northern gardens when winter thaws (which bring them into bloom) are followed by a return of freezing temperatures. If late winter and early spring tend to bring fluctuating temperatures in your area, plant winter hazel in a sheltered spot.

COTINUS

C. coggygria, Smokebush

WHERE TO PLANT:	Prefers full sun but will grow in partial shade. The ideal soil is a moist, well-drained loam, but smokebush tolerates many types of soils, even dry, rocky ones. It is not fussy in regard to pH, and is hardy from Zones 4 or 5 to 8.

COTINUS—*Continued*

WHEN TO PLANT:	Smokebush is easy to transplant; set out nursery plants in spring or fall.
HEIGHT AND SPREAD:	From 10 to 15 feet tall and as wide.
PROPAGATION:	Nursery plants. Seeds need scarification and are difficult to germinate at home, and cuttings do not root easily.
PLANTING TIPS:	This plant is noted for its summer flowers, which have long pinkish hairs that give them a fluffy appearance—like puffs of smoke. Smokebush looks best when planted in groups on the lawn or in a shrub border.

COTONEASTER
C. horizontalis, Rock cotoneaster
C. lucidus, Hedge cotoneaster

WHERE TO PLANT:	*C. horizontalis* grows best in full sun; *C. lucidus* is fine in either full sun or partial shade. Both species thrive in well-drained soil of average fertility and adapt to a range of pH, although they seem to prefer slightly alkaline soils. *C. lucidus* likes a slightly richer soil, but will also tolerate dry soil and seashore conditions. *C. horizontalis* is hardy from Zones 4 to 7, and *C. lucidus* from Zones 3 to 7. *C. horizontalis* needs good air circulation.
WHEN TO PLANT:	Set out container-grown or balled-and-burlapped plants in spring.
HEIGHT AND SPREAD:	Rock cotoneaster grows 2 to 3 feet tall and 5 to 8 feet wide; hedge cotoneaster reaches 10 to 15 feet tall and 6 to 10 feet wide.
PROPAGATION:	Softwood cuttings. Take softwood cuttings of *C. horizontalis* anytime in summer; early July is the best time to take cuttings of *C. lucidus*. The best softwood cuttings are tip cuttings severed right at a node. They root best with bottom heat. Low-growing young shoots can be layered in late summer (simple layering). Seeds are difficult to germinate.
PLANTING TIPS:	Rock cotoneaster is a low, spreading plant good for covering bare patches in sunny borders, and can be planted in rock gardens. Hedge cotoneaster is useful in shrub borders and as a hedge.

Once established, cotoneasters don't like to be moved.

Cotoneasters are quite susceptible to fire blight, which is almost impossible to cure. To reduce the incidence of this disease, plant in sunny, dry locations with excellent air circulation.

CRATAEGUS
C. species, Hawthorn

WHERE TO PLANT:
Full sun, in any well-drained soil of average fertility. Hawthorns tolerate either acid or alkaline pH. They are generally hardy from Zones 3 to 7.

WHEN TO PLANT:
Set out balled-and-burlapped plants in early spring.

HEIGHT AND SPREAD:
Approximately 20 to 30 feet tall by 20 to 35 feet wide.

PROPAGATION:
Grow nursery plants; hawthorns are difficult to propagate at home. Seeds collected from fruit can take as long as 2 years to sprout.

PLANTING TIPS:
Hawthorns are effective as specimen trees or planted in groups. They can also be grown as screens or, because of their long thorns, as barrier hedges. The trees can tolerate urban conditions that prove too stressful for many other trees.

DAPHNE
D. *cneorum*, Rose daphne
D. *odora*, Winter daphne

WHERE TO PLANT:
Partial shade, in moist but well-drained soil rich in organic matter, with a pH of 6.0 to 7.0. Winter daphne can tolerate more shade. Rose daphne is hardy from Zones 4 to 7; winter daphne from Zones 7 to 9.

WHEN TO PLANT:
Set out container-grown plants in early spring or early fall.

HEIGHT AND SPREAD:
Rose daphne is a low, spreading plant, growing 6 to 12 inches tall and 2 or more feet across. Winter daphne is taller, growing to 3 or more feet tall and 5 feet across.

PROPAGATION:
Softwood cuttings. Take softwood cuttings of D. *cneorum* in July or hardwood cuttings in November. Take softwood cuttings of D. *odora* in late July.

DAPHNE—*Continued*

PROPAGATION:
(continued)

Cuttings of rose daphne should root readily, but winter daphne roots more quickly when the cuttings are dipped in rooting hormone (they should produce roots in about 2 months). Daphne cuttings appear to root best in moist sand. Daphnes can also be grown from seed, which must be stratified for 3 months before sowing.

PLANTING TIPS:

These diminutive evergreen shrubs are valued for their fragrant flowers. *D. cneorum* bears its pink flowers in spring, and is a good plant for rock gardens, or for use as a ground cover. *D. odora* opens its pinkish purple blossoms in February or March.

Mulch daphnes in summer to keep the roots moist. A winter mulch will help protect the plants from damaging winter winds.

DEUTZIA

D. gracilis, Slender deutzia

WHERE TO PLANT:

Full sun to partial shade, in any reasonably fertile garden soil. Slender deutzia tolerates a range of pH and is hardy from Zones 4 to 8.

WHEN TO PLANT:

Set out nursery plants in spring or fall.

HEIGHT AND SPREAD:

From 2 to 4 feet tall by 3 to 4 feet across.

PROPAGATION:

Softwood or hardwood cuttings. Take softwood cuttings anytime during the growing season. Take hardwood cuttings in fall.

PLANTING TIPS:

Slender deutzia is a low-growing plant with a mounded form. It bears white flowers in spring. Plant it in a shrub border or massed as a hedge. It is easy to grow.

EUONYMUS

E. alata, Winged euonymus
E. fortunei, Wintercreeper

WHERE TO PLANT:

Full sun, partial shade, or shade, in moist but well-drained soil of average fertility. Euonymus tolerates a range of pH, from acid to alkaline. Winged euonymus grows well in all but very dry soils;

wintercreeper in all but very wet ones. *E. alata* is hardy from Zones 3 to 8; *E. fortunei* from Zones 4 to 8 or 9.

WHEN TO PLANT:
Set out balled-and-burlapped or container-grown plants in spring or fall.

HEIGHT AND SPREAD:
Winged euonymus can reach 15 to 20 feet in height with an equal spread. Wintercreeper grows only 6 to 8 inches high unless supported on a structure, and individual stems may grow as long as 10 to 15 feet.

PROPAGATION:
Softwood or hardwood cuttings. Take softwood cuttings in summer or hardwood cuttings in fall.

Softwood cuttings root best in moist sand.

PLANTING TIPS:
Winged euonymus is excellent planted as a hedge or screen, in groups, in a border, or even as a specimen plant. Its leaves turn bright red in fall.

Wintercreeper is an easy-to-grow ground cover that can also be grown as a low hedge or trained up a wall. Numerous cultivars are available, with foliage variegated with white or gold.

FAGUS

F. grandifolia, American beech
F. sylvatica, European beech

WHERE TO PLANT:
Full sun is best, although partial shade is also acceptable. Beeches thrive in well-aerated, moist but well-drained soil of average fertility, with a pH of 5.0 to 6.5. They do not like soil that is waterlogged or compacted. American beech is hardy from Zones 3 to 9, and European beech from Zones 4 to 7.

WHEN TO PLANT:
Set out balled-and-burlapped plants in spring.

HEIGHT AND SPREAD:
American beech grows to 50 to 70 feet tall, with an equal spread. European beech grows 50 to 60 feet tall, with a spread of 35 to 45 feet.

PROPAGATION:
Seeds. Collect seeds when they ripen in fall and sow immediately outdoors. Or stratify seeds of American beech for 3 months, or seeds of European beech for 3 to 5 months, at about 41° F and plant them the following spring. American beech may send up suckers from its roots; these can be dug up and planted.

FAGUS—*Continued*

PLANTING TIPS:
The stately beeches are among the most beautiful of all shade trees and deserve to be planted as specimens on an expansive lawn. European beech is the more handsome species. American beech has shallow roots that make it difficult to grow lawn grasses beneath its branches.

FORSYTHIA

F. × intermedia, Border forsythia

WHERE TO PLANT:
Full sun. The best soil is fertile and light, but forsythias are not fussy and will grow in just about any soil of average fertility as long as it is well drained. They tolerate a range of pH, and are hardy from Zones 4 to 8.

WHEN TO PLANT:
Set out bare-rooted or balled-and-burlapped plants in spring or fall.

HEIGHT AND SPREAD:
From 8 to 10 feet high by 10 to 12 feet wide.

PROPAGATION:
Softwood cuttings are easy to root, and suckers transplant very easily. Take softwood cuttings in summer, hardwood cuttings in fall. Or simply uproot suckers and transplant them.

PLANTING TIPS:
The bright yellow flowers of forsythia are a familiar sight in lawns and shrub borders in early spring. The plants are also handsome when planted as informal hedges or massed on banks. Because shrubs grow quite vigorously and need plenty of room, they are not suitable as foundation plantings.

FOTHERGILLA

F. gardenii, Dwarf fothergilla
F. major

WHERE TO PLANT:
Full sun to partial shade, in well-drained sandy or peaty loam rich in organic matter, with an acid pH. *F. gardenii* is hardy from Zones 5 to 8; *F. major* from Zones 4 to 8.

WHEN TO PLANT:
Set out balled-and-burlapped or container-grown plants in spring or fall.

HEIGHT AND SPREAD:	Dwarf fothergilla grows 2 to 3 feet tall with an equal spread. *F. major* reaches a height of 6 to 10 feet and a spread of 2 to 5 feet.
PROPAGATION:	Cuttings, although they sometimes go dormant. Take cuttings from suckers or roots anytime during summer. Take softwood cuttings in June or July. Cuttings taken from suckers or roots do best when given bottom heat.
	Softwood cuttings root best when dipped in rooting hormone before planting. When the cuttings have rooted in fall, leave them in the flats and harden them off. The rooted cuttings may go dormant. After they enter dormancy, store them over winter in a cold frame or other protected location where the temperature can be maintained at 34° F. Remove the flats to a warm greenhouse in February or March. When new growth appears, repot the young plants.
PLANTING TIPS:	Grow fothergilla in a shrub border, in foundation plantings, or in groups. They are good companions to azaleas and rhododendrons. Plants have white flowers in spring and brilliant autumn foliage.

FRANKLINIA

F. alatamaha

WHERE TO PLANT:	Full sun is best (although partial shade is acceptable), in moist but well-drained soil rich in organic matter, with an acid pH. Franklinia is hardy from Zones 5 to 9.
WHEN TO PLANT:	Set out balled-and-burlapped or container-grown plants in spring or fall.
HEIGHT AND SPREAD:	From 10 to 20 feet tall with a spread of 6 to 15 feet.
PROPAGATION:	Cuttings root easily; they do best if dipped in rooting hormone before planting. Take cuttings in late summer or fall. To start from seed, sow seeds as soon as the fruit ripens—do not allow them to dry out.
PLANTING TIPS:	Franklinia is a small tree or large shrub that makes a handsome specimen tree for lawns of modest size. It bears showy white flowers in summer.

FRAXINUS

F. americana, White ash
F. pennsylvanica, Green ash

WHERE TO PLANT:
Full sun, in deep, moist but well-drained soil. White ash can tolerate soils that are somewhat rocky or that tend toward dryness. Green ash is tolerant of dry conditions and salty soils, although in the wild it is often found growing along streams and in other moist places. Both species are not particular about pH, and both are considered hardy from Zones 3 to 9.

WHEN TO PLANT:
Set out nursery plants in spring or fall.

HEIGHT AND SPREAD:
White ash grows 50 to 80 feet tall and as wide. Green ash grows to 50 or 60 feet, with a spread of 25 to 30 feet.

PROPAGATION:
Seeds. Collect seeds when they ripen. Seeds need a warm period followed by a cold period in order to germinate. Stratify seeds of white ash for 1 month at 68 to 85° F, then for 2 months at 41° F. Stratify seeds of green ash for 2 months at about 68° F, then for 4 months at 32 to 41° F.

Ash cultivars are propagated by budding onto seedling understocks.

PLANTING TIPS:
Because of its smaller stature, green ash is the better choice for most home situations—white ash needs lots of space.

GINGKO

G. biloba

WHERE TO PLANT:
Full sun, in deep, sandy, moist but well-drained soil. Gingko tolerates a range of soils and can withstand soils with a high salt content. It is not fussy in regard to pH and tolerates polluted air. Hardy from Zones 3 to 9.

WHEN TO PLANT:
Set out nursery plants in spring or fall.

HEIGHT AND SPREAD:
From 50 to 80 feet tall by 30 to 40 feet wide.

PROPAGATION:
Seeds or softwood cuttings. Seeds are borne by female trees only. Collect seeds when fruit ripens, around the middle of fall, and sow them outdoors right away. Or stratify them in moist sand for about

2½ months at 60 to 70° F, then for 2 to 3 months at about 41° F. Seeds do not store well.

You may also take softwood cuttings in June, dip them in rooting hormone, and place them in moist medium under mist; they should root in about 2 months.

PLANTING TIPS: Gingko is a big, durable tree that grows well in urban conditions, although it needs a lot of space.

Female trees bear messy fruit with an extremely unpleasant smell. Plant male trees only.

GLEDITSIA

G. triacanthos var. *inermis*, Thornless honey locust

WHERE TO PLANT: Full sun, in moist, fertile soil with an alkaline pH. Honey locust will tolerate drought and salty or limestone soils. It is hardy from Zones 3 to 9.

WHEN TO PLANT: Set out nursery plants in spring or fall.

HEIGHT AND SPREAD: From 30 to 70 feet tall with an equal spread.

PROPAGATION: Buy young trees from a nursery; honey locust is difficult to propagate at home. Cultivars are commercially propagated by budding or grafting onto selected rootstocks.

PLANTING TIPS: Honey locust has open, lacy foliage that allows grass to flourish underneath the tree. It is a handsome tree for planting in lawns. This variety blooms in May or June.

HAMAMELIS

H. × intermedia, Witch hazel

WHERE TO PLANT: Full sun to partial shade, in moist but well-drained soil rich in organic matter, with an acid pH. This species, a hybrid between *H. mollis* (Chinese witch hazel) and *H. japonica* (Japanese witch hazel), is hardy from Zones 5 to 8.

WHEN TO PLANT: Set out balled-and-burlapped plants in spring or fall.

HEIGHT AND SPREAD: From 15 to 20 feet tall.

HAMAMELIS—*Continued*

PROPAGATION: Cuttings or layering. Take softwood cuttings in June. Layer the plant in summer.

PLANTING TIPS: Witch hazel opens its fragrant flowers with their ribbonlike petals in late winter, January to March. Flowers of this hybrid species are usually red, yellow, or orange; some cultivars produce bicolored flowers. If fragrance is your primary concern, plant *H. mollis*—it has the most fragrant flowers of all the witch hazels.

Grow witch hazel as a specimen plant, in groups, or in a shrub border.

HIBISCUS

H. syriacus, Rose of sharon

WHERE TO PLANT: Full sun to partial shade. The ideal soil is moist but well-drained and rich in organic matter. But the plant will grow in most soils that are neither very wet nor very dry. Rose of sharon tolerates a range of pH (5.5 to 7.0 is best) and holds up well in hot weather. It is hardy from Zones 5 to 8.

WHEN TO PLANT: Set out nursery plants in spring or fall.

HEIGHT AND SPREAD: From 8 to 12 feet high by 6 to 10 feet wide.

PROPAGATION: Softwood cuttings taken in June or July. Cuttings usually root easily when treated with rooting hormone before planting.

PLANTING TIPS: Rose of sharon has attractive summer flowers and is useful in shrub borders, or planted singly or in groups on a lawn. It self-sows with abandon in many gardens and can become a pest.

HYDRANGEA

H. macrophylla, Bigleaf hydrangea

WHERE TO PLANT: Full sun to partial shade, in moist but well-drained soil rich in organic matter. Grown in soil with a pH of 5.0 to 5.5, the plant will produce blue flowers; a pH of 6.0 to 6.5 will cause the flowers to be pink. *H. macrophylla* is hardy from Zones 6 to 9. It can tolerate seashore conditions.

WHEN TO PLANT:	Set out container-grown plants in spring or fall.
HEIGHT AND SPREAD:	From 3 to 6 feet tall and as wide.
PROPAGATION:	Softwood cuttings taken from late spring to midsummer (late May through July) from nonflowering shoots. Hardwood cuttings can be taken in fall.
PLANTING TIPS:	The big, round flower heads of hydrangea are seen in summer beds and borders. The bushes can be planted in a shrub border, or with perennials and annuals. Since this shrub may be killed back to the ground in the northern zones, it is not suitable as a foundation shrub there.

ILEX

I. aquifolium, English holly
I. opaca, American holly

WHERE TO PLANT:	Partial shade is best, but full sun is also acceptable. Hollies thrive in loose, moist but well-drained, fertile soil with an acid pH. Good drainage is very important, as is an acid soil; the leaves may yellow in very alkaline soils (an indication of chlorosis). Do not plant holly in an exposed location where it will be subject to strong winds. It does not grow well in dry soils, although it does tolerate polluted air. American holly is hardy from Zones 4 to 9, and English holly in Zones 5 to 9.
WHEN TO PLANT:	Set out balled-and-burlapped plants in spring.
HEIGHT AND SPREAD:	From 20 to 40 feet high by 18 to 40 feet wide. Holly is a medium to slow grower. A tree 40 feet high may easily be more than 50 years old.
PROPAGATION:	Softwood or hardwood cuttings. Take hardwood cuttings in fall, dip them in rooting hormone, and plant them in moist sand in a cool greenhouse or in a cool room under lights. For best results with cuttings, wound them and treat them with rooting hormone before planting. Holly is slow and difficult to grow from seed, taking 2 or more years to germinate.
PLANTING TIPS:	In order for your hollies to produce red berries you must plant a male tree for every two or three female trees, to ensure good pollination.

(continued)

ILEX—*Continued*

PLANTING TIPS:
(continued)

Plant holly in small groups, or as hedges or screens.

Hollies take a long time to establish themselves, so water new plants regularly throughout their first season in the garden.

Both species described here are evergreen; English holly is a more beautiful plant but American holly is hardier.

KALMIA
K. latifolia, Mountain laurel

WHERE TO PLANT: Full sun to partial shade, in moist but well-drained soil rich in organic matter, with a pH of 5.0 to 6.0. Mountain laurel appreciates cool soil; mulch in spring and summer to help conserve moisture and keep the root zone cool. Hardy from Zones 4 to 9.

WHEN TO PLANT: Set out nursery plants in spring or fall.

HEIGHT AND SPREAD: From 7 to 15 feet tall with an equal spread.

PROPAGATION: Buy nursery plants. Starting from seeds or cuttings is difficult for the home gardener.

PLANTING TIPS: Mountain laurel's clusters of pink or white flowers are lovely additions to shady shrub borders in late May or early June. The plants can also be planted in groups or masses on a lawn.

KOELREUTERIA
K. paniculata, Golden-rain tree

WHERE TO PLANT: Full sun, in any good garden soil. This tree tolerates many kinds of soils and a range of pH, including alkaline conditions. It will grow through hot weather and drought, and withstands windy conditions and polluted air. Golden-rain tree is hardy from Zones 5 to 9.

WHEN TO PLANT: Set out balled-and-burlapped plants in spring or fall.

HEIGHT AND SPREAD: From 30 to 40 feet tall and equally wide.

PROPAGATION: Root cuttings taken in early winter (December) while the tree is dormant. Seeds are difficult to germinate under home conditions.

PLANTING TIPS: This tree is especially noteworthy for its hanging panicles of yellow flowers in summer—yellow is an unusual color for tree blossoms. Plant golden-rain tree as a specimen on a lawn.

KOLKWITZIA
K. amabilis, Beautybush

WHERE TO PLANT: Full sun, in well-drained soil of average fertility. Beautybush tolerates a range of pH and is hardy from Zones 4 to 8.

WHEN TO PLANT: Set out balled-and-burlapped plants in spring or fall.

HEIGHT AND SPREAD: From 6 to 10 feet tall and not quite as wide.

PROPAGATION: Softwood cuttings taken in summer. The best are tip cuttings taken at a node. Although this shrub can be started readily from seed, plants grown from seed often display flowers of an inferior color. For best results, propagate with cuttings.

PLANTING TIPS: Beautybush bears pink flowers in May or June.

LAGERSTROEMIA
L. indica, Crape myrtle

WHERE TO PLANT: Full sun, in moist but well-drained soil rich in organic matter, with a pH of 5.0 to 6.5. Crape myrtles are generally hardy from Zones 7 to 9, but can often survive farther north in a protected location.

WHEN TO PLANT: Set out balled-and-burlapped or container-grown plants in spring or fall.

HEIGHT AND SPREAD: From 15 to 25 feet tall and 10 to 20 feet wide.

PROPAGATION: Seeds or hardwood cuttings. Take softwood cuttings in summer, or hardwood cuttings in fall. Sow seeds in spring (plants grow readily from seed but flower color may vary).

PLANTING TIPS: A favorite among southern gardeners, crape myrtle bears its pink, white, or purple flowers in late summer. Plant it as a specimen or in groups.

Seeds need light to germinate; press into soil gently but do not cover.

LARIX

L. decidua, Common or European larch

WHERE TO PLANT:	Full sun, in moist but well-drained soil. Hardy from Zones 2 to 6.
WHEN TO PLANT:	Set out balled-and-burlapped or container grown plants in spring or fall.
HEIGHT AND SPREAD:	From 70 to 75 feet high by 25 to 30 feet wide.
PROPAGATION:	Seeds. Collect seeds when they ripen. Seeds will sprout with no pretreatment, but to achieve maximum germination, stratify them for 1 to 2 months at 30 to 40° F.
PLANTING TIPS:	Tall, handsome, deciduous trees for northern gardeners, larches are best planted as specimens on broad lawns. Larches have needles and cones but are not evergreen.

LIGUSTRUM

L. amurense, Amur privet
L. japonicum, Japanese privet
L. sinense, Chinese privet

WHERE TO PLANT:	Full sun to partial shade, in practically any soil except one that is constantly wet. Japanese and Chinese privet can tolerate more shade than Amur privet. Privets are not demanding in terms of pH. Amur privet is hardy from Zones 3 to 7; Chinese and Japanese privet in Zones 7 to 10.
WHEN TO PLANT:	Set out bare-rooted plants in early spring or fall.
HEIGHT AND SPREAD:	Amur privet grows 12 to 15 feet tall and 10 to 15 feet across; Japanese privet grows 6 to 12 feet tall and 6 to 8 feet wide; Chinese privet reaches 10 to 15 feet high and 8 to 10 feet wide.
SPACING:	To grow privet as a hedge, set plants 3 feet apart.
PROPAGATION:	Take softwood cuttings in summer. Softwood cuttings root easily; they root best if tip cuttings are taken right above a node, with a long internode between the cut end and the first pair of leaves.
PLANTING TIPS:	Privets are classic hedge plants. They are durable and can withstand shearing and urban conditions. Amur privet is grown in the North; the other two species in the South. Japanese privet is also used for topiary.

LIQUIDAMBAR

L. styraciflua, Sweetgum

WHERE TO PLANT:	Full sun, in deep, moist soil of average fertility, with a pH of about 6.0 to 6.5. The tree is hardy from Zones 5 to 9.
WHEN TO PLANT:	Set out balled-and-burlapped plants in spring.
HEIGHT AND SPREAD:	From 60 to 75 feet high by 40 to 50 feet wide.
PROPAGATION:	Softwood cuttings taken in summer. Take cuttings with a heel and choose shoots with lots of leaves. You may also collect seed when it ripens in fall and stratify it for 1 to 3 months at about 40° F before planting.
PLANTING TIPS:	A good tree for large lawns, also planted in parks and as a street tree, the sweetgum has pretty autumn foliage and distinctive seedpods.

Make sure the tree has plenty of space for its extensive root system, and give the roots time to reestablish themselves after transplanting. Keep the soil evenly moist throughout the first summer after transplanting.

Although sweetgum looks attractive planted along streets, it has little tolerance for pollution and will not do well in congested urban areas.

LIRIODENDRON

L. tulipifera, Tulip tree, Yellow poplar

WHERE TO PLANT:	Full sun, in deep, moist but well-drained loam. Prefers a slightly acid pH but tolerates higher pH as well. Tulip tree is hardy from Zones 4 to 9.
WHEN TO PLANT:	Set out balled-and-burlapped plants in spring.
HEIGHT AND SPREAD:	From 70 to 90 feet high by 35 to 50 feet wide. Yellow poplars grow rapidly. A six-year-old tree may be 20 feet high.
PROPAGATION:	Cuttings or seeds, but it is difficult to propagate at home. Softwood cuttings taken in midsummer are somewhat successful.

LIRIODENDRON—*Continued*

PLANTING TIPS:
This big tree is best planted as a specimen on a large lawn. It bears 5-inch yellow cup-shaped flowers in the spring. The flowers are difficult to see from the ground but attractive from a balcony or upper-story window.

LONICERA

L. fragrantissima, Winter honeysuckle
L. × heckrottii, Goldflame honeysuckle
L. japonica, Japanese honeysuckle
L. tatarica, Tatarian honeysuckle

WHERE TO PLANT:
Full sun to partial shade, in moist but well-drained, loamy soil. Honeysuckles tolerate many other soils as well, except for soggy soils, and can adapt to either acid or alkaline pH, from 6.0 to 8.0. Winter, goldflame, and Japanese honeysuckles are hardy from Zones 4 to 9, although goldflame grows best from Zone 5 south. Tatarian honeysuckle is hardy from Zones 3 to 9.

WHEN TO PLANT:
Set out bare-rooted plants in early spring or fall; they transplant easily.

HEIGHT AND SPREAD:
Winter honeysuckle grows 6 to 10 feet tall with an equal spread; Goldflame honeysuckle grows to 10 feet tall; Japanese honeysuckle grows 15 to 30 feet tall; Tatarian honeysuckle grows 10 to 12 feet tall by 10 feet wide.

PROPAGATION:
Softwood cuttings. Take softwood cuttings in June and root them in a mist chamber. Collect seeds when they ripen and stratify them for a month or two at about 40° F. Divide in fall.

PLANTING TIPS:
Honeysuckles are shrubs or woody vines known for their sweetly fragrant flowers. They are lovely planted on banks and slopes, trained on trellises, or grown on walls.

Winter honeysuckle bears highly fragrant white flowers in March or early April. Goldflame honeysuckle is red when in bud; the buds open to reveal gold centers, and the outside of the flowers turn pink as they age.

MAGNOLIA

M. grandiflora, Southern magnolia, Bullbay
M. soulangiana, Saucer magnolia
M. stellata, Star magnolia

WHERE TO PLANT: Full sun is best for saucer and star magnolia, although they will also tolerate partial shade; southern magnolia does fine in sun or partial shade, and will thrive with just a few hours of sun a day. All three magnolias grow best in deep, fertile, moist but well-drained soil rich in organic matter, with a pH of 5.0 to 6.5. Southern magnolia tolerates wet soil; star magnolia holds up well in hot summer weather; saucer magnolia is tolerant of air pollution. Southern magnolia is hardy from Zones 6 to 9; saucer magnolia from Zones 4 to 9; star magnolia from Zones 3 to 8.

WHEN TO PLANT: Set out balled-and-burlapped or container-grown plants in early spring.

HEIGHT AND SPREAD: Southern magnolia grows 60 to 80 feet tall with a spread of 30 to 50 feet; saucer magnolia reaches 20 to 30 feet with an equal spread; star magnolia grows 15 to 20 feet tall, with a 10- to 15-foot spread.

PROPAGATION: Softwood cuttings or seeds. Take softwood cuttings in June, when next year's flower buds have formed. Cuttings should root in about a month if you wound them and dip in rooting hormone before planting. Root the cuttings in a mist chamber; preferably in moist sand. Cuttings can be difficult to overwinter. Root them as early as possible so they will be well established by winter. At the onset of cold weather, wrap the flat of cuttings in plastic and put it in a refrigerator or another location where temperatures are just above freezing. Plant out in spring when new growth begins.

Collect seeds when they ripen and stratify for 3 to 6 months at 32 to 40° F before planting, or sow immediately outdoors. Or layer low-growing shoots in summer. Magnolias can also be propagated by budding.

PLANTING TIPS: Magnolias are handsome as specimen trees, planted in small groups, or planted near buildings. Southern magnolia bears fragrant white flowers in May or June; saucer magnolia has large-petaled flowers of white tinged with pinkish purple in March or

MAGNOLIA—*Continued*

PLANTING TIPS:
(continued)

April; star magnolia covers itself with starry white fragrant flowers in early spring. Southern magnolia, the largest and most stately of these trees, should be planted where it has room to spread.

One drawback to magnolias, especially saucer magnolia, is that fallen flower petals are messy on sidewalks or lawns beneath the branches.

Late spring frosts can damage the buds of saucer and star magnolias, so avoid planting in a southern exposure (which could advance the blooming time) in the North. Southern magnolia blooms later, but needs protection from strong winter winds in Zones 6 and 7.

MALUS

M. species and cultivars, Crab apple

WHERE TO PLANT:
Full sun, in moist but well-drained loam that is rather heavy in texture, with a pH of 5.0 to 7.0. Crab apples will also adapt to other soils. Hardiness varies with species, but most are hardy from Zones 3 or 4 to 8. They do not grow well in the Deep South and Southwest.

WHEN TO PLANT:
Set out bare-rooted plants in spring or fall.

HEIGHT AND SPREAD:
Crab apples can grow from 15 to 50 feet tall, but most reach a height of 20 to 25 feet and a width of 20 to 25 feet.

PROPAGATION:
Budding or whip and tongue grafting. Bud or graft in mid- to late August. Some species can be propagated from softwood cuttings. Take softwood cuttings from the middle of June to the end of July.

PLANTING TIPS:
Flowering crab apples are among the most beautiful of all trees in spring, when they are covered with heavenly pink or white blossoms. Their relatively small size makes them useful in even small yards. Planting crab apples as specimen trees is the best way to show them off.

Hybrids are usually grafted onto other apple species; commonly used understocks include *M. baccata*, *M. robusta*, and *M. sieboldii*.

Crab apples are quite susceptible to fungal diseases that cause them to defoliate by midsummer. Be sure to select varieties that have resistance to the two most common diseases—scab and rust. Three cultivars noted for disease resistance are 'Centurion', 'Henningi', and 'Professor Sprenger'.

OXYDENDRUM

O. arboreum, Sourwood

WHERE TO PLANT:
Full sun to partial shade, in moist but well-drained soil rich in organic matter, with a pH of 5.5 to 6.5. Sourwood has some tolerance for dry conditions, but it cannot stand polluted air. The tree is hardy from Zones 5 to 9.

WHEN TO PLANT:
Set out balled-and-burlapped plants in spring or fall.

HEIGHT AND SPREAD:
From 25 to 30 feet tall by 20 feet across.

PROPAGATION:
Softwood cuttings. Take softwood cuttings with a heel in July. For best results dip cuttings in rooting hormone and plant in a moist medium of equal parts sharp (builder's) sand and peat moss.

You can also collect and sow seeds as soon as they ripen in fall. Seeds germinate best under mist. Grow the seedlings indoors under lights.

PLANTING TIPS:
Sourwood is a lovely specimen tree that bears drooping panicles of fragrant white flowers in early summer. It has attractive autumn foliage as well.

PHILADELPHUS

P. coronarius, Mock orange

WHERE TO PLANT:
Full sun to partial shade. The ideal soil is moist but well-drained and rich in organic matter, although mock orange is quite tolerant. It is also adaptable to a range of pH. This species is hardy from Zones 4 to 8.

WHEN TO PLANT:
Set out bare-rooted plants in early spring or fall.

HEIGHT AND SPREAD:
From 10 to 12 feet tall and as wide.

PHILADELPHUS—*Continued*

PROPAGATION: Cuttings or division. Take softwood cuttings in June or July, and hardwood cuttings in autumn. Cuttings root best when dipped in rooting hormone before planting. Divide in autumn. Plants can also be propagated from suckers or by simple layering. You can also collect and sow seeds as soon as they ripen.

PLANTING TIPS: Mock orange is a good plant for a shrub border. In late spring its slender branches are full of fragrant white flowers.

PICEA

P. abies, Norway spruce and varieties

WHERE TO PLANT: Spruces thrive in full sun to partial shade, in deep, moist but well-drained, sandy loam but tolerate other soils as long as they have good drainage. Best pH is 5.0 to 6.0. Spruce suffers from drying winds and sun in winter, so try to plant it on a north slope or other protected spot. Hardy from Zones 2 to 7.

WHEN TO PLANT: Set out balled-and-burlapped plants in spring or fall; make sure the root ball does not dry out during transplanting.

Named varieties can be propagated by grafting in a greenhouse in January.

HEIGHT AND SPREAD: The species form of Norway spruce can grow as tall as 150 feet, but some of the dwarf varieties grow just 1 or 2 feet high. The spread ranges from half to double the height of the tree depending on the variety.

PROPAGATION: Seeds and cuttings. Sow seeds of species outdoors in late spring, and keep the planting area shaded and watered throughout the first year of growth.

Take hardwood cuttings with a heel in autumn and plant in sharp (builder's) sand in December. Keep the sand evenly moist, and root the cuttings under lights or under glass, where the temperature is about 70° F. The cuttings should strike roots in about 12 weeks. After they have rooted, remove them from the sand and plant them in pots of a fertile, light, well-drained soil mix. Plant seedlings outdoors in late spring. Spruce cuttings are sometimes hard to root because of the sticky resin they contain; it might help to dip the end of the cutting in hot (130 to 150° F) water for a few minutes before placing in the rooting medium.

PLANTING TIPS: Norway spruce is among the most widely grown evergreens in the United States. The species and taller varieties are handsome specimen trees, and make effective windbreaks and screens. The dwarf varieties are well suited to rock gardens.

PIERIS

P. japonica, Japanese pieris, Japanese andromeda

WHERE TO PLANT: Full sun to partial shade, in moist but well-drained soil rich in organic matter (especially peat), with an acid pH (4.0 to 5.0). Hardy from Zones 5 to 8, and can often be grown in Zone 4 if given winter protection.

WHEN TO PLANT: Set out balled-and-burlapped or container-grown plants in spring or fall.

HEIGHT AND SPREAD: From 9 to 12 feet tall with a spread of 6 to 8 feet.

PROPAGATION: Seeds and cuttings. Sow seeds in moist medium as soon as they ripen; seeds germinate in 2 or 3 weeks. Take cuttings in June. For best results treat cuttings with rooting hormone and root them under mist.

PLANTING TIPS: Japanese pieris is an attractive specimen shrub, with panicles of small white flowers in early spring (March or April).

PINUS

P. species, Pine

WHERE TO PLANT: Pines tolerate a range of soils and various adverse conditions. *P. sylvestris* (Scotch pine) and *P. nigra* (Austrian pine) can grow in many kinds of soils. *P. mugo* (mugo pine), *P. pungens* (prickly pine), *P. banksiana* (scrub pine), and *P. thunbergiana* (Japanese black pine) prefer sandy soils. *P. nigra*, *P. pungens*, and *P. thunbergiana* are good trees for seaside gardens because they are not bothered by salt spray. *P. nigra* and *P. thunbergiana* grow well in city conditions. Most pines need soil that is well drained. In both summer and

PINUS—*Continued*

WHERE TO PLANT:
(continued)

winter, they are sensitive to drying winds, which can cause the needles to turn brown. Plant on a north slope or other sheltered location to avoid problems. Hardiness varies according to species, with most being hardy from Zones 2, 3, or 4 to 7. The best pH is 5.0 to 6.0.

WHEN TO PLANT:

Set out balled-and-burlapped plants in spring or fall; do not let the root ball dry out during transplanting. Sow seeds of species outdoors in spring, when all danger of frost is past.

HEIGHT AND SPREAD:

Pines come in a tremendous range of sizes and forms, from 15 feet high by 25 feet across, to 100 feet tall by 30 feet across. There are also dwarf varieties growing just a few feet tall.

PROPAGATION:

Grow species from seed. Stratification requirements vary among the species. Named varieties can be propagated by grafting.

All of the pines mentioned here produce seeds that require no stratification.

PLANTING TIPS:

Pines are lovely landscape trees, attractive when planted as specimens, in groups, or as screens. Dwarf cultivars can be planted in borders, foundation plantings, and rock gardens.

When choosing pines to plant on a small property or near a house, remember that some species become extremely large and may provide unwanted shade during winter.

PLATANUS

P. acerifolia, London plane tree
P. occidentalis, Sycamore, Buttonwood

WHERE TO PLANT:

Full sun to partial shade, in deep, fertile, moist soil. Sycamores will tolerate a range of soils and pH, and can grow in very alkaline soils. Hardy from Zones 4 to 9.

WHEN TO PLANT:

Set out nursery plants in spring.

HEIGHT AND SPREAD:

Sycamore grows 75 to 100 feet tall with an equal spread; London plane tree can reach heights of 140 feet and a width of 75 feet.

PROPAGATION:

Seeds. Sow seeds outdoors as soon as they ripen or stratify for 2 months at about 40° F.

PLANTING TIPS:

London plane tree is one of the best street trees for cities, withstanding dryness, wind, and polluted air.

Sycamores are also good street trees, but do best in small town or rural environments. They have interesting, peeling bark and distinctive round seed heads, which may prove to be messy on a lawn or paved area.

PRUNUS
P. species, Flowering cherry

WHERE TO PLANT:

Full sun, in any well-drained soil of average fertility. Cherries are not fussy about pH. Many are hardy from Zones 3 to 8. One of the best species, *P. serrulata* (Japanese cherry), is hardy only as far north as Zone 5.

WHEN TO PLANT:

Set out bare-rooted or balled-and-burlapped plants in early spring.

HEIGHT AND SPREAD:

Varies with species, from 10 or 15 feet tall to 40 or 50 feet tall with an equal spread.

SPACING:

If planting in groups, plant 20 to 25 feet apart in all directions.

PROPAGATION:

For best result with named varieties, purchase nursery plants. You can grow species from seed. Collect ripe seeds in summer and stratify them for 2 to 3 months at about 40° F before planting. You can also take softwood cuttings in summer. Cuttings do not always root reliably, although dipping them in rooting hormone will help.

PLANTING TIPS:

Flowering cherries are breathtakingly beautiful landscape trees, lovely planted as specimens or in groups. They are covered with pink or white flowers in spring.

A winter mulch of compost or well-rotted manure is beneficial.

Cherries as a group are quite prone to insect and disease attack. While a few species may live 30 to 50 years, others commonly succumb to disease before they are 20 years old. Plant trees where subsequent removal will not disfigure the yard or garden.

QUERCUS

Q. alba, White oak
Q. nigra, Water oak
Q. palustris, Pin oak
Q. virginiana, Live oak

WHERE TO PLANT: Full sun, in deep, fertile, moist but well-drained soil with a pH of 5.5 to 6.5. Water oak needs a wet location, and most oaks can tolerate fairly wet soils. Live oak tolerates a range of soils, even heavy, compacted soils, and withstands salt spray. Hardiness varies: white oak is hardy in Zones 3 to 9; water oak in Zones 6 to 9; pin oak in Zones 4 to 8; live oak in Zones 7 to 10.

WHEN TO PLANT: Set out balled-and-burlapped plants in spring or fall.

HEIGHT AND SPREAD: White oak grows up to 100 feet tall with a spread of 50 to 80 feet; water oak reaches a height of 50 to 80 feet and a spread of 30 to 60 feet; pin oak grows 60 to 70 feet tall and 25 to 40 feet wide; live oak attains a height of 40 to 80 feet with a 60- to 100-foot spread.

PROPAGATION: Seeds. Sow seeds outdoors as soon as they ripen in fall. If you must store the seed, stratify it in the refrigerator over winter. The acorns may sprout during storage, but you can still safely plant them in spring as long as you keep the soil moist after planting.

PLANTING TIPS: Oaks are big, stately, long-lived trees for large landscapes. Different species have particular qualities to recommend them. Water oak is widely grown in the South as a shade or street tree. Pin oak is also popular for shade and street planting, and has beautiful red autumn foliage. The magnificent live oak, often festooned with Spanish moss, is seen all over the Southeast, planted along streets, on broad lawns, and near the mansions of old plantations.

RHODODENDRON

R. species and hybrids, Azalea, Rhododendron

WHERE TO PLANT: Full sun to partial shade (provide more shade the further south you live), in cool, light, moist but well-drained soil rich in organic matter and with an acid pH of 4.5 to 6.0. A light soil is helpful because the plant's shallow roots need plenty of air. Peat moss is an excellent source of organic matter for soil where azaleas and rhododendrons will be grown. Choose a location where plants are protected from strong winds and afternoon sun.

Hardiness varies greatly among species and hybrids. Ghent, Knaphill, Exbury, Robin Hill, and Dexter hybrids are the hardiest azaleas, and grow well in the Northeast and mid-Atlantic regions. P.J.M. hybrids are also hardy and are grown successfully in these areas and the upper Midwest. Belgian and Southern Indian azaleas are least hardy and are widely planted in the South. The Catawbiense hybrids dislike extreme heat and cold and do very well along the West Coast from Seattle as far south as San Francisco.

WHEN TO PLANT:
Set out balled-and-burlapped plants in spring or late summer to early fall.

HEIGHT AND SPREAD:
Azaleas and rhododendrons range in size from 2-foot-tall dwarfs to shrubs or small trees 20 feet tall. In most cases the spread is about equal to the height of the plant.

PROPAGATION:
Semi-hardwood cuttings, leaf cuttings, seeds, or mound layering. Rhododendron cuttings are hard to root; seeds work better if you are growing species. Sow seeds of species in February. Take semi-hardwood cuttings from July to early September, when the current season's growth has matured enough to root well. Mound-layer in spring. Mound layering works best with deciduous azaleas. Some deciduous azaleas can be grafted in winter.

To start species rhododendrons or azaleas from seed, scatter the fine, dustlike seeds on top of a flat full of moist peat or ground sphagnum moss. Mist to settle the seeds into the medium. To maintain humidity cover the flat with polyethylene and keep it at a temperature of around 55° F. When shoots poke through the soil, take off the plastic and place the flat where the seedlings will get lots of light and good air circulation. When the seedlings are big enough to handle, transplant them to new flats containing a mixture of sand, peat moss, and pasteurized garden soil.

To start azalea cuttings, first make the cuttings 3 to 4 inches long. Wound the cuttings as described under Acer. Remove one or two lower leaves, dip the cuttings in rooting hormone, and insert them in a flat of moistened rooting medium (see page 56 for recipes for media). Make sure the medium is thoroughly moist but not soggy.

RHODODENDRON—*Continued*

PROPAGATION:
(continued)

Give the cuttings bottom heat, or place them under an automatic mist system (see page 55 for information on mist propagation). Stop misting when rooting occurs (in 1 to 2 months), and transplant the rooted cuttings to pots or a nursery bed.

To propagate from leaf cuttings, use leaves that have an axillary bud, and take each cutting with a heel that includes the bud. Plant in a propagating frame or flat given bottom heat, indoors or in a greenhouse.

PLANTING TIPS:

Azaleas and rhododendrons are lovely in large or small landscapes. Their beautiful flowers appear in spring, and their foliage remains attractive all season. The flowers come in two color families: white, pink, rose-pink, and crimson; and white, yellow, orange, and scarlet to brick red. Use them in foundation plantings, in woodland gardens, or in groups or masses in large landscapes. Dwarf cultivars can be included in mixed borders and rock gardens.

There are no blanket rules for telling azaleas and rhododendrons apart, but in general, most rhododendrons are evergreen and have large leaves; many azaleas are deciduous, and most of them have small leaves. There are many hybrid groups of azaleas. Study nursery catalogs carefully to determine which are best suited to your area.

Because of their shallow roots, do not cultivate the soil around azaleas and rhododendrons. Mulch to keep the roots cool and to hold moisture. Also, do not plant close to tenacious surface-feeding trees and shrubs such as honeysuckle, lilac, privet, birch, cherry, and maple.

Some evergreen azaleas shipped from nurseries were grown in pure peat moss and arrive with their roots in a ball of peat; such plants can experience severe shock when planted in the garden. To minimize shock, make sure the peat is thoroughly moist at planting time. Carefully draw some of the lower roots out of the root ball to help ease the transition into garden soil. Some growers recommend making three or four vertical cuts about ½ inch into the bottom of the root ball with a sharp knife to stimulate new roots to grow.

ROSA

R. species and cultivars, Rose

WHERE TO PLANT:
Full sun (roses grow best with 6 hours of unobstructed sunlight a day); morning sun is preferable to afternoon sun, if you have a choice. Soil should be deeply dug, reasonably fertile, well-drained, and rich in organic matter. The perfect pH is about 6.5, but roses grow well in a range of pH from 5.5 to 7.0. Roses cannot tolerate soggy soil; if your drainage is poor, plant in raised beds or, as a last resort, install drainage tiles. If possible, prepare the soil a season ahead of when you expect to plant.

Do not plant roses close to large shrubs and trees whose roots may compete with them for moisture.

To reduce the incidence of disease, make sure your roses are in an open spot where they will get plenty of air circulation.

WHEN TO PLANT:
Plant bare-rooted and packaged roses and roses preplanted in cartons in early spring as soon as the soil can be worked, while the plants are still dormant. Plant container-grown roses from spring to early summer or in fall.

SPACING:
In mild climates, the Pacific Northwest, West Coast, Deep South, and Southwest (Zones 8, 9, and 10), space hybrid teas and grandifloras 3 to 4 feet apart, floribundas 2½ to 3½ feet apart. In the mid-South, South Central States, and along the East Coast (Zones 5, 6, and 7), space hybrid teas and grandifloras 2½ to 3 feet apart; floribundas 2 to 3 feet apart. In the North Central states and parts of the Northeast (Zone 4), plant hybrid teas, grandifloras, and floribundas 2 to 2½ feet apart. In the coldest parts of the North Central States and New England (Zone 3), plant hybrid teas, grandifloras, and floribundas 1½ to 2 feet apart. Plant climbing roses 6 feet apart in all zones. Plant shrub roses to be grown as hedges 2 to 3 feet apart. Plant miniatures 1 to 2 feet apart.

PROPAGATION:
Shield budding. The best way to cut the bud shield is to make the first cut upward, then make a crosswise cut above the bud to remove the shield.

Species roses may also be propagated through softwood cuttings. Take softwood cuttings in summer. Cuttings from side shoots perform more satisfactorily than tip cuttings.

ROSA—*Continued*

PLANTING TIPS:

Roses are usually shipped from nurseries as bare-rooted plants. Plant them within 24 hours of receiving them. If you cannot plant for 2 or 3 days, open the package, sprinkle the plants with water, reclose the package, and put it in a cool place. If you must wait longer than a couple of days to plant, remove the roses from their packages, soak the roots in water for a few hours (never longer than 8 hours), and then heel them into a vacant spot in the garden, as described on page 97. Do not hold the plants longer than 2 weeks.

If you cannot plant container-grown roses right away, put them in a shady spot and keep them watered. In locations where winter temperatures drop to 0° F and lower (Zones 3 to 7), set plants so the bud union (the knob where the green top meets the brown main stem and roots) is 1 to 2 inches below the soil surface. In warm climates (Zones 8 to 10) plant with the bud union 1 to 2 inches above the soil surface.

Before planting bare-rooted roses, carefully inspect the plants and cut off any shriveled, broken, or damaged canes (branches) and roots. Most nurseries prune their plants before shipping, but if your plants are unpruned, cut back long canes to 1 foot above the bud union, and cut off any canes thinner than a pencil and any canes that cross over one another.

Dig the planting hole deep and wide enough to comfortably accommodate all the roots without bending them. (This usually means a hole 12 to 15 inches deep and 15 inches to 2 feet across.) Mix a shovelful of compost or peat moss with the soil in the bottom of the hole. Make a mound of soil in the bottom of the hole and set the plant on it; make sure the bud union is at the correct depth for your area. Spread the roots down and over the sides of the soil mound. The main roots should not overlap one another. Begin filling the hole with soil, carefully working it in around the roots with your fingers. When the hole is about two-thirds filled with soil, fill the hole to the top with water to settle the soil around the roots. After the water drains away, fill the rest of the hole with soil, rock the plant gently back and forth a few times, and water again, thoroughly.

Make a mound of soil about 8 inches high around the stem. If you are planting in fall, the soil mound will provide winter protection. If you are planting in spring, this mound will help hold moisture and ease the plant's transition to the garden. Remove the soil mound as leaf buds start to develop on the stems (do it gradually over a period of a week). Cover the rose bed with a 2-inch mulch of buckwheat hulls, salt hay, or other loose material to help conserve water, keep down weeds, and prevent water from splashing onto stems (which can encourage disease).

To plant roses preplanted in biodegradable cardboard containers, tear the sides of the box before setting the plant in the hole. This will prevent root problems in case the container is slow to decompose after planting.

To plant container-grown roses, make the planting hole a minimum of 6 inches larger and deeper than the size of the container. Water regularly for 3 weeks after planting—until the plants become established in the garden. To aid removal of roses in metal containers, have the nursery cut the container before you bring it home.

Be sure to install a trellis, fence, or other support before you plant climbing roses.

SPIRAEA
S. × *bumalda*
S. prunifolia var. *plena*, Bridal-wreath
S. × *vanhouttei*, Bridal-wreath

WHERE TO PLANT: Full sun, in any moist but well-drained soil of average fertility. Spiraea tolerates a range of pH. All the species listed here are hardy from Zones 3 or 4 to 8.

WHEN TO PLANT: Set out nursery plants in spring or fall.

HEIGHT AND SPREAD: *S.* × *bumalda* grows 2 to 3 feet tall and 3 to 5 feet across; *S. prunifolia* reaches 4 to 9 feet in height with a spread of 6 to 8 feet; *S.* × *vanhouttei* grows 6 to 8 feet tall, and spreads 10 to 12 feet.

PROPAGATION: Softwood cuttings taken in June or July. *S.* × *bumalda* responds well to mound layering.

If your bushes have arching branches, you can peg the tips to the ground and layer them in summer. Spiraeas may also be propagated by division and by seeds. Sow seeds outdoors as soon as they ripen.

SPIRAEA—*Continued*

PLANTING TIPS:
Spiraeas are lovely planted in masses, and can be used as borders or low screens. They bear clusters of small white flowers in late spring.

Spiraeas are easy to grow, durable plants that need little care. *S.* × *vanhouttei*, the most widely grown bridal-wreath, holds up well under city conditions.

SYRINGA

S. vulgaris, Common lilac

WHERE TO PLANT:
Full sun, in well-drained soil rich in organic matter, with a pH near neutral. Hardy from Zones 3 to 7.

WHEN TO PLANT:
Set out nursery plants in spring or fall. Dig and replant suckers in early fall.

HEIGHT AND SPREAD:
From 8 to 15 feet tall by 6 to 12 feet wide.

PROPAGATION:
Suckers or softwood cuttings. Semi-hardwood and hardwood cuttings also work. Take softwood cuttings in summer, semi-hardwood cuttings in late summer, or hardwood cuttings in fall. Mound-layer older plants in summer.

Commercial growers sometimes cleft-graft lilac scions onto privet roots, but the process is time consuming and complicated, and not the best method for home gardeners.

PLANTING TIPS:
Syringas are classic plants for shrub borders, blooming in spring in white and shades of lilac and purple. Their spikes of flowers possess an intoxicating fragrance. Lilacs can also be planted as specimens or in groups.

Lilacs flourish best in soil that has been manured; dig in a 4-inch layer of well-rotted manure every other autumn.

TAXUS

T. baccata, English yew
T. canadensis, Canadian yew, Ground hemlock
T. cuspidata, Japanese yew
T. × *media*

WHERE TO PLANT:
Yews can grow in full sun, partial shade, or shade. They require fertile, moist but very well-drained soil, and they tolerate a range of

pH. Excellent drainage is critical. Give them a spot where they will be protected from strong winds, especially in winter. Drying winds can desiccate the needles and turn them yellow or brown. English yew is hardy only in Zones 6 and 7; Canadian yew from Zones 2 to 6; Japanese yew in Zones 4 to 7; *T. × media* in Zones 4 to 7.

WHEN TO PLANT:　Set out balled-and-burlapped plants in spring.

HEIGHT AND SPREAD:　English yew grows 35 to 60 feet tall and 15 to 25 feet wide; Canadian yew is 3 to 6 feet tall and 6 to 8 feet across; Japanese yew can be up to 40 feet tall (but most of the cultivated varieties are lower, bushy shrubs), *T. × media* varies in height from 6 to about 20 feet, and the spread varies depending on the cultivar.

PROPAGATION:　Cuttings. Take cuttings from late summer through winter, as described on pages 62–64, and root them in a cold frame or greenhouse.

Yews can also be propagated from seed, but the resulting plants may differ significantly from the original. Plants started from seed also grow slowly.

PLANTING TIPS:　Yews are excellent planted in groups or masses, as hedges, or in foundation plantings. They thrive along the Atlantic Coast and in the Pacific Northwest, where summer weather is humid, often foggy, and not too hot. English yew in particular dislikes hot, dry weather.

English yew is rarely grown in the species form, which is a tall tree. Instead, look for low, shrubby varieties such as *T. adpressa*, *repandens*, *stricta*, and *variegata*.

If you plant nursery trees, make sure they are in balled-and-burlapped form, with a substantial soil ball around the roots. Yews resent transplanting, and their roots dry out quickly.

THUJA
T. occidentalis, American or Eastern arborvitae
T. orientalis, Oriental arborvitae

WHERE TO PLANT:　Full sun is best, but partial shade is also acceptable. The best soil is fertile and moist but well drained. American arborvitae is hardy from Zones 2 to 7 and marginally hardy in Zone 8. Oriental

THUJA—*Continued*

WHERE TO PLANT: *(continued)*	arborvitae is hardy from Zones 5 or 6 to 9. American arborvitae grows best in Zones 7 and north, and Oriental arborvitae in Zones 7 and south.
WHEN TO PLANT:	Set out balled-and-burlapped plants in spring or fall.
HEIGHT AND SPREAD:	American arborvitae grows 40 to 60 feet tall and 10 to 15 feet across, although there are several smaller dwarf varieties. Oriental arborvitae grows 18 to 25 feet tall with a spread of 10 to 12 feet, and also has some dwarf varieties.
PROPAGATION:	Propagate American arborvitae from cuttings taken over the winter from new wood. Cuttings root best if taken with a heel. Propagate Oriental arborvitae from seed that has been stratified for 2 months at 40° F. Cuttings of Oriental arborvitae are more difficult to root than those of American arborvitae.
PLANTING TIPS:	Plant arborvitaes as specimens in foundation plantings or as a hedge. They are also useful as windbreaks.

TILIA

T. americana, American linden, Basswood
T. cordata, Littleleaf linden

WHERE TO PLANT:	Full sun to partial shade, in deep, fertile, moist but well-drained soil. Lindens will also tolerate soils that are drier or heavier, and they are adaptable in terms of pH. These are large trees that need lots of space. American linden is hardy from Zones 2 to 8, and littleleaf linden from Zones 3 to 7.
WHEN TO PLANT:	Set out nursery plants in spring or fall.
HEIGHT AND SPREAD:	American linden grows 60 to 80 feet tall with a spread of 30 to 50 feet; littleleaf linden is slightly smaller, 60 to 70 feet tall and spreading 30 to 45 feet.
PROPAGATION:	Purchase nursery plants. Although lindens can be started from seed, they produce seeds with an extremely tough seed coat and complex dormancy requirements. It is difficult for a home gardener to germinate linden seeds successfully. Commercial growers also bud lindens onto seedling rootstocks, but it makes more sense for home growers to order nursery plants.

| PLANTING TIPS: | Lindens are handsome shade and street trees, with big heart-shaped leaves and clusters of small white to yellowish flowers in early summer. |

TSUGA
T. canadensis, Canadian or Eastern hemlock
T. caroliniana, Carolina hemlock

WHERE TO PLANT:	Full sun to partial shade or shade, in fertile, moist but well-drained soil rich in organic matter and with an acid pH. Hemlocks are forest trees and like cool soil. They do not like hot, dry, windy conditions, and do not grow well in the Midwest. They cannot tolerate air pollution and will not thrive in urban locations. Canadian hemlock is hardy from Zones 3 to 7; Carolina hemlock, from Zones 4 to 7.
WHEN TO PLANT:	Set out balled-and-burlapped plants in spring.
HEIGHT AND SPREAD:	Eastern hemlock grows 40 to 70 feet tall and 25 to 35 feet across; Carolina hemlock reaches 45 to 60 feet in height with a spread of 20 to 25 feet.
PROPAGATION:	Grafting or layering. Seeds have complex dormancy needs which are difficult to accommodate at home.
PLANTING TIPS:	Hemlocks are handsome when planted on broad lawns. They are dense trees and little else will grow readily beneath their branches. *T. canadensis* can be grown as a hedge or screen.

VIBURNUM
V. species

| WHERE TO PLANT: | Full sun to partial shade, in well-drained soil that tends toward moistness. Viburnums prefer an acid pH but are tolerant. Hardiness varies with species. Some examples: *V. × burkwoodii* is hardy in Zones 3 to 8; *V. carlesii* from Zones 4 to 7; *V. plicatum* var. *tomentosum*, doublefile viburnum, from Zones 5 to 8; *V. tinus* from Zone 7 (or sometimes Zone 6, if given winter protection) to Zone 10. |

VIBURNUM—*Continued*

WHEN TO PLANT:
Set out balled-and-burlapped or container-grown plants in spring or fall. Viburnums can be handled in bare-rooted form when small; plant these in early spring.

HEIGHT AND SPREAD:
Viburnums range in size from 2 to 3 feet up to 30 feet tall. *V. × burkwoodii* grows 8 to 10 feet tall and 6 to 7 feet wide; *V. carlesii* grows 4 to 5 feet tall and 4 to 8 feet across; *V. plicatum* var. *tomentosum* reaches 8 to 10 feet in height with a spread of 9 to 12 feet; *V. tinus* grows 6 to 12 feet tall and is slightly narrower than its height.

PROPAGATION:
Softwood cuttings taken in June or July root easily. Viburnum cuttings are sometimes difficult to overwinter. To avoid problems, try to root the cuttings early in the season so they are well established by winter. Wrap the flat in plastic and store the cuttings over winter in the refrigerator or another location where the temperature is just above freezing. Plant the cuttings outdoors in spring.

Growing from seed is complicated. Collect seeds when ripe. They need 3 to 5 months of warm stratification until the radicle—first tiny root—emerges from the seed. After the radicle emerges, transfer the seeds to 3 months of cold stratification and then plant them out.

PLANTING TIPS:
Viburnums are easy to grow. They have attractive white flower clusters—snowball-shaped in some species—and in most cases, pretty autumn foliage. Plant them as specimens, in groups, in shrub borders, or along walkways or driveways. They tolerate air pollution and are suited to city conditions.

Most viburnums bloom in spring, but *V. tinus* flowers in February, or earlier in the southern parts of its range.

WEIGELA
W. florida

WHERE TO PLANT:
Full sun, in any well-drained soil of average fertility. Plants tolerate a range of soils and pH. They withstand pollution and grow well in urban conditions. Hardy from Zones 4 to 8.

WHEN TO PLANT:	Set out bare-rooted plants in early spring or fall, container-grown plants anytime in spring or fall.
HEIGHT AND SPREAD:	From 6 to 9 feet high by 9 to 12 feet wide.
PROPAGATION:	Softwood cuttings root easily; the best are tip cuttings taken slightly above a node, with long internodes. Take softwood cuttings anytime in summer, June to August. Plant them in moist sand in a cold frame or in a shady corner of the garden. You can also sow seeds outdoors as soon as they mature.
PLANTING TIPS:	Weigela is an attractive, easy-to-grow shrub to plant in groups on the lawn, or in a shrub border.

ZELKOVA

Z. serrata

WHERE TO PLANT:	Full sun, in deep, moist but well-drained soil. Zelkova is undemanding in terms of pH, and hardy from Zones 5 to 8.
WHEN TO PLANT:	Set out bare-rooted or balled-and-burlapped plants in early spring or fall.
HEIGHT AND SPREAD:	From 50 to 80 feet tall with an equal spread.
PROPAGATION:	Seeds and softwood cuttings. Collect seeds when they mature. They will usually germinate with no pretreatment, but for best results stratify seeds in the refrigerator for 2 months before planting. Softwood cuttings are best taken from seedlings rather than older plants; take them in summer.
	Cuttings taken from seedlings root best when dipped in rooting hormone.
PLANTING TIPS:	Zelkova is a big, stately tree similar in shape to the American elm, which it is increasingly being planted to replace. It tolerates wind and dry conditions once it is established, and is a good tree for planting in lawns and parks and along streets.

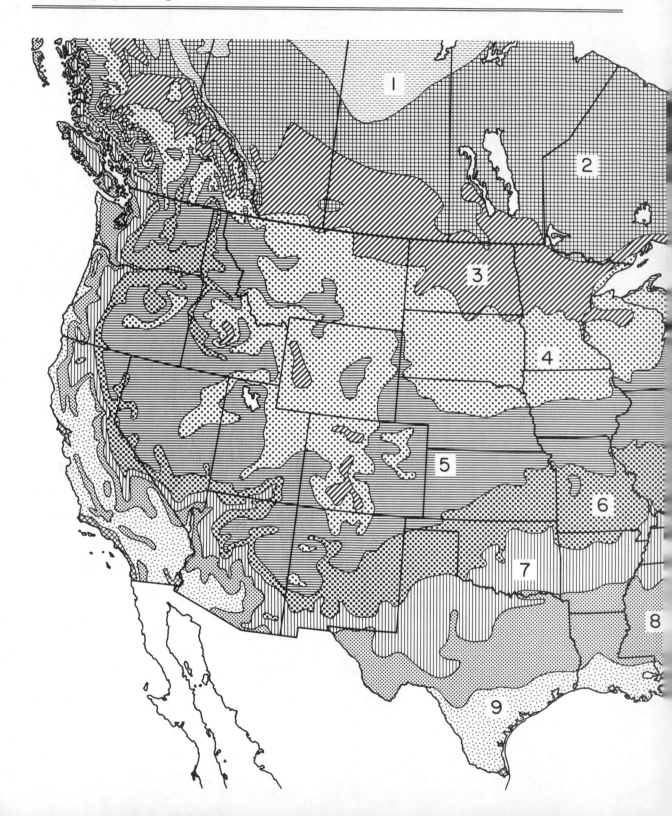

APPROXIMATE RANGE
OF AVERAGE ANNUAL
MINIMUM TEMPERATURES

ZONE

1	BELOW -50°F
2	-50° TO -40°
3	-40° TO -30°
4	-30° TO -20°
5	-20° TO -10°
6	-10° TO 0°
7	0° TO 10°
8	10° TO 20°
9	20° TO 30°
10	30° TO 40°

100   0   100 200 300 400 500

MILES

INDEX

Page references in *italic* indicate tables. **Boldface** references indicate illustrations.